John Lingard, Townsend Young

Introduction to English history

arranged for the use of schools, with continuation to the reign of Queen Victoria

John Lingard, Townsend Young

Introduction to English history
arranged for the use of schools, with continuation to the reign of Queen Victoria

ISBN/EAN: 9783741176272

Manufactured in Europe, USA, Canada, Australia, Japa

Cover: Foto ©ninafisch / pixelio.de

Manufactured and distributed by brebook publishing software (www.brebook.com)

John Lingard, Townsend Young

Introduction to English history

INTRODUCTION
TO
ENGLISH HISTORY,

FROM THE TEXT OF

THE REV. JOHN LINGARD, D.D.

ARRANGED FOR THE USE OF SCHOOLS,

WITH CONTINUATION TO THE

REIGN OF QUEEN VICTORIA.

BY TOWNSEND YOUNG, LL.D.

DUBLIN:
JAMES DUFFY, 15, WELLINGTON-QUAY,
AND
22, PATERNOSTER-ROW, LONDON.
1867.

PATTISON JOLLY,
STEAM-PRESS PRINTER,
22, WEST ESSEX-ST., DUBLIN.

PREFACE.

....

THE sanction of experience has long established the utility of handbooks of this design. They have been found useful not only for educational purposes, but even for private reading. They are little machines of great power; but like other machines, their efficiency depends almost entirely on the nicety of their construction. To possess this essential character, they should be faithful to the original, clear, and interesting. It is my duty to state briefly what I have done, or endeavoured, in these respects. Following Dr. Lingard's text, its cardinal points have been selected; the doing of which has been facilitated by familiarity with the subjects and experience of what is fit for youth.

To obtain clearness, the order had to be adjusted so that detatched parts when brought together may exhibit an event or transaction as a complete statement in an intelligible form. An abstract of this kind, if too strictly controlled by dates, would be very disjointed. Instead of its being a help to the memory, which is the chief intention, it would embarrass; and instead of gratifying curiosity would prove a discouragement.

To be pleasing when there is so little room to be anything but useful, is a matter of some difficulty. It can be attained only by avoiding a dry style, and dressing the facts in an easy, flowing garment, which improves their figure, and makes them welcome guests. I have taken pains to bestow on the narration as much simple and appropriate grace as I could command. Nothing is more injurious to future taste than an early acquaintance with faulty writing; yet, it must be confessed, that our schoolbooks are, in general, sad specimens of crude composition and flat diction.

A few particulars respecting the *Norman Conquest* have been drawn from sources of known authority. The reigns connected with the period of the *Reformation* have been merely condensed. There was no need of doing any more, except to preserve whatever was important; not forgetting that this part of my author is universally esteemed the most valuable and the most happily executed. The long reign of George III. required but a plain chronicling of the events. For Victoria's reign and the two which precede it, I have had to depend almost entirely on my own industry.

The questions are in a manner very different from the *old school*. Their superiority is obvious. When you ask a pupil about a *person* or a *place*, you instantly catch his attention, jog his memory, and call his understanding into play; in fact, you are making a historian of him. To be ready for such questions, he *must* read. *Suggestive* interrogatories promote laziness, and never make a good historian. The mode I have given is the principal feature of the *Competitive Examination* papers. It saves a great deal of time; and is always triumphant in the hands of a *smart* teacher.

Dublin, 20*th Sept.*, 1867.

CONTENTS.

Chap.		Accession.	Page.
I. Roman Britain,			1
II. Anglo-Saxon Period to Alfred,			7
III. Anglo-Saxon and Danish Periods,			11
IV. Manners and Customs of the Anglo-Saxons,			18
V.	THE NORMAN LINE.		
1. William I., The Conqueror,		1066	20
2. William II., Rufus,		1087	22
3. Henry I., Beauclerc,		1100	24
4. Stephen of Blois,		1135	28
VI.	LINE OF PLANTAGENET.		
5. Henry II.,		1155	29
6. Richard I., Cœur de Lion,		1189	33
7. John,		1199	40
8. Henry III.,		1216	44
9. Edward I.,		1272	46
10. Edward II.,		1307	51
11. Edward III.,		1327	54
12. Richard II.,		1377	60
13. Henry IV.,	⎫	1399	65
14. Henry V.,	⎬ Lancaster	1413	67
15. Henry VI.,	⎭	1422	68
16. Edward IV.,	⎫	1461	70
17. Edward V.,	⎬ York	1483	71
18. Richard III.,	⎭	1483	72

CONTENTS.

VII. HOUSE OF TUDOR.

19. Henry VII.,		1485	72
20. Henry VIII.,		1509	73
21. Edward VI.,		1547	97
22. Mary I.,		1555	103
23. Elizabeth,		1558	111

VIII. HOUSE OF STUART.

24. James I.,		1603	131
25. Charles I.,		1625	136
THE COMMONWEALTH.			142
26. Charles II.,		1660	148
27. James II.,		1685	153
28. William III. and Mary II.,		1689	157
29. Anne,		1702	160

IX. HOUSE OF BRUNSWICK.

30. George I.,		1714	162
31. George II.,		1727	164
32. George III.,		1760	167
33. George IV.,		1820	172
34. William IV.,		1830	179
35. Victoria,		1837	182
☞ Questions on the Principal Points of English History.			190

INTRODUCTION TO
DR. LINGARD'S
HISTORY OF ENGLAND.

CHAP. I.—ROMAN BRITAIN, FROM B.C. 53, TO A.D. 449.

JULIUS CÆSAR, the famous Roman general, was engaged in the conquest of Gaul, which name then included France and Belgium, when he formed the design of invading Britain. At that period there existed some trading intercourse between those countries. From the Gallic merchants Cæsar had heard accounts of Britain, whose white cliffs were visible from where he then was, amongst the Morini (the people of Picardy.) On the 26th August, fifty-five years before the Christian era, the Roman expedition set sail, and landed near Deal; or, as some think, near Folkstone. To this event we owe the first historical notice of Britain by an eye-witness; for Cæsar, who conducted it, wrote a history of his wars, and in his book has left much interesting information concerning the country and people whose conquest he had undertaken. There is, however, in three Greek writers, earlier mention of this remarkable island, by four centuries; and it was well known for its tin mines 450, B.C. On the decline of this product in Spain, the Phœnician merchants of Cadiz and Carthage had recourse to Britain for their supplies. Indeed, so attractive had this commerce become that, at the very earliest period referred to, the country had received the appellation of "The Tin Islands."

The invasion was vainly resisted by the natives, whom Cæsar says he came to punish for the assistance they had given to the Gauls. All that he acquired, however, was the submission of a few chiefs; when, seeing the insufficiency of his forces, and the destruction of several of his galleys by a tempest, he returned to Gaul, after the brief stay of one month. Having there, during the winter, completed preparations for a fresh visit, he set out next summer, July 15th, 54 B.C., with an army of 30,000 men on board 800 galleys, for the reduction of Albion, a name derived from the white cliffs on its southeastern coasts. After the defeat of Cassivelaunus, the principal chieftain of the Britons, and the imposition of an annual tribute, the Romans crossed over once more to the continent in the September of the same year; Cæsar having merely shown them the island, as the historian Tacitus observes.

From Julius Cæsar's book on *The Gallic War* we learn the most interesting and trustworthy information of the ancient Britons. Cloth was manufactured by the tribes along the Thames, who were of Belgic origin, and more civilised than the rest of the inhabitants. These were clad chiefly in undressed skins; or they went nearly naked, the body being generally dyed with woad, a plant which gave it a blue colour. Their dwellings were wicker huts, plastered with clay, and thatched with conical roofs, resembling those of their continental neighbours. The towns were little more than encampments, of greater or less compass, consisting of an assemblage of such rude habitations. As all barbarians show a fondness for useless or silly ornaments, they had theirs. The more considerable personages wore chains of iron or brass suspended from the neck, and rings of the same metals on the second finger of each hand. For weapons they had the spear, the knife, and the arrow. In great contests, as with the Romans, they made use of chariots, whose axles were armed with scythes, capable of inflicting terrible wounds by their rapid rotation. In the southern parts they had a simple knowledge of tillage, which enabled them to raise more corn than was wanted for immediate consumption; but, in the middle and remote districts, neither agriculture nor manufacture appears to have been known. The flesh of wild animals and of cattle entered largely into their diet; and, we are told by Cæsar, that they kept geese and hares for pleasure, although they did not use those creatures for food. However simple their primitive mode of life, yet their polished invader did not regard the southern tribes as absolute barbarians. He even expresses his admiration of their war-chariots drawn by trained horses; and also of the skill displayed in the defences of their towns and fortifications. There is, besides, reason to believe that, at the commencement of the Christian era, the Britons exported corn, cattle, slaves and peltry, iron, tin, and lead. The precious metals have been also included, but the assertion is hardly credible. A further advance in civilisation is mentioned, that is, coined money; but this is still less probable, until the Roman settlement was regularly effected.

Much is not known concerning the form of government or civil polity. The ruling powers appear to have been divided among the chieftains of the several tribes, amounting at one time to, at least, forty. This division of authority was sometimes increased, by the father in possession sharing it amongst his heirs. The widow sometimes succeeded her deceased prince, and led her warriors to battle. As the ideas concerning the right of succession were loose, it was often set aside by the ambitious and popular. The rivalry of neighbouring tribes and states gave rise to petty wars, petty conquests, and perpetual uneasiness. Intestine factions ever flourished; and their savage liberty led to their speedy subjugation.

The national religion was called Druidism, from the Greek word *drus*, an oak; which tree and its parasite the mistletoe, were objects of the profoundest veneration. They also adored gods, similar in their attributes to some of the false deities of Greece and Rome. Human victims were sometimes sacrificed by the priests, called Druids; who possessed boundless influence; acted as physicians and judges; and lived a sort of mysterious life in the gloom of the forest and the cavern. They also pretended to be familiar with a sacred knowledge, for which the vulgar were disqualified, and which they accordingly communicated only to illustrious pupils. This knowledge embraced fate, the will of the gods, the starry influences, the laws of creation, the virtues of plants, and the forecast of the future. They taught, moreover, the great doctrine of the immortality of the soul; but they combined with it the old oriental fiction of its transmigration. They had acquired a continental celebrity, and their instruction was sought by the Druids of Gaul and others. The principal seat of their superstition was the Isle of Anglesey; where the priests, priestesses, sacred groves and altars were devoted to unsparing destruction by the Roman commander Suetonius, A.D. 78. Those of the priests who practised poetry and music, were called bards.

After Cæsar's departure Britain was free from Roman intrusion for nearly a century. Neither of the emperors, Augustus nor Tiberius, found an opportunity of undertaking its subjection. Adminius, a banished son of Cymbeline, one of Cassibelan's successors, surrendered the island, as if it were his patrimony, to Caligula. This imperial madman conducted a large army to Boulogne. Having marshalled it on the sea-coast, he had himself rowed in his galley to a short distance from the shore. On his return, he announced to the legions that they had conquered the ocean, and ordered them to collect, as trophies of their victory, the shells on the beach. But his successor, Claudius, was more serious. Instigated by another exiled chief, he despatched an expedition under Aulus Plautius, who was bravely resisted by Caradoc, or *Caractacus*, as the Romans called him. But the emperor himself, with reinforcements, having joined Plautius, A.D. 43, the British chief was forced to submit. Claudius returned to Rome, which he entered in triumph; having given the command of the legions between Plautius and Vespasian, who was afterwards emperor. But Caractacus, unable to bear his humiliation, soon broke out into hostilities, which he contrived to wage for nine years, with various fortunes. He was at last completely overthrown by Ostorius Scapula, the successor of Plautius. Into his hands the unfortunate prince was betrayed by his stepmother, to whom he had fled for concealment. As he and his family were led captives through Rome, he gave utterance to his astonishment at the Romans for coveting the hovels of Britain, who had such palaces at home. Claudius, seated on an elevated throne, beheld the mournful procession of his fallen foes; and, moved with noble compassion, ordered the British hero to be set free. Resistance had not entirely ceased with the capture of Caractacus; but Suetonius Paulinus followed up previous victories, till he had almost exterminated the Druids and their institutions by the sack and burning of Anglesey.

On his return thence he had to face Boadicea, queen of the Iceni, whom the seizure of her patrimony by the Roman procurator, had driven into insurrection. She burnt London and Verulam, now *St. Alban's;* but, ultimately vanquished, she poisoned herself, A.D. 61, in the reign of Nero. Vespasian and his son Titus, the conqueror of Jerusalem, greatly distinguished themselves by their military exploits in Britain; but the conquest of the island was not completed till the arrival of Agricola, A.D. 78. His wise and merciful administration produced more permanent effects than the prowess of his legions, could have effected. The leaders were attracted from their fastnesses to reside in the towns seized or founded by their civilized masters, who now began to teach the arts of life, to create an admiration of their government and discipline, and to sow the seeds of a superior intelligence and inquiry. He was the first to make the incursive Caledonians feel the weight of the Roman arms; having defeated their general Galgacus in his endeavours to defend the passes of the Grampians. His immediate successors were busied for a period of thirty years in efforts to bring the island to a still more orderly state, so as to make it harmonize with the other dependencies of the empire. The desultory attacks of the Caledonians, however, greatly retarded the progress of improvement, till the emperor Hadrian came over to repress them. For this purpose, he caused a rampart of earth to be constructed, sixty miles in length, from the Tyne to Solway Firth, A.D. 121; and to introduce more order into the public administration, the island was constituted a province of the empire.

During the reign of Hadrian's successor, Antoninus, Lollius, the governor of Britain, erected another fortification, A.D. 138, from the Forth to the Clyde, to check the inroads of the northern tribes, whose temporary quiet was usually employed in making preparations for a fresh revolt. In honour of the emperor this was called the *vallum* of Antoninus. For the same purpose, it was found necessary to strengthen Hadrian's line of defence by a stone wall a few paces in advance of it. It is known as the Picts' Wall; or, the Wall of Severus, during whose visit to the island, it was constructed. It extended sixty-eight miles, and was twelve feet high, and eight feet thick. It coursed over mountains and through valleys, and has left remains which are still viewed with surprise. Severus was an old and decaying man when he took the command of the British legions; and died at York, A.D. 211.

A state of tranquillity ensued which lasted for seventy years, when the Franks and Saxons began to infest the shores, which the empire, inwardly distracted and weakened, was ill able to protect. The emperor Dioclesian, however, showed his solicitude, by appointing Carausius, with the title of "Count of the Saxon shore," to the command of the Roman fleet. But this able soldier was led into a treasonable correspondence with the enemy. He revolted; assumed the title of highest dignity, that of Augustus; and invaded Gaul. His acquisitions there were soon wrested back by the activity of the emperor Constantius; and his life was forfeited to the treachery of his ambitious colleague, Allectus. This usurper died some time before Constantius had landed to dethrone and punish him. Under the mild administration of this governor, the natives enjoyed most of the blessings of peace; but the general persecution proclaimed by Dioclesian did not fail to reach the Christian portion.

The introduction of Christianity into Britain is involved in much obscurity. Some assert that it was first preached by St. Peter; and others by St. Paul; but Dr. Lingard confesses that the testimony in favour of either is slender and unsatisfactory. There is no need of any excess of zeal in deciding the first apostleship, especially when the evidence is defective or doubtful. It is much more important to trace the progress of the faith, with the fidelity due to every kind of history, than to frame a narrative from ill-supported and improbable statements. It is not doubted but that within very few years from the Ascension, Christian converts made their appearance, and multiplied in many places at a remote distance from Rome. It is probable that several of these had received their gift in that city; and, perhaps, from the very lips of those illustrious Apostles; and it is equally probable that such favoured persons often became active evangelists themselves, although without any ministering or sacerdotal power. Indeed, it is certain that the first disciples secretly propagated the faith with devout earnestness; so that, like the Baptist, they may have been the precursors of the more public and distinguished preachers, invested with priestly or episcopal functions. Some particulars, however, little short of absolute fact, connected with early British Christianity, are very interesting. Claudia, wife of Pudens, the senator with whom St. Paul lodged, was a British lady, and the supposed daughter of Caractacus, whose family were exiles when the Apostle was in Rome. Pomponia, wife of the proconsul Plautius, who has been mentioned in connection with the Roman conquest, was also a Christian. As persecution had not visited Britain until a late period, the Christian doctrine made so much progress as to have penetrated among the northern tribes before the close of the second century. Before the close of the third we can discover the outlines of a regular hierarchy; and, in the Council of Arles, A.D. 314, among the bishops present, we find Elborius of York, Restitutus of London, and Adelphius of Lincoln.

It was a few years before this date that Dioclesian's persecution fell on Britain. The native protomartyr St. Alban suffered at Verulam in 303. Two years after, on the resignation of Dioclesian and Maximian, Constantius and Galerius assumed the purple; and religious freedom was again permitted. One of the new emperors was that Constantius Chlorus, the humane governor of Britain, who, by Helena, a presumed native, was the father of Constantine the great, the first Christian emperor, and the most remarkable man that ever bore that title. Constantius died, A.D. 306, at York, where his son was born. Before his parent's decease he had arrived from the Continent in time to be recommended to those legions, whose hardy valour soon made him undisputed master of the Roman empire.

For more than half a century after this event, the Britons enjoyed protection and rest; but as decay seized the extremities of the empire, the northern tribes revived their encroachments, and put an end to public quiet and security. Those tribes are known in history as the Picts and Scots; the former being probably the Caledonians under an altered appellation; and the latter, a colony from the north of Ireland, then called Scotia; originally led by Fergus the First, who, so successfully pushed his conquests and alliances, as to have become the founder of the Scottish monarchy, which lasted for about twelve centuries. The armies of the Roman provinces were required to defend Italy, and even the capital itself, against crowds of barbarians, pouring forth from the banks of the Rhine and the Danube, and the shores of the Baltic and of the German Ocean. At length, in the reign of Honorius, the Britons were left totally undefended; and when aid was sought from the emperor against their northern enemies, they were told to provide for themselves. Whereupon, by a fierce and resentful effort, they deposed the Roman magistrates, and drove back for a time the Picts and Scots.

Rivalry for power, and the dissensions bred by it, again invited the aggressions of the northerns. The weakness caused by internal feuds was increased by a famine and pestilence. The natives, no longer capable of unaided resistance, became the prey of their neighbours. In such extremities Vortigern, one of the British princes, engaged the assistance of the brothers Hengist and Horsa, who commanded a Saxon fleet, at that time cruising in the channel, A.D. 449. The Saxons landed at Ebbsfleet, and were cantoned in the island of Thanet.

CHAPTER II.—ANGLO-SAXON PERIOD TO ALFRED.
FROM A.D. 449 TO 901.

FOR some time Hengist and Horsa served their employer faithfully; but, having received large reinforcements from home, they formed the design of securing territory for themselves. As, no doubt, an excuse for a rupture was vigilantly sought, the Saxons flew to arms on being refused a supply of provisions. A battle was fought at Aylesford, in which Vortigern lost a son, and Hengist his brother. But the Saxon was so far successful as, at his death, to leave Kent to his son Oisc. Ælla, a new adventurer, and a countryman of Hengist, landed in 477; and, after thirteen years of warfare, founded the kingdom of Sussex. Other Saxon leaders established in quick succession the several principalities or petty kingdoms, denominated altogether the *Saxon Heptarchy*. These, in addition to Kent and Sussex, were Essex, East Anglia, Bernicia and Deira, Wessex and Mercia. One of the kings was generally honoured with a precedency, and distinguished by the name of *Bretwalda*, or Britain-weilder.

ETHELBERT, king of Kent, was Bretwalda, when Augustine was sent by Pope Gregory the Great to convert the Saxons. He was baptized on the feast of Pentecost, A.D. 597. This prince became a very zealous convert, and endowed some sees. A difference arose between the native bishops and Augustine on points of discipline. A conference was held, but it did not end satisfactorily. The laws of Ethelbert, the earliest code on our records, were very merciful; life itself was valued at a fine called *were*.

The history of the Saxon princes is a continued scene of perfidy and murder. The Church, however, was not without some distinguished ornaments. Gildas, the most ancient British historian, flourished in the sixth century. Venerable Bede, a native of Monk Wearmouth, Durham, educated by the monks of Jarrow, was learned in all the sciences that survived the fall of the Roman empire; and author of "The Ecclesiastical History of the Angles." He died in 735. His pupil, Alcuin, who was invited to the court of France by Charlemagne, where he became the instructor of his patron, wrote on scientific and theological subjects, and closed a brilliant career in 804.

But of all the royal heptarchists the kings of Wessex were destined to act the most conspicuous part. In 688, king Caedwalla was converted by the preaching of St. Wilfrid. This noble enthusiast would not be satisfied without receiving baptism at the hands of the Pontiff himself; and was baptised in the great church of the Lateran by Pope Sergius III., by the name of Peter. Before the expiration of the period for wearing the white baptismal robes, he died, and was buried in the basilica of St. Peter. His conversion contributed largely to the diffusion of the faith. It was followed by that of his people, who spread over eight of the most considerable of our southern shires.

EGBERT, who in his youth had had the opportunity of studying the arts of government in Charlemagne's court, succeeded to the crown of Wessex, A.D. 800. By his arms and address he brought the several Anglo-Saxon nations to acknowledge his authority, and combined five of them into one great monarchy, about the year 828. In 834, the Danes of Jutland and the Baltic Islands, who had made themselves known by previous descents on the English coasts, landed on the banks of the Dart, and plundered the neighbouring country. The last exploit of Edgar was the defeat of the Danes in Cornwall during the following year. He died in 837, and was buried in Winchester, then considered the capital of England.

ETHELWOLF succeeded; and married Osberga, by whom he had four sons: Ethelbald, Ethelbert, Ethelred I. and Alfred. He went on a pilgrimage to Rome, in 855, and died at Stambridge, in Essex, 857. The sons just named, reigned in succession, without the occurrence of any important event beyond the repeated aggressions of the Danes. Ethelred died in 871; in which year, Edmund king of East Anglia was murdered by the Danish pirates, for refusing to renounce Christianity. He was canonized, and the place of his death and burial has been since called *St. Edmund's Bury*.

ALFRED, deservedly surnamed *The Great*, was in the twenty-second year of his age when he came to the sovereignty, in the midst of the troubles and confusion caused by the Danes. His education was defective; his self-government by no means wise or rigorous; but his affections were kind, and his mind noble and penetrating. He was born at Wantage in 849; and at the age of five years displayed such beauty and vivacity, that a father's fondness sent him to Rome, to be crowned at that early age by the Sovereign Pontiff. The Danes continued to make descents, and to extend their merciless depredations. Their forbearance was sometimes purchased by the native princes, and even by Alfred himself; but it was never certain; for their rapacity was regardless of faith and honour, as well as of ruth and honesty. Before long, the entire realm, with the exception of the districts north of the Tyne, and south of the Thames, came under their dominion. Alfred, unable to oppose the Danes by land, resolved on trying his fortune on the seas. His hopes were raised by the capture of a Danish ship of war. This success was followed by the retirement of the foe into Mercia. They soon, however, re-appeared in Wessex, and Alfred fled to a retreat in Somersetshire. There he patiently awaited a favourable opportunity to summon his followers to a meeting in Selwood Forest. Preparations were arranged for an attack on the Danes, then in the neighbourhood, under the command of Gothrun, who was defeated, and put to flight. He subsequently surrendered on treaty, by which he and thirty of his officers agreed to embrace Christianity. The victorious king acted as sponsor to his fallen enemy, whose future fidelity presented a striking contrast to the established character of his nation.

The immediate sequel of this treaty was a tranquillity which lasted for fifteen years, and was turned to the best account by the king in the regulations and improvements introduced into agriculture, the national defences, and the civil policy of the country. He caused fifty castles to be erected on the seacoast, as checks to the Danish pirates; greatly augmented the navy, and gave it considerable superiority over the hostile fleets by the increased strength and dimensions of his new vessels. But it was his zeal for justice and learning that so endeared this prince to his people and their posterity; and has preserved his name a treasure in the memory of mankind. He composed a code of laws, in which the most salutary statutes of Ethelbert, Ina, and Offa were incorporated. By inculcating impartiality; by punishing corruption and other judicial irregularities; by imposing fear and respect on those in power or office; by restraining insolence, and protecting the weak; he showed the advantages of legal tribunals, of strict and equal justice; restored the efficiency of trial by jury; and brought it into a repute which has recommended it to all the people, though not to all the governments, of Europe.

Equally wonderful and unwearied were his efforts to acquire knowledge himself, and to diffuse it among his subjects. The continual violence and devastations of the Danes had retarded every species of improvement, but especially that of the mind. In his time there was scarcely a scholar in Wessex who knew Latin. The prince himself was in his thirty-ninth year when he commenced the study of that language, from which he afterwards translated Bede's *Ecclesiastical History*, Boece's *Consolations of Philosophy*, and other instructive writings. He also drew together learned men from all quarters, one of the most remarkable of whom was Grimbold, provost of St. Omer. By their aid he opened several public schools. The school at Oxford was destined to be the germ of that renowned university, which has been long a brilliant gem in the crown of literature. In short, Alfred laid himself out for a life of practical philosophy and paternal government; and deliberately designed that it should be a pattern in wisdom and good works to all his successors. Few, very few, have imitated that pious pattern. The worth of the prince is of less esteem than the glitter of the chair he sits on.

But while he was thus civilizing his country, and bettering its social state, the plundering propensities of the Danes and Northerns again broke out. Hastings, the most renowned of their leaders, or, as they were called, Sea-kings, landed in Kent, with a large force in the year 892. The invader was defeated, but not without a fierce struggle. His wife and children fell into the hands of the victor, who mercifully restored them on condition that Hastings and his followers should leave the kingdom. Many of them sought an asylum in Normandy, where their countrymen had already founded a colony and planted their name; while others were permitted to settle in East Anglia and Northumbria.

Alfred died at Farringdon, Oct. 28, 901, in the fifty-second year of his age, and was interred at Winchester. By his wife, Elswitha, a Mercian princess, he left two sons and three daughters, among whom he divided his lands; but his money he bequeathed chiefly for charitable and religious purposes. He was succeeded by his second son Edward.

CHAP. III.—ANGLO-SAXON AND DANISH PERIODS,

FROM A.D. 901 TO 1066.

EDWARD I., surnamed *The Elder*, was crowned at Kingston, in Surrey. His title was disputed by Ethelwald, the son of Alfred's elder brother. Ethelwald was an orphan child when his rights were set aside by the *Witenagemot*, or national assembly of the Wise, in favour of the maturer qualifications of his uncle; a kind of policy, not unusual at this period; but which often entailed the evils of a disputed succession. The contest between those rivals, lasted for a long time. The death of Ethelwald, who fell in battle, put an end to it. This event afforded Edward the opportunity of completely mastering the northern Danes, incorporating Mercia, and abolishing all traces of a separate government. He also imposed a tribute on Wales; and compelled the Scots to acknowledge him as their chief. After a fortunate reign of twenty-four years in which he displayed much ability and vigour, he died at Farringdon, in 925; and was buried at Winchester. His successor, was his eldest son, Athelstan.

ATHELSTAN, who from the complete establishment of his power, has been called the first monarch of all England, was crowned at Kingston, by Anthelm, archbishop of Canterbury. On the death of Sightric, he invaded Northumbria, and drove out the Danish princes. But one of them, Anlaf, organised a powerful league against him, composed of Danes, Normans, Scotch, and Irish. The defeat of the allies at Brunanburgh, in Northumbria, completed and confirmed the sway of the English king. One of his sisters was married to Hugo, father of the founder of the *Capetian* Kings of France.

This able, just, and charitable prince died, midst universal regret and admiration in the year 941; and was succeeded by his brother Edmund I. then in his nineteenth year.

EDMUND I. soon experienced the restless daring of the Danes, relieved from the terror of his predecessor's arms. After quelling their revolt, he fell beneath the knife of Leof or Liofa, an outlaw; leaving two sons, Edwin, and Edgar, whose rights were, on account of infancy, postponed by the nobles and clergy. For the same reason, the claims of Athelstan's children were passed by, and his brother Edred chosen by the thanes and ecclesiastics.

EDRED was crowned in the year 946, and reigned ten years. He made Osulf, one of his generals, earl of Northumberland, which he divided into shires; and rebuilt Glastonbury abbey, of which the celebrated Dunstan became abbot.

EDWY now, A. D. 955, came into his rights at the age of seventeen, by general consent. St. Dunstan, from his opposition to the King's partiality for his beautiful cousin Ethelgiva, was driven into exile. The Archbishop of Canterbury succeeded in driving out this romantic lady whose conduct, at all events, subsequent to Edwy's marriage, does not appear to have been blameless. She is thought to have been put to death by the Mercians; who also compelled the king to divide his territory with his brother Edgar. In this prince the unity of the realm was restored by the sudden death of Edwy in 959.

EDGAR immediately recalled Dunstan, and promoted him from one see to another, till that of Canterbury became the reward of his courage and consistency. He received the surname of *the Peaceable*, from the uniform quiet, which marked his government. In the administration both of church and state affairs, he evinced foresight, vigilance, and high integrity of purpose. He founded fifty Benedictine monasteries to minister to the necessities temporal and eternal of the poor, to extend education, and to promote agriculture and arts of rural life. To rid the Welsh of wolves, he changed their money tribute into one of three hundred heads of those destructive animals to be presented yearly. He was twice married. The story told by William of Malmsbury of his second wife Elfrida, is looked on as a romantic fable. He was not crowned till the fourteenth year of his reign. He died in 975, two years after the ceremony; and was succeeded by his son Edward, surnamed the *Martyr*.

EDWARD II., at the age of thirteen, mounted the throne by the aid of Dunstan, in spite of a strong party, created by his step-mother Elfrida, in favour of her son Ethelred, who was but seven years old. He perished in the fourth year of his reign, by the hands an assassin, instigated it is supposed, by his step-mother. The deed was perpetrated at the door of her residence, Corfe Castle, while the king was taking a drink on horseback, after the fatigues of the chase.

ETHELRED obtained quiet possession in 978, at the age of ten. The Danes, having observed what little love subsisted between the king and his subjects, renewed their old enterprises. The public calamities and discontent were increased by a scarcity of food, a pest among the cattle, and a fatal dysentery among the people. He conceived the inhuman project of a general massacre of the Danes, which was carried into execution the 13th November, 1003. To avenge this slaughter, Sweyn, whose sister had been one of the victims, landed the following year with a formidable force. After having amply gratified his wrath, by four years' havoc, he consented to desist on receiving thirty six thousand pounds of silver; which was raised by a tax called Danegelt; and was the first levied on land. But a repetition of hostilities was the natural consequence of such a bargain with barbarians. A large fleet, which had been collected together for the defence of the nation, having been dispersed by mixed misfortunes—a defection of several captains, and a violent storm—Sweyn boldly resolved on the conquest of the whole island. Many towns submitted, and the king fled, 1014; but in the mid of his career the Dane died. Ethelred was reinstated. Canute or Cnute, the son of Sweyn was compelled to retire; but returned the following year with a large fleet. This event hastened the death of the king, whose constitution had been for some time declining fast. After a calamitous reign of thirty-eight years, by which he gained the surname of *The Unready,* he ended life in 1016; and was succeeded by Edmund, his son by his first wife, Elgiva.

EDMUND, surnamed *Ironsides,* maintained his cause against Canute so valiantly that the latter readily agreed to a division of the country into two independent sovereignties. The Saxon prince survived this compact only seven months, when his decease left Canute monarch.

CANUTE, surnamed *The Great,* was destined to be not only one of the greatest princes of his time, but also one of the best on the records of history. He was master of England, Denmark, Norway, and Sweden, regions inhabited by the hardiest and most enterprising spirits in Europe. At first he was jealous, vindictive and despotic; but he was cautious and politic; and of an understanding so sound that he was not long in discovering his errors, and not averse from hearing them censured. He sent Edward's children out of the kingdom, and thought it advisable to marry Emma, the widow of Ethelred. Perhaps it is to the influence of this lady, that we should attribute Canute's total change of behaviour. The principles of Christian justice and charity, soon became visible in him. His conduct and administration warmed the affections of his English subjects into enthusiasm. A story is told that as he was sitting on the sea shore at Southampton, he commanded the flowing tide to advance no further, and affected to await its obedience. As the water reached him, he turned on his attendants, and made an observation that served at once to rebuke the flatteries of dependents, to exalt the Omnipotent Majesty, and to exhibit the arrogance and feebleness of man. Canute paid a religious visit to Rome, in 1026, and died in 1035. He left by Emma, a son, Hardicanute, and a daughter Gunihlda; and also, by Alfgive, two illegitimate sons—Sweyn, who became king of Norway; and Harold, of England.

HAROLD, surnamed *Harefoot,* from his swiftness, was raised to the throne by a powerful party, notwithstanding the juster rights of Hardicanute. His intrusion did not last long, for he died in 1039, and was succeeded by the better claimant, with whom, however, a subdivision had been previously arranged, in order to avert a civil war. Emma's sons, by her first husband, Ethelred, were the true heirs. One of them, Alfred, was inveigled over from Normandy on a pretence of supporting his claims; treacherously seized; and condemned to lose his eyes. Of this cruelty he died.

HARDICANUTE, as soon as tidings of Harold's death reached him, hastened home and was acknowledged without delay or dispute. He wreaked his vengeance on the remains of his predecessor, which he caused to be disinterred. The motive he assigned was the murder of Alfred, his half brother; but his indignation was easily appeased by the present of a ship from Godwin, who had the chief part in entrapping the prince. He died while drinking at a marriage-feast in Lambeth, 1041. He was the last of the Danish kings, a race who had usurped the sceptre for twenty-eight years.

EDWARD *The Confessor*, son of Ethelred and Emma, was called to the throne by the unanimous voice of the citizens of London. The rightful heir was the son of Edmund Ironside; but he was far away in Hungary. At the time of his election, Edward was forty years of age, twenty-seven of which had been spent in exile in Normandy. His natural disposition was amiable; and he improved it by the serious cultivation of moral principles and practical piety. At his accession he experienced some uneasiness from three powerful chiefs, Godwin, Leofric, and Siward; upon whose mutual jealousies depended his immediate security. From a sense of insecurity, as it is justly supposed, he married Editha, earl Godwin's daughter, in 1044. He declared that she might enjoy the honours of a queen, but not the rights of a wife; a declaration variously explained. Edward had acquired a partiality for the Normans, which he had not the prudence to conceal. His preference provoked the national hatred of the Anglo-Saxon thanes. Earl Godwin, his son Harold and others, rose in arms, and advanced against the Normans of Herefordshire; but they were deserted by their adherents, and fled. The Norman families had invited William, duke of Normandy, to their assistance. On his arrival he found the insurgents had dispersed; so he went back laden with magnificent presents from the king. Godwin and Harold sued for pardon and obtained it. The earl did not long survive. It is related that, one day at table, the king having hinted at the share Godwin had in Alfred's death, the earl wished that the next morsel he ate might kill him, if he had any part in the crime. The wish was fatal; and the king bestowed the vacant earldom on Harold, his brother-in-law.

This nobleman was now the most powerful of English subjects. His position easily excited the duke William's jealousy, who justly gave him credit for ambitious views corresponding with his own. An accident put him in the way of trying and thwarting Harold. The latter was shipwrecked on the coast of Normandy. William, taking advantage of his helpless state, exacted from him homage as his future lord. It is also asserted that Harold swore, on holy relics, that he would promote William's succession on the death of Edward. The king's death soon put the sincerity of this oath to the test. He died January 5th, 1066, to the inexpressible grief of all his subjects, and was buried in Westminster Abbey, whose completion, long an object of his solicitude, he barely lived to witness. His bones were enshrined in a golden casket, set with gems, by order of the *Conqueror*. He was canonized by Pope Alexander III., in 1163. Henry III. honoured his remains with a new and more costly shrine. So venerated was this pious monarch, and such an impression had the equity and mercy of his administration made on his subjects and their posterity, that for ages after, when the people complained of oppression and sued for their rights, they never thought of demanding more than the restoration of "the laws and customs of the good king Edward." The idea of a character so perfect is easily conceived and easily delineated. To know how he lived, and how he was beloved; what he did, and how it was appreciated; is quite enough to fill the mind with such a variety of pleasing images and coloured fancies, as anticipates the nicest efforts of language.

It was in this reign that Macbeth killed Duncan, and usurped the throne of Scotland. Edward espoused the cause of Malcolm, the lawful heir, and sent to his aid Siward, earl of Northumberland, who defeated Macbeth at Dunsinnane in Perthshire.

HAROLD II., favoured by a report, put into circulation by his party, of his having been nominated by the deceased king as his successor, was immediately proclaimed. The first opposition he met with proceeded from his brother Tostig, who sought to regain his power in Northumbria, with the aid of Hardrada, king of Norway. Harold defeated the confederates in the bloody battle of Stamford Bridge, in which

THE NORMAN INVASION. 17

both of his opponents perished. The victory had been scarcely won when news came to him of the landing of William on the coast of Sussex. Harold had peremptorily refused fulfilling his oath to the duke, on the plea of its having been extorted. The latter came to wrest, by means of a large army, what, perhaps, he never seriously expected to obtain quietly. The battle which was destined at once to decide this memorable argument, was fought within nine miles of Hastings, at a spot called Senlac, since known as *Battle*, October 14th, 1066. The Anglo-Saxon forces, all on foot, were massed on a declivity, and commanded by the three brothers, Harold, Gurth, and Leofwin. There, with their bows, bills, and axes, they awaited the attack of the Normans. About nine in the morning William put his army in motion to assault the enemy on his vantage ground. His archers and bowmen composed the first line; his heavy infantry in coats of mail the second; behind those were arranged the knights and men-at-arms. The last were troops to which the adversary had nothing to oppose. Yet their strength was economized; it was brought into play only at the critical juncture: at all events not until some good service was taken out of the two lines in advance. The English fought with great courage and firmness. They gained some advantages, which they too eagerly pursued. They were also drawn away from their solid order by two or three well-managed feints. It was upon those occasions that their discipline and equipments were brought to bear; and then they told with overwhelming effect. But corslet and helmet must give way to the battle-axe wielded by multitudes. The left wing of the Normans fled. The duke was reported to have fallen. The wavering of doubt and dismay began to spread, when William rode through the ranks bareheaded, helmet in hand, shouting and encouraging; and arresting that fatal stagger which preludes flight and ruin. The fury of the contest slackened and raged through several hours of terrible slaughter, during which both of Harold's brothers fell. The defeat of his first advantages deprived him of all hope of advance. For a long time he could do no more than maintain a dauntless front, and resist the repeated onslaughts of his steel-cased assailants. The issue that could not be avoided, was precipitated by the fall of Harold, who was killed by an arrow which entered the eye. This disaster happened about sunset, and was soon followed by the dispersion of the remnant of the Anglo-Saxon army. Of the carnage we have no reliable ac-

C

count. The Normans amounted to 60,000; and, if it be true that they lost one-fourth, which is not improbable in so bloody and protracted a fray, the loss on the other side may be estimated at thrice that number.

With Harold and his brother perished all the nobility of the south of England. His mother, even for a great ransom, was refused his body, which William desired to be buried on the beach, observing that, " as he guarded the coast while alive, let him guard it after death." His remains, however, were stealthily removed to the church of Waltham, of which he was the founder.

Thus ended the Anglo-Saxon period, which lasted for more than six centuries.

CHAP. IV.—MANNERS AND CUSTOMS OF THE ANGLO-SAXONS.

OF Saxon institutions, the most important were derived from the Germans, as they are described by Tacitus. From him we learn, that every chieftain was surrounded by retainers, who honoured him in time of peace, and accompanied him in his wars. To fight by his side was a duty; to survive his fall a disgrace. When the northern hordes went forth on their military expeditions, or in search of new settlements, it was this artificial connection, reciprocally binding the lord and the vassal, that held them together. Its consequences gradually developed themselves, as the tribes became fixed in their new habitations; and ultimately took the feudal form, with all its obligations of homage, suit, and service. The feudal system existed among the Saxons, though not in its most oppressive features, before the Norman Conquest. Its fundamental principle was, that of all the ties which society had invented, the most sacred was that which bound together the lord and the vassal.

Amongst the Anglo-Saxons the free population was divided into the *eorl* or noble, and the *ceorl* or ignoble. The *cyning* or king, occupied the first place; he was lord of the principal chieftains, and, through them, of their vassals. The great tenants of the crown were summoned at Easter, Whitsuntide, and Christmas, to pay homage to the king; and feasted for eight days at his expense. He was supreme judge, and revised appeals from all other courts.

The *ealdormen* or earls, ranked next to the king and royal family. They governed districts, then and still, called shires;

and sometimes more shires than one. They presided with the bishops in the shire courts, and saw the law carried out; they also led the men of the shire to battle. The *thanes* were a numerous and distinguished order, and next in rank to the earls. Of them there were two classes; the greater were thanes of the king; the less, thanes of the earl. For various administrative purposes, the king appointed other officers called *reeves*; such as the *borough-reeve*, the *port-reeve*, the *shire-reeve*, or sheriff.

In criminal cases, the accused was at liberty to prove his innocence, by the purgation of *lada*, or swearing; or by the *ordeal*, or judgment of God. In support of his own oath, he produced his compurgators, who swore that "they believed his oath to be upright and clean;" and the compurgators themselves should be resident within the jurisdiction of the court, blameless freeholders, and known to all present for *true men*. The number of those compurgators or jurors varied according to the custom of the locality. In Wessex, the party could choose thirty, of whom fifteen were rejected by the judges; in East Anglia and Northumbria, forty-eight, of whom half were appointed by ballot. If they corroborated his oath by their own, he was acquitted; if not, he may appeal to the ordeal, or proof by hot water, or by fire.

The principal crimes were homicide and theft. When the murderer was taken he could not be put to death for thirty days. If by that he failed to pay or give security for the *were*, or fine, at which murder was legally rated; he might be put to death by the relatives of the murdered man.

During the whole Anglo-Saxon period, the traffic in slaves prevailed. They were disposed of in the public market; and it is supposed that a slave was valued at four times as much as an ox. While the export of native slaves was prohibited, the import of foreign ones was not hindered. The Northumbrians are said to have carried off their own countrymen, even their relations and friends, to make sale of them at foreign ports. The people of Bristol were the last to relinquish this infamous commerce. Their agents travelled through every part of the country to make purchases, especially for the Irish market, where there was a quick sale with good prices. The unwearied preaching of Wulstan, bishop of Worcester, at last overcame the cupidity of the Bristol merchants, and they abandoned this guilty but profitable trade.

It is very difficult to trace the early municipal polity of the

Anglo-Saxons; for the history of their ancient towns and boroughs is lost in the gloom of ages. It is only towards the close of the Saxon dynasty that the materials for speculation or enquiry begin to appear. From all that can be gathered it seems that the principles of government which existed in the surrounding country, prevailed likewise in the towns. In both the lord and the tenant are seen. The lord is accompanied by his reeve and his court; possesses his right of tollage; and claims his rents, fines and forfeitures. On the other hand, the tenant holds of his lord by every variety of service, from that which was deemed honourable, to the lowest and most humiliating. In the towns, however, the inhabitants gradually acquired advantages denied to their equals in the country. They had the benefit of markets, for the sale of their wares and merchandise; they were protected by their numbers and union from robbers and banditti; and formed one body politic with common rights and interests. They had their hall or hanse-house for meeting and deliberating; they exercised the power of passing by or borough laws for the improvement of their borough; and possessed by lease or purchase, houses and lands for their common benefit.

The principal magistrate was the *wic-reove*, or provost, who in the more populous towns was an officer of great importance, and sometimes reckoned amongst the noblest in the land. He collected the revenue of the king or lord; and exercised within his borough the same authority as the sheriff did within his shire. London, Winchester, York, and Exeter, possessed powers and privileges which frequently determined affairs of state, and influenced the most important political events; and the liberties of England are, perhaps, as much indebted to the hereditary spirit of the corporation of London, as to all the parliaments that ever sat at Westminster.

CHAP. V.—THE NORMAN LINE.
1. WILLIAM I., surnamed THE CONQUEROR.

William was the illegitimate son of Robert, the fifth duke of Normandy, by Herleva or Arlette, daughter of a tanner of Falaise. He succeeded his father in the dukedom by consent of the Norman barons. His wife was Matilda, daughter of Baldwin, count of Flanders.

After the battle of Hastings, Edgar, grandson of Edmund Ironside, who was the rightful heir, and surnamed *Etheling*, in mark of his noble descent, was called to the throne by the

Londoners. William immediately marched on the city, and subdued its hostility. He was crowned in Westminster Abbey, by the archbishop of York, on Christmas-day, 1066. As a recompense for the loss of the succession, he bestowed considerable tracts of land on Edgar, who acquiesced in his condition, although there were many conspiracies and revolts in his favour. Those were repressed with great vigour and speed; and punished with unrestrained fury. To the vengeance of William it is said that 100,000 victims were sacrificed. The best part of the north of England was laid waste; so that for years, not a cultivated spot was to be seen, between York and Durham. To put as much hindrance as possible in the way of nocturnal conspiracy, he commanded that all persons should be within doors by sunset, and that all domestic fires should be put out at the tolling of an evening bell, called Curfew, (*couvre-feu*) from the injunction. What the Conqueror did by necessity and for precaution, may be excused; but as he was naturally cruel, rapacious, and arbitrary, he paid no respect to the persons, the properties, or the feelings of his new subjects. He appropriated immense tracts, belonging to the thanes and earls, to his parks and forests, which he multiplied in every direction, driving out like a worthless herd, the immediate tenants and servants without pity or remorse. He made a forest, which is called aforesting, of the whole country between the Avon and the bay of Southampton, for the more convenient amusement of his court; and passed the most barbarous laws to secure the game to the favoured few. The district thus devastated, covered thirty square miles, and is known still as the New Forest.

Malcolm, king of Scotland, married to Margaret, sister of Edgar, whose cause he espoused, was completely defeated by William. Having thrown himself on the victor's mercy, he was allowed to retain his crown; but, as a vassal.

Provoked by a derisive jest of the French king, William invaded France. At the burning of the town of Mantes, his horse trod into hot ashes, and, plunging, bruised the rider against the pommel of the saddle. The injury was fatal. On his death-bed, in presence of the clergy and nobles, he left Normandy to his eldest son, Robert, as his right; England, to William, his second son; and a legacy of 5,000 crowns to Henry, the youngest. Those children had been giving him a great deal of uneasiness, by their mutual jealousies, and their disobedience to himself. Robert rebelled openly, and seized Normandy. His father proceeded to recover it. At the siege of Gerberoi, 1077, parent and son, unknown to each other, met in mortal combat. They were reconciled by Matilda.

Never had a vanquished people to endure such vehement and indiscriminate a tyranny as William exercised over the Anglo-Saxon nation. The whole race, of whatsoever rank, were excluded from all offices of trust and honour. Even the native bishops, under various pretexts, were removed to make way for Normans or other foreigners. Lanfranc, a Piedmontese, superseded Stigand in the archsee of Canterbury; he was indeed worthy of his dignity. Other appointments were also well filled; but this does not remove the injustice of the motive. The use of the vulgar tongue was forbidden in legal proceedings and in the courts of judicature. The feudal laws, which were grievously oppressive to a people who had enjoyed the mild institutions of the Confessor, were introduced. To make the process of taxation easy he caused an account to be taken of all the property in the kingdom, and put together in a book, called *Doomsday Book*, and still preserved in the Rolls' Library. To overawe his new subjects he built several castles and strongholds, among others, Norwich, Winchester, York, Nottingham, Hereford, and the Tower of London.

William of Normandy was under the middle size; strongly built; inclined to be fat; of a stern aspect, but commanding presence. He was brave, hardy, overbearing, and violent. He neither spared person in his passion; nor property in his cupidity. But as a prince and a politician, he was not surpassed by any man of his time. He laid the foundations of the firmest monarchy, the widest empire, and the greatest people of which history presents a record.

He lingered a few weeks after his hurt; died at Rouen, Sept. 9th, 1087; and was buried at Caen.

2. WILLIAM II., surnamed RUFUS.

William, who got his surname from the *red* colour of his hair, hastened from the bedside of his father, to England, where, upon promises of good government made to the Norman nobles, he was crowned at Westminster, by Lanfranc, Sept. 26, 1087.

Odo, bishop of Bayeux, his father's half-brother, raised up a powerful party among the Normans, in favour of Robert's claims; but they were defeated; for Rufus won over the English to his side by liberal and tempting promises. Odo was driven from England, and the estates of his adherents divided among William's friends.

Robert's bad administration caused much discontent in Normandy; of which Rufus took advantage with the intention of seizing the dukedom. The brothers, however, came to an agreement, which bound them to oppose Henry, whom they drove into Bretagne. The duke shortly after mortgaged his territory for five years for 10,000 marks, (each 13s. 4d.,) to enable him to join the first Crusade, which Peter the Hermit was then preaching, under the approbation of Pope Urban the Second.

The reign of Rufus was an uneasy and turbulent one. He had to repel an invasion of the Scots under their king Malcolm III. Malcolm was besieging the Castle of Alnwick, when the garrison offered to surrender to the king in person. Robert de Mowbray presented the keys on the top of a spear; and as Malcolm reached for them, the weapon was thrust through his eye, (1093.) The story goes that this murderous act was the origin of the name Percy (*pierce-eye*), the family name of the dukes of Northumberland. William's barons were frequently in revolt, exasperated by the exactions, oppressions, and violence of their faithless, expensive and debauched monarch. He allowed no rest to church or state. He bullied the bishops, seized the revenues of vacant sees; and devoted them to profligate indulgences.

In the year 1095, while in expectation of death, he sent for Anselm, abbot of Bec, in Normandy. At the persuasion of his bishops, but much against the will of this pious and prudent man, he made Anselm archbishop of Canterbury, of which see he kept the temporalities since Lanfranc's death, in 1089. In the dispute about the papacy, between Clement and Urban, the claims of the latter were acknowledged by Anselm. But William, that he may enjoy the vacant sees more securely, sided with neither; and ordered the archbishop to be tried for treason and deposed; but this command the bishops refused to obey. The king formed a project to thwart the uncompromising prelate. He acknowledged Urban; sent to Rome for the *pallium*; but, as no one would either buy it or take it, he had to bestow it on Anselm. But there is a more likely version of this matter. As Anselm's election had not yet been confirmed by the pope, he asked for permission to go to Rome to receive the badge of distinction from the hands of the Pontiff. He had for answer that he may do as he pleased, but that his lands would be seized in case of his absence. He departed; and, as he did not return till recalled by Henry, it is probable that the journey for the pallium was a contrivance to get beyond the tyrant's reach.

William lost his life by an arrow, while hunting in the New Forest, August 2, 1100. Sir Walter Tyrrell is said to have shot the arrow, but whether by accident or design, has not been ascertained. Years after, when the admission of the accident could have been made without fear or danger, he denied it on solemn oath. The body was carted to Winchester, and buried without religious rite. He died unmarried.

In his reign the Tower was surrounded with a wall, and Westminster Hall built for a royal banqueting room. This was pulled down, and rebuilt by Richard II. In the last year of his reign, four thousand acres of land, left by earl Godwin to the monks of Canterbury, sunk under the sea. These are known as the Goodwin Sands, and are frequent scenes of shipwreck.

3. HENRY I., surnamed BEAUCLERC, The *Scholar*.

No sooner had Henry heard of his brother's death, than he rode to Winchester, and secured the royal treasures. He caused himself to be proclaimed and crowned without delay; and to secure public favour, he promulgated a charter of liberties; extended the privileges of the citizens of London; restored its ancient immunities to the Church; promised to put in force the customs of Edward the Confessor; relaxed the most obnoxious of the feudal laws; and to crown all, married Matilda, daughter of Malcolm, king of Scotland, and niece of Etheling. But Henry's security was soon threatened by Robert, who had returned from the Holy War to his duchy, within a month after the catastrophe of Rufus. Into war his own inclinations were precipitated by Flambard, the disreputable bishop of Durham, who had escaped from the prison into which Henry had thrown him. Robert landed at Portsmouth, and was on his way to Winchester, when overtaken by the king. The latter sent a messenger, requesting a conference; and an agreement was entered into, by which Robert relinquished his claims on England, in consideration of a pension of 3,000 marks, the restoration of the castles in Normandy, and the recall of all forfeitures against his adherents. But Robert, having been treacherously seized while on a visit to his friends in London, and deprived of his pension by way of ransom, set projects on foot which brought Henry to Normandy; and ended in the defeat and capture of the projector at the battle of Tinchebray, Sept. 28, 1106. Robert was confined in Cardiff Castle; where, at the age of eighty, death closed a lenient captivity of twenty-eight years. The belief that an attempt to escape was punished with the deprivation of eyesight is without sufficient evidence.

To understand the protracted dispute between Henry and Anselm some explanation must be given of the *right of investiture*. According to ancient usage, the election of bishops depended on the suffrages of the clergy and the provincial prelates. Various circumstances tended to introduce innovations into this practice; and especially the conversion of barbarous nations, among whom the missionary had generally to shape out his own diocese, without the interference of any civil authority. On the other hand, in civilised nations, and especially in the dawn of the feudal system, the *temporalities* of a see, that is its lands and revenues, were regarded as lay property: and consequently, as such vested in the crown. Since no one could enter into those temporalities without the consent of the crown, the king claimed the right of presenting the *ring* and the *crozier*, the acknowledged emblems of episcopal jurisdiction; and this ceremony is what is denominated the right of *investiture*. But kings went further. A diocese being considered a spiritual fief, it was against the prince's interest that such fiefs should fall into the hands of his enemies. Under pretence of securing himself, the real motive being the acquisition of patronage, he claimed the right of *nominating* to the see, and then of investing with ring and crozier.

As Anselm persisted in refusing collation by taking the emblems from the hands of the king, he was banished. But Henry having the fear of Pope Paschal's excommunication before his eyes, brought about an accommodation; before receiving their temporalities, fealty and homage, as being civil duties, were to be exacted from every clergyman; and the king disclaimed the right of investiture, as the *ring* and *crozier* were signs only of spiritual jurisdiction.

The unfortunate duke Robert left an heir to his rights, his vicissitudes, and his failures. His name was William. He was invested with the duchy in 1116, being then about fifteen years old, by Louis VI. of France. This king formed a confederacy in his favour, which was defeated, three years later, by Henry, at the battle of Brenville. By the treaty which followed, Normandy was added to the English crown; and accordingly Henry's son, William, did homage for it to Louis. But the accidental death of this prince gave a new life to the claims of Robert's son.

After an absence of four years, Henry prepared to return to England. At Barfleur he was solicited by a Norman mariner, one Fitz-stephen, for the honour of carrying him in his new vessel, "*The White Ship*," (La Blanche Nef.) He informed the king that it was his father who carried over Henry's, when he sailed for the conquest of England; and that he held his fee for performing such service. The vessel the king had already chosen he did not change; but to *The Blanche Nef* he entrusted his son, then in his eighteenth year; two natural children, Richard and Adela; his niece and her husband, the earl of Chester, and a knightly retinue of one hundred and twenty persons. The ship was wrecked, 1120, on sunken rocks, near the place called *Ras de Catteville*, the disaster being attributable to the intemperate jollity of the crew; or, according to the Saxon writers, to the judgment of Heaven, since the sea was perfectly calm, and the prince had been heard to declare his intention of yoking the Saxons to the plough. Bérauld, a butcher of Rouen, alone survived to give an account of this calamity. William left a widow, who was barely in her twelfth year, and had been a wife but six months. She was daughter to Fulk of Anjou, whose alliance was sought to detach him from the interests of Robert's son. The king was deeply affected by the news of his loss; and, it is said, that he was never afterwards seen to smile.

Fulk of Anjou, to whom the return of his daughter's dowry was refused, soon showed himself an active partisan on William's side. His youngest daughter Sibylla was affianced to him, and the earldom of Mans given. But Henry suddenly appeared in Normandy, and scattered Fulk's powerful confederacy.

The sagacious Fulk, conjecturing that William was born to ill luck, now withdrew Sibylla; but Louis made up the disappointment by bestowing his sister-in-law and considerable fiefs bordering Normandy, on the precarious son of Robert. To these gifts was shortly added the earldom of Flanders, which Louis had helped to rescue from Burchard de L'Isle, the murderer of Charles the Good. To this gift William had a just claim, as the representative of Matilda, his grandmother, daughter of Baldwin V.

DEATH OF HENRY II.

Queen Matilda having died in 1118, Henry gave his hand to the young and beautiful Adelais of Louvain, niece of Pope Calixtus II. As this union brought him no heirs he settled the crown, with the consent of the states of his kingdom, on his daughter Matilda, widow of the emperor Henry V. of Germany. He then gave her in marriage to Geoffrey of Anjou, who succeeded his father Fulk, when the latter accepted the shadowy title of King of Jerusalem. As this union was contracted without consulting the English and Norman barons, these conceived themselves released from their fealty to Matilda. At all events they made the proceeding an excuse for holding correspondence with Stephen, earl of Boulogne, son of Adela, the king's sister ; with William, earl of Flanders, son of duke Robert ; or with Robert, earl of Gloucester, Henry's natural son, a bold, brave, ambitious man. Henry's knowledge of the designs of those parties made him very uneasy ; but from the chief disquietude, that occasioned by William, he was speedily relieved. The Flemings rose against an earl given them without their concurrence, and chose Henry Landgrave of Alsace. William defeated them and their English and Norman allies under the walls of Alost ; but he received a wound in the hand from a pike, which shortly after mortified, and caused his death, 1127. The nature of his affairs still demanded the king's presence in Normandy, where he was seized with his last illness, brought on, it is said, by a surfeit of lampreys. He died at St. Denis Le Froment, 1135, a year after his brother Robert ; and left his daughter, Matilda, heir to all his possessions. He was buried in the abbey of Reading, of which he was the founder.

As his character is easily inferred from the transactions in which we have seen him engaged, it is only necessary to observe that its leading feature was duplicity in both its forms, concealment or pretence. When Bloet, bishop of Lincoln, one of his principal justiciaries, was told that the king had spoken of him in the most flattering terms, he exclaimed that he was undone, for he never heard his majesty praise a man whom he did not intend to ruin. His apprehensions were justified by the sequel. The prelate had boasted that the monastery he was building should equal Reading. The words were carried to the king, who stript his justiciary of his office and his wealth ; and who, perhaps, would have deprived him of his see, had not death anticipated him. It must also be remembered that in the distribution of royal favours during this long reign, no services, no talents, could expiate in an Englishman the original sin of his nativity.

4. STEPHEN OF BLOIS.

Henry's nephew, Stephen, was count of Blois, in right of his father; and earl of Boulogne, in right of his wife Matilda. He had received many favours of the late king, and was the first to take the oath of fealty to Matilda, when Henry had assembled the nobles for that purpose at Windsor, in 1126. He now took the earliest opportunity to break it.

He had long been the most popular nobleman in England; had many adherents amongst the clergy and the people; his brother was the influential bishop of Winchester; and he was aware of the strong repugnance of the barons to hold their fiefs of a female sovereign. Accordingly he lost no delay in hastening to London, Winchester, and other places where he was welcomed and proclaimed. He was crowned, with the least possible delay, at Westminster, Dec. 26th, 1135, and lived through a turbulent reign of nine years, undistinguished by any event of more than ordinary occurrence. By abstaining from plundering the Church, from oppressing laymen, and from levying *danegelt*, he greatly strengthened his popularity; by a prodigal distribution of the royal treasures, he attracted crowds of supporters; and by his courtesy, affability, and kindness often disarmed an adversary.

Matilda's uncle, David I., king of Scots, was the first to assert her rights. He invaded England, and compelled the inhabitants of Carlisle, Alnwick and Newcastle to take the oath to Matilda. But his forebearance was easily won. He was also uncle to Stephen's wife. On receiving the towns of Carlisle, Doncaster, and Huntingdon, for which his son Henry did homage, he withdrew from what he thought, perhaps, a perilous position. But he reappeared in the cause of the empress in 1138, provoked, it is supposed, by Stephen's refusal to give him the earldom of Northumberland. But he suffered a terrible defeat at Northallerton, in an engagement called the Battle of the Standard, from the rude signal hastily set up on the occasion: a ship's mast surmounted by a cross. It was by the energetic exertions of Thurston, the aged archbishop of York, that this rising was quelled.

In September, 1139, Matilda landed on the coast of Suffolk, with one hundred and forty knights; and was soon joined by her half-brother Robert, duke of Gloucester. The battle of

DEATH OF STEPHEN.

Lincoln was soon fought, in which Stephen became Robert's prisoner, and was conveyed to Bristol Castle.

Change of fortune brings on a change of friends. Many of the most influential of Stephen's party deserted to the empress; among others, his brother Henry, bishop of Winchester. In this city her coronation was performed in the year 1141. Thence she proceeded to London, where her entry was attended with general acclamation; and order taken for the repetition of that ceremony. Meanwhile, her disdain, arrogance, and exactions alienated her best friends. When Stephen offered to relinquish his pretensions, on condition of his son Eustace being secured the earldoms of Boulogne and Moretoil, her great partisan the bishop of Winchester, who brought the proposal, was haughtily refused. An attempt to levy exorbitant tallage on the citizens of London brought the crisis. They rose, drove her out, and made way for the rival queen.

Henry of Winchester again veered with the breeze of prosperity; and hoisted Stephen's standard on his palace, which he fortified, as well as on Winchester Castle. Gloucester laid siege to it; but his rear having been attacked by the London army, his troops were routed, and himself captured. He and Stephen were now exchanged; and the civil war, with various fortune, long continued to waste the country. Normandy remained quiet, having peaceably accepted Geoffrey of Anjou. With the consent of his people he wisely ceded the duchy to his son Henry, who, in 1152, landed in England. Shortly after Stephen's only son, Eustace, sickened. His death led to an accommodation. The crown was to be worn by Stephen during life; and afterwards to devolve on Henry. This pacification was cordially kept during the few months which Stephen survived it. He was buried near his wife in Faversham Abbey, Kent, of which she was the founder.

CHAP VI.—LINE OF PLANTAGENET.

5. HENRY II. Henry was only in his twenty-first year when he ascended the throne, while in full possession of Touraine and Anjou; Maine and Normandy; and Poitou, and Aquitaine. The last two estates he had acquired by his wife, Eleanor, the lately-divorced wife of Louis VII. of France. He was crowned at Westminster, Lincoln, and Worcester.

One of Henry's earliest acts was to compel Malcolm IV. of

Scotland to exchange the three northern counties for the earldom of Huntingdon. The most memorable events of his reign are his contention with Becket, and the invasion of Ireland.

Becket, a Norman diminutive of *Beck*, was the son of a citizen of London, who had followed a Norman lord to the Crusades, and had, while a captive, gained the affections of a Saracen chief's daughter. This damsel found her way to London and her lover, with no other means of discovery than the name of the city and of her Christian knight; which she made resound through the streets till her efforts succeeded. Their son, Thomas à Becket, was educated at Oxford and Paris. He rose rapidly from one preferment to another till he became chancellor and tutor to the king's son, and finally archbishop of Canterbury. After entering into his see, he entirely changed his mode of life. He had before lived sumptuously, and with a degree of splendour and ostentatious display that astonished all, and excited the envy and malignity of some. He now prescribed for himself simplicity, abstemiousness, and self-denial. The enmity created by his talents and magnificence were not silenced by his virtues, his munificence, and his charity. The sycophants about the court poisoned the king's ears, and disposed him to strip and humble his friend and minister at the earliest opportunity. One was at hand, if not contrived. For ages there had been none qualified to preside in law-courts but ecclesiastics; as few, even among the barons, could either read or write, till about the close of the thirteenth century. The highest legal functions were usually discharged by the dignitaries of the Church. As a matter of course, clerical offences came under the cognizance of clerical judges, if no special jurisdiction had ever been reserved to their courts for the trial of such offences. Such reservation, however, was plainly expressed by canons, in which the civil authority had for ages acquiesced. But a spirit had arisen against the ecclesiastical courts. Whether of reform or aggression it matters not. Indeed at the present time the whole question is not much interesting or instructive; still it is right that Becket's conduct should be honestly viewed. An attempt was made by the king and his advisers to remove clerical offences from the ecclesiastical courts; that is, from trial by men who yet officiated in the ordinary courts; who for centuries were almost the only persons qualified to hear and decide causes. Becket resisted the proposed innovation; he stood upon his rights; he defended ancient privileges. He fought for established usages; which, in his opinion, it was not necessary to abolish, in order to check any abuses. Whatever may be said of his obstinacy, it was certainly without arrogance; while it was animated with the purest principles, and sustained with the loftiest moral courage. Had civil liberty such defenders, such martyrs, the foundations of the constitution would not be laid in the ignorance, destitution, and crime of half the population.

To arrange the matters in dispute a council was called at Clarendon, at which certain "Constitutions" were drawn up and signed by the king, the prelates, and thirty-seven barons. At the entreaty of his brethren, who feared for their lives, Becket added his name. If little that is objectionable can now be discovered in the *Constitutions of Clarendon*, the fact has no weight against Becket. What should be kept in view is—those Constitutions were an invasion of the rights and privileges of his order, long promulgated in the canons, long acknowledged by the state, and long confirmed by custom. After all, was he not still factious? He cannot be deemed factious, who, in defence of his principles, stands almost *alone*.

At a council held at Northampton, the king had several charges against Becket; but the primate denied the jurisdiction of the court, and declared his intention of appealing to Rome. He left the kingdom, and had an interview with pope Alexander III. at Sens, where he was met by a deputation of English bishops and barons sent to counteract him. Alexander condemned ten of the articles. Henry began to get alarmed, and became apparently reconciled to his primate, who, after six years' absence, returned to Canterbury, amid the rejoicings of clergy and people. He was, however, continually exposed to the injuries and insults of his enemies. At last, four knights, instigated, it is said, by some incautious exclamation of the king, bound themselves by oath to murder him, and effected their purpose while he stood, aware of their intention and refusing concealment, though at hand, between two of the altars of his cathedral. Thomas à Becket was assassinated Dec. 29, 1170, in the 53rd year of his age. The king soon after did penance at his tomb, which after his canonisation, became one of the most frequented pilgrimages in Europe.

After the tragical fate of Becket, the king returned from Normandy, and prepared an army for the conquest of Ireland, where a handful of Welsh adventurers, led by the earl of Pembroke, had already achieved wonderful success. The earl, better known by his surname Strongbow, was invited to that island by Dermot, king of Leinster, who had been expelled for his crimes. He sought out Henry in Aquitaine, and offered to do homage for his kingdom, on condition of getting help towards its recovery. This proposal was very agreeable to the English monarch, to whom speculations about Ireland were no novelty; for, sixteen years before, he obtained a grant of that island from the Englishman Nicholas Brakespeare, then pope Adrian IV., under the pretence of reforming religious abuses, extirpating vice, and instructing the ignorant. Most of those who, under Strongbow, joined in this enterprise, were desperate men of ruined fortunes. The first landing took place in the early part of the summer of 1169, under the half-brothers, Robert Fitz-Stephen and Maurice Fitz-Gerald; from the latter of whom the earls of Kildare and the dukes of Leinster, descended. Wexford became their first prize. Strongbow soon followed with a large re-inforcement, and captured Waterford and Dublin. As a reward Dermot gave him his daughter Eva, for wife, and nominated him his successor; which he shortly became by the decease of his father-in-law. In the year 1172 Henry with five hundred knights and a numerous body of archers crossed over to Ireland, to secure to himself the fruits of the new conquests. The native princes, except those of Ulster, came in to do him homage in considerable numbers; but he left in 1194, without having acquired any additional territory. That year the ominous letter of Adrian was produced in an Irish synod, to overawe the clergy, and check the spreading defection of the native princes. A treaty followed between Henry and Roderick O'Connor, who acknowledged Henry as king of Ireland, and was himself satisfied to be "king under the English crown." After Henry's departure Cork and Down were acquired by the adventurers; but little else was done towards the enlargement of English dominion. Indeed, Ulster remained unsubdued till the exile of the earls of Tyrone and Tyrconnell, in 1603; that is, for better than four centuries after the invasion.

Henry was the father of a remarkable family of eight children, by his queen Eleanor. His eldest, William, died in his infancy. Henry, who was married to Margaret, daughter of Louis VII, and crowned during his father's lifetime, died before he succeeded. Geoffrey, was killed at a tournament in Paris, 1186. Richard and John came to the throne. Maud, or Matilda, married Henry, duke of Saxony, and became ancestress of George 1st. of Hanover. Eleanor was married to the king of Spain, and Johanna to the king of Sicily.

Henry's contests with his sons, and their confederates, especially Louis VII, and William, the Lion, king of Scotland, occupied a great deal of his time. The latter fell into his hands at the siege of Alnwick, in 1174, while on his pilgrimage at the tomb of St. Thomas à Becket. The king sent him prisoner to Falaise, and did not release him, till the supremacy of the crown of England was acknowledged by the Scot performing an act of homage. Between Louis and him, after various hostilities, truces and breaches, a reconciliation was effected, which lasted till the death of both monarchs put an end to all jealousies. Louis died in 1180, and Henry in 1189. The death of the latter occurred at Chinon in Normandy; his remains were deposited in the convent of Frontevraud in Anjou.

This king evinced great political skill, caution, and cunning. He was envious and vindictive; and had no regard for his honour or his oath. To exhibit his power, or gratify his malice, he raised or ruined those who came near him. He scrupled at no means of getting rid of an obnoxious party. He never forgave any opposition to his will, his cupidity, or his ambition; and at the slightest opposition, he was ready to give way to a fit of ungovernable fury. Had he been less employed he would probably have been much more vicious. He had one virtue, which he turned to the service of crime, this was temperance.

6. RICHARD I., CŒUR DE LION.

The Lion-hearted, from his great bravery, was in the thirty-second year of his age, at the time of his coronation at Westminster, Sept. 3, 1189. He had a fine person and appearance. Although his temper sometimes gave way to haughtiness and cruelty: yet he never lost the character of being frank and generous, but he was not always magnanimous; while he was often unjust, and sometimes mean.

According to an agreement between Richard and Philip (II) Augustus, to join the crusaders, they mustered their forces at Vezelai, and proceeded by different routes to Sicily, where Richard's brother-in-law, the usurper Tancred, ruled. Many were the misunderstandings which took place from time to time between the English king and his friends, which were terminated by convenient but not cordial adjustments. One of these differences arose from Richard's refusing to fulfil his contract with Adelais, or Alice, the sister of Philip. As he assigned sufficient reason for his conduct, and also agreed to make a pecuniary compensation which Philp disgracefully accepted, he was freed from his obligation; and was soon after married to Berengaria, of Navarre.

The leagued princes set out at last for their final destination. Their first success was the surrender of Acre, the release of fifteen hundred Christian captives, and the restoration of the holy cross. Philip hastily abandoned further enterprises; and having sworn not to attack England, returned to France followed by the scorn and execrations of the crusaders. The sultan, Saladin, having failed to execute the late treaty, about 6000 Saracens were, as had been threatened, butchered before his eyes. On his march to Jaffa, Richard signally defeated the sultan. He advanced to within a short distance of Jerusalem—where was "the holy sepulchre," the object of all those vast armaments—when he found his inability to undertake its siege. He reverted to the coast; and a truce for three years was concluded with the infidels. Ascalon was to be dismantled, and the pilgrimage to the sepulchre to be safe and free.

Richard now turned his face towards home, preceded by the fame of his heroism, and endeared to all the chivalry and enthusiasm of Europe. In a few months he won renown which, for centuries after, swept the chords of the lyre, inflamed equally the breasts of the brave and of the devout, and furnished romance with countless fancies and enchantments. On his voyage he fell into the hands of pirates; whom he prevailed over to land him at Zara, in Sclavonia. He had now no other alternative than to make his way back by Germany. He journeyed in disguise; but was discovered and imprisoned by Leopold, duke of Austria, whom he had offended in Palestine, and who gave him up to Henry VI., emperor of Germany, on being promised a share of his ransom. Richard was conveyed from Vienna to Worms, where he was secured in a fortress. When the tidings of his captivity came to France, king Philip offered a sum equal to his ransom, to get possession of him: a proposal which could not be accepted without consulting the German Diet, or assembly of nobles and clergy. This body would not part with the prisoner, but determined to try him for making a truce with the Saracens, for insulting the duke's flag in the Holy Land, and for his alleged murder of the Marquis of Montferrat. Nothing could surpass the rage of Louis. He declared war against the emperor; and, at the same time, made the most tempting offers to the captive's brother, John, Earl of Mortain; to whom he promised to guarantee Normandy, and to aid in seizing England, if he would become his ally, and marry his degraded sister, Alice, an alliance revolting even to John. The Earl of Mortain made no special bargain, but took advantage of Philip's nefarious friendship; and, on pretence of Richard's death, exacted the oath of fidelity from his officers. The king obtained knowledge of those doings through some Norman abbots, and the seal of his chancellor, William de Longchamp, whom John had expelled. Meantime the diet decreed his ransom at one hundred thousand pounds, and the annual payment of five thousand for his kingdom as a fief of the empire.

John, having failed to seduce the great body of the bishops, barons, and public functionaries from their allegiance, went over to Philip, declared himself to be his liege-man for England, gave him up considerable portions of the continental domains, and swore to marry Alice, as soon as he should become king of England. But Richard, after many complaints, sent to his subjects of their slowness and neglect, was liberated by the diet on giving hostages for what remained of his ransom undischarged .This event took place at the end of two years' imprisonment. Philip and John did their best to hinder it. They offered the emperor seventy thousand marks of silver to prolong the durance for a year; or one thousand pounds of silver for every successive month of the monarch's detention; or one hundred and fifty thousand marks for handing him over to themselves. The tempted emperor would have broken his word, but the diet were more mindful of their honour, and perhaps of the Christian hero's deeds to consent to any breach of faith. Yet Richard's perils were not all over. It was the stormy season, and he was detained weather-bound at Antwerp for an entire month, during which the emperor's avarice overcame his respect for the diet, and determined him to seize and sell the king. The design was discovered by one of the hostages left to ensure the ransom. Richard was forewarned in time to make good his escape.

When Cœur de Lion arrived at Sandwich, he found that his false brother had been driven out; the barons besieging the traitor's castles, and the bishops excommunicating him and his adherents. However pleased he may have been with the fidelity of his subjects, certainly he was not very grateful. After his second coronation he annulled the sales of royal domains, made to forward his eastern expedition, under the pretence that such sales were simple pawns or mortgages. He, indeed, directed the holders to compare what they had paid with what they received, and that he would make recompense for any loss out of his own pocket. But no one had courage to send in an account. The domains were given up without any compensation in return. As for the English race, after having been weighed down by taxes for the king's deliverance, they were further burdened for that of the of the hostages left in Germany, and the war which was now to be waged against Philip and John.

Richard's first successes in Normandy prompted the base Earl of Mortain to betray his allies. To grace his perfidy, he caused to be imprisoned a great number of French knights whom he had invited to a feast. But the king, although reconciled to him by the intercession of their mother, neither rewarded his services, nor trusted in his professions. Philip was obliged to conclude a truce, and thereby leave his antagonist at liberty to punish the Aquitanian insurgents, headed by the Viscount of Limoges and the Count of Perigord. The truce, however, was scarcely affirmed when it was broken, through the intrigues and incitements of the able and restless Bertrand, lord of the castle of Haute-Fort, that famous warrior and *troubadour*, who, animated by an ardent patriotism, "at all times wished the kings of France and England to be at war with one another." It was this active agent, who, by his satirical verses and skilful management, persuaded Philip to violate the recent truce and royal oath. Saintonge now became the field of battle. The two kings, at the head of their armies, met at Mirabeau; he of England supported by Normans, English, and Augevins, with the men of Touraine, Maine, and Saintonge; and he of France, backed by the French, Burgundians, Champenois, Flemings, and Berrichons. Archbishops, bishops, and abbots were seen to pass between the camps, vainly trying to bring about an accommodation. The king of France was the haughtier; he would be satisfied with nothing less than the oath of vassalage for Normandy, Guienne, and Poitou; but observing symptoms of defection among the Champenois, who had touched Richard's silver, he sent the clergy to offer peace without the offensive conditions. Peace was made. The two kings swore to a ten years' truce, and dismissed their troops.

It was the English king's turn to be the perjuror, instigated by the ingenious and indefatigable de Born, and other intriguers, he fell suddenly on the French provinces near his own. The bishops again interfered, and a conference was fixed at which Richard gave his rival the lie, and called him a recreant, to the delight and comfort of honest Bertrand de Born, to whom the civilities of the interview, furnished a lucky theme for chafing both parties. At this time, however, Philip was afraid to stir, but Richard went forth, and took, plundered or burnt his boroughs and cities. As the latter discovered that little was ultimately gained by those ravages, he grew weary, and offered his rival, as the basis of a more durable peace, his sovereignty over Auvergne, for an equivalent political advantage. The offer was accepted, and Philip acquired a seigniory, that hated his race and refused his authority. When therefore Richard thought proper to break the truce, the count Auvergne called also the *dauphin*, from the device of a dolphin worn on his shield, raised the standard of insurrection against his new lord paramount. Then the English king basely left them to their fate; and then Philip laid waste the country, putting all to the fire and sword. The Auvergnats had quickly to sue for peace. Within a brief period, the truce between the two kings expired, and the personage of France, again attacked his rival's territories. Richard crossed the channel, and sent a message to the dauphin, who did not deem it advisable to depend on him a second time.

In this manner, for a space of eight years, bargain and breach followed each other by turns, while their respective subjects groaned under the frivolous ambition of those despicable creatures. The native English especially, were ground to pieces, not only by excessive, but unequal taxation. Of the citizens of London, who were entitled to take part in the assemblies held in their council-hall, for the assessing of rates, the majority were of foreign extraction. This circumstance, combined with hate and contempt, power and threats, was enough to give the rates, in general, an oppressive leaning on one side. Richard's exactions never ceased, so that the rates not only impoverished and irritated those of his own race, but drove them to contrive exemptions and escapes for themselves, at the expense and fury of the unprotected and unpitied English. Injustice and ruin spread discontent, and fomented a spirit of resistance. Wrong and reflection breed patriots, and one now appeared, the first in our annals, who undertook to defend the people by legal weapons. His name, William Longbeard, which merits to shine beside those of Langton and Hampden, is part of his history. As a contrast to the Normans, the natives were proud of a long beard. This distinction was not always worn with impunity; but some were bold enough to show it in defiance. Among these was William, who enjoyed competency by the industry of his parents, and used it in pursuing such legal studies as would be most beneficial to the common cause. To his favourite fashion he owes his surname. He employed his knowledge of the laws in defending the poorer citizens against the legal embarrassments and vexations to which they were exposed by the rich; the most frequent of which was the unequal division of assessments. His efforts drew round him the affections of all who had suffered by, or were exposed to the foul play of the dominant party.

This remarkable man the last representative of the hostile feelings of the two races left by the Conquest, appeared as usual, in the municipal council, A.D. 1196. The chief burgesses had given their votes so that the lighter portion of the contribution should fall on themselves. Longbeard stood out against them. To the taunts of treason and rebellion he replied,—"Those are the traitors to the king, who exempt themselves from paying what they owe him, and defraud his exchequer; and I will denounce them to him myself." For this purpose he crossed the sea, and was well received by Richard, whose promise of redress, however, was soon forgotten. But to torture in some way, Hubert, archbishop of Canterbury, and grand justiciary, published an ordinance forbidding any commoner of London to quit the city on pain of imprisonment as a traitor. Some tradesmen who thought it no harm to go to the fair of Stamford, were put up. The populace, alarmed for their safety, formed secret societies, of which William Longbeard was the soul, and which included, it is said, fifty thousand members. The humbler classes assembled openly, to give ear to the impassioned parables, and picturesque eloquence of their leader. But this man let slip his opportunity; he did not strike while the iron was hot, and so became the victim of that old and fatal error, irresolution.

His adversaries were beforehand with the tardy tribune. A parliament was called, and William summoned, before which he appeared, attended by such multitudes, that open proceedings against him were dropped, and his private ruin determined on. Artful emissaries were sent among the people; false promises and false alarms were spread; on the one hand, public enthusiasm cooled; while on the other apprehensions began to seize the advocates of insurrection. The end was not remote. Two Norman citizens engaged to watch William, and take him by surprise. Secretly attended by their partisans they dogged him; till finding him one day with only a few friends they fell on him, and drove him into the church of St. Mary de L'Arche. The news ran rapidly through the city, but William's friends were dismayed by the armed bands which presented themselves in every direction. Whether it was this pusillanimous fear, or regard for the hostages which they had some time before been induced to give the justices for their good behaviour, no movement was made to rescue the popular favourite and his few friends, who had barricaded themselves in their sanctuary. Out of this he was driven by setting the edifice on fire. Wounded and tied to the tail of a horse, he was dragged through the streets, to the Tower of London, presented there to the archbishop, and ordered with his nine companions for immediate execution. If the cause makes the martyr, he deserves, says Matthew of Paris, to be reckoned amongst the martyrs; who defended the truth, and protected the poor. The gallows on which he was hanged was removed in the night time, as a relic. Guards had to be placed over the spot where it had been erected, to put a stop to the perpetual removal of portions of the sacred earth, or to obstruct the patriotic pilgrims who came there to pray, and who were sometimes imprisoned and scourged.

Richard perished in an ignoble quarrel with one of his barons. Vidomar, viscount of Limoges, found a treasure on his estate, and offered part to the king, who insisted on the whole, and proceeded to enforce his demand. While besieging Vidomar, in his castle of Chaluz, the king was wounded in the shoulder by an arrow. When the place was taken by storm, the garrison were hanged as robbers, with the exception of Gourdon, the archer who hit the sovereign. Through the unskilful treatment by the surgeon, mortification set in, and the sufferer prepared for death. Having ordered Gourdon or Jourdain, before him, the king gave him his liberty, and one hundred shillings to take him home. But Marchadee, one of the generals, detained the youth, and had him flayed alive.

Richard expired at the age of forty-two, in the year 1199, having bequeathed his heart to Rouen, and his body to Fontevraud, where he had directed it to be buried, as a mark of repentance, at his father's feet.

7. JOHN, surnamed LACKLAND.

At Richard's death, the lawful heir was his nephew Arthur, son of Geoffrey, who had been killed in a tournament. John took immediate steps to seize the ancient patrimony of the Plantagenets, and dispossess the young duke of Bretagne, then in his twelfth year. But Arthur's rights were supported by the loyal feelings of the natives, and the selfish promises of the king of France. John was acknowledged without any debate in England, as well as in Normandy and Aquitaine. The accession of this feeble prince stimulated the designs of Philip, into whose hands Arthur and his mother Constance had placed Bretagne and its dependencies for security. Seeing that the king of France had appropriated those territories given in trust, Arthur fled for safety to his uncle, by whom he was received with a delusive show of kindness, and from whom he found it expedient to make a precipitate retreat, to escape incarceration. He had no where to go but to his previous patron, who now to serve his own purposes, betrothed him his youngest daughter Mary, a child five years old, and confirmed him in the full possession of Bretagne, and proclaimed him count of Anjou and Poitou.

It was at this juncture that Hugh de la March, whom John had deprived of his betrothed, headed a fierce revolt of the barons of Poitou and Limousin. Philip, whose policy had been influenced by this event, despatched Arthur with an army to besiege the town of Mirabeau, which was easily taken. While besieging the castle in which Eleanor, widow of Henry II. was then shut up, John suddenly fell on the confederates, and made Arthur and most of the leaders of the insurrection prisoners. He carried them all into Normandy. Arthur soon disappeared. Some say he died in the castle of Rouen; some that he was killed accidentally in an attempt to escape; and others that he was stabbed by his uncle on the sea shore near Cherbourg; but these are all mere conjectures; which, however, do not weaken the suspicions attached to John.

The Bretons deeply lamented the fate of their young duke, and appealed to Philip for vengeance; who accordingly cited the king of England as his vassal, to appear before him and the peers of France, and answer for the disappearance of his nephew. John disobeyed, and his lands were declared forfeited. A sudden irruption of all the neighbouring states poured in as

Normandy, and in less than a twelve-month, there remained to John, only Rouen, Verneuil, and Château Gaillard, and these soon followed.

Thus, after a separation of two hundred and ninety-two years, all those rich provinces were re-annexed to the French crown; and for his consolation John obtained a truce for two years. But rest seemed as disagreeable to him as war was disastrous. His disputes with Rome immediately began. In 1205, the junior monks of Canterbury clandestinely elected Reginald, their sub-prior, to that see; while the others chose, at the king's command, De Grey, bishop of Norwich. On the dispute being referred to the Pope, he selected a more suitable man than either, and an Englishman, then residing in Rome, Cardinal Langton. John swore he should never set foot in his kingdom. The pontiff put the kingdom under an interdict. The churches were closed; the sacraments, except to infants and the dying, withheld; the dead buried without Christian rite, in horrid silence, and in unconsecrated ground. The minds of men were appalled—their hearts stricken down—the face of society dimmed with a sullen woe—and its frame loosened by the sudden removal of the sacred bonds of religion and public prayer. The light of the gospel seemed put out by an instantaneous breath; and the hand of Egyptian darkness drawn over the eyes of piety; which, when they looked inwardly saw its nourishment snatched away; its springs dried up; and all the divine consolations of humanity banished from the afflicted land by the impious contumely of a reprobated prince.

This sad state lasted a year, when the Pope thought to bring John to his senses by excommunicating him. This sentence was borne for four years, and recourse was had to the expedient of freeing his subjects from their oath of fealty, and soliciting the aid of all Christian princes in dethroning him. Philip complied, and prepared a numerous army; but John unexpectedly attacked him, and gained such advantages as led to terms with the pontiff. Langton was to be admitted, the exiled bishops restored, and the interdict and excommunication revoked, May 13, 1213. On the following day, the king, surrounded by the prelates and barons, put into the hands of Pandulph, the legate, a charter, surrendering to Pope Innocent the kingdoms of England and Ireland, as fiefs of the Holy See. He then took the usual oath of fealty; and then the barons wisely bethought of demanding their rights from his suzerain. The Pope supported his liege, and the barons transferred their allegiance to Philip's son, Louis.

John now determined to carry the war into France. The barons refused to accompany him, pleading that he had not yet fulfilled his treaty with the pope, and that the eccleciastical censures were still continued. John submitted; and those penalties remitted on the return of the bishops. He fancied himself quite righted, and sailed for the continent, but the barons did not follow. Langton hated tyrrany and seized the moment. He formed a league among the nobles, and swore them to conquer or die in defence of their liberties. For a time their prospects were gloomy. Their king, at the head of 100,000 men, gained some advantages in France. Philip opposed him with a much inferior force; but accomplished his ruin by the decisive victory at Bouvines. A truce for five years was agreed on.

Meanwhile Langton made the draught of *Magna Charta*. The barons presented their demands at the ensuing Christmas court. The king put them off till Easter. Both parties appealed to Rome, and that court went with John. When the festival arrived the barons appeared in arms at Stamford, where they awaited an answer from the king who was at Oxford, and sent them a stern denial. The barons elected Robert Fitzwalter, commander of "the army of God and of the Holy Church," and took possession of London and other places. A conference was now sought, the scene of which was fixed at Runnymede, between Staines and Windsor; and there, on the 18th of June, 1215, *Magna Charta*, the most memorable document in our records, received the royal signature. Yet it is not easy to say what rights were gained by it, or what abuses prevented. It may be viewed as an outpost, whose gain or loss was of no decisive advantage; but which to one party was of great importance as a rallying point.

The arrival of mercenary soldiers tempted John to disregard his compact; and both sides flew to arms. News arrived that the Pope had annulled the charter, and recommended the barons to submit for the present to the king, and meantime to lay demands before him for a fair settlement. His holiness ordered Langton to excommunicate the refractory; but the archbishop declined. On the renewal of the war, the king of Scots came to aid the barons. John advanced to meet him; and on his way to the north, destroyed by every species of devastation all that lay within his reach. The hapless population had not a safe market place, unless churchyards, which possessed, as such, the privileges of sanctuary.

Again the barons offered the crown to Louis, the dauphin, who was married to John's niece. Louis was excommunicated. On the ground that the Pope had not been truly informed the French bishops, assembled in synod at Melun, refused to carry out a similar sentence against king Philip. Pending the dispute, Innocent died, and John thus lost his best friend. Louis embarked at Calais with a fleet of six hundred and eighty ships. John retired at his approach, and joined the legate at Bristol. Philip was received in London by the barons and citizens of London, who did him the usual homage. He appointed Simon, the primate's brother, chancellor, and won all ranks by his affability. But if his opponents commanded the open country, still the king held the most important fortresses; and the arrival of the legate, Gualo, re-animated the spirits of himself and his friends. His castles of Dover and Windsor greatly retarded Louis. By the advice of the earl of Nevers, supposed to have been perfidious, the barons raised the siege with the intent of surprising John while at Cambridge. He eluded them; and full of chagrin, they returned to Dover, leaving him to reduce Lincoln, and distribute the lands of the confederates among his followers. His prospects began to brighten, and those of Louis to grow dusky. The Cinque Ports intercepted Louis's supplies. Associations against him were spreading through Kent, Hants, and other counties. English earldoms were conferred on French favourites, to the mortification of the jealous barons. To add to his difficulties the adventitious king wasted time in inactivity; and many of his powerful supporters privately negociated for the royal pardon.

John, with increasing strength and confidence, returned through Grimsby and Spalding to Lynn, which was his principal depôt, and proceeded over the Wash to Cross Keys. But as he reached the land, and looked back, he saw his baggage, money, and insignia swallowed up in a whirlpool, caused by the afflux of the tide and the current of the Welland. That night he repaired to the convent of Swineshead, where he was seized with fever, which has been variously attributed to anxiety, to surfeit, or to poison. Within six days after, he died at Newark, leaving his eldest son, Henry, his heir, and his body for interment at Worcester. His death took place, October 19, 1216, in the forty-ninth year of his age. He was three times married.

8. HENRY III., OF WINCHESTER.

At the accession of Henry he had but completed his tenth year. He was just old enough to understand that the best part of his kingdom was swayed by a rival, whose cause was still the more popular, and whose vassals were the neighbouring princes of Scotland and Wales. His coronation was performed October 28, 1216, in the cathedral of Gloucester, by the legate, Gnalo, and the bishops of Winchester, Exeter, and Bath. The guardianship of the minor, and of his kingdom, was entrusted to the wise and valiant earl of Pembroke, earl marshal.

The confirmation of the Great Charter in a grand council, assembled at Bristol under the auspices of the earl, tended to detach many of Louis's adherents, and to damage his cause. Other vexations ensued. The French prince was beaten at Lincoln; and shortly after his fleet was dispersed off the coast of Kent by the justiciary, Hubert de Burgh. He was soon glad to leave, having secured an amnesty for his allies, and the ransom and release of all prisoners. Magna Charta was again confirmed; the king a second time crowned; and his elder sister, Jane, married at York, to Alexander II. of Scotland.

Henry often led his army into Wales, although Llewellyn, its sovereign, was his brother-in-law. He chastised his successor, David, for offering to become the vassal of Innocent IV. Two princes, elected as joint successors to David, became voluntary vassals of the English king.

Louis, who had promised to restore Normandy, whenever he should succeed to the crown, endeavoured instead to aggrandize himself at Henry's expense. The papal legate effected an armistice. Before it expired, Louis was succeeded by his son, Louis IX. whose early troubles exposed him to Henry's reprisals. The latter assembled a large army, and, in 1230, crossed over to France; and the war continued with varying fortune, till 1259, when the wearied monarchs patched up a peace.

The extensive appointment of foreigners to church livings had long been a cause of complaint, as well as the heavy tax levied by the court of Rome, under the name of *tallage*. Those abuses were in some degree redressed. But Henry's partiality to foreign counsellors proved his ruin. It caused an insurrection in 1233, which was not suppressed until they had been dismissed. On his marriage, 1236, with Eleanor, daughter of Raymond, count of Provence, they again swarmed, and monopolized the highest offices.

Simon de Montfort, earl of Leicester, the king's brother-in-law, took advantage of this grievance. Under his influence a great council assembled at Oxford, June 11, 1258. This was subsequently known as *the mad parliament*. The barons engaged in the cause with an oath of fidelity to one another. No less than twenty great functionaries were deprived of office; and their posts filled by the chief reformers. A committee was appointed to draw up instructions for the public administration, who promulgated some excellent rules, and divested the king of his principal prerogatives. Royal orders issued without the consent of the lords of the council, were looked upon as crimes against the state. Those encroachments on the regal authority may have been at that time dangerous and treasonable, when the responsibility of ministers was not defined or recognised; but they would now be regarded as in the spirit of the constitution, when ministers are held accountable for all the public acts of the sovereign.

At length, in 1261, Henry attempted to recover his authority. The barons resolved to hold theirs; but the appeal to arms was averted for the present by an agreement to wait for the return of prince Edward, who was attending a tournament in France. Edward apparently sided with the barons, who agreed to a conference with which they were dissatisfied. It was then proposed to refer the dispute to the king of France, or to the king's brother, Richard, earl of Cornwall, who had been elected king of the Romans. Leicester, dissatisfied with the decision which had been arrived at, withdrew to France; but he soon returned on the king's appearance there also.

Leicester lost no time in reorganizing the previous association. His party gained several advantages. It was again resolved to choose the French for umpire; the contending parties presented themselves before Louis at Amiens. When his decision was pronounced, the barons proclaimed it a sheer absurdity; and hostilities were immediately set on foot in the old way. Henry unfurled his standard at Oxford, and reduced several of the strongholds of his rebellious barons. He made Leicester's second son, Simon, with many other eminent parties, prisoners at Nottingham, where he was joined by Comyn, Bruce, and Baliol, the future aspirants to the Scottish crown. But the battle of Lewes soon followed, May 14, 1264. In this Leicester was victorious, and the king and prince Edward fell into his hands; and with them the entire power of the state.

To silence obloquy and strengthen himself against the partisans of the court, he cultivated popularity, and sought public sanction for all his proceedings. If he had an ambitious object in view, he approached it by constitutional steps; and the people gained by the measures he took, perhaps, to make himself their master. His character may be left to the public opinion of his time, which has transmitted to us a reformer of abuses, a protector of the poor, and the saviour of his country. But he had attained a position always attended with danger. It begets rivals, enemies, and traitors; and such easily procure friends and instruments. Derby was found corresponding with the royalists; Gloucester raised the royal standard. But the spilling of blood was for a time deferred. A short lull was effected by a hollow reconciliation; and it was employed in planning Edward's escape; which was accomplished by the connivance of Thomas de Clare, brother to Gloucester.

The immediate consequence was the battle of Evesham, in which Montfort and his eldest son, Henry, fell, August 4, 1265. Their estates were given to the king's second son, Edmund *Crouchback*. Leicester's cause languished through the next two years. When quiet was restored by Edward's activity and conduct, he proceeded to join St. Louis in the seventh crusade, 1270. After some success in the Holy Land, which afforded sufficient indications of a military genius, he made ready for his return to England, in obedience to letters from his father, whose strength was rapidly declining. Notwithstanding his expedition in coming home, he was not a witness of the king's last moments. Having reigned fifty-six years, he died, Nov. 20, 1272; after living without much blame or praise. Two sons, Edward and Edmund, and two daughters, Margaret, queen of Scotland, and Beatrice, duchess of Bretagne, survived Henry III.

9. EDWARD I., surnamed LONGSHANKS.

Henry's eldest son, was in his thirty-fifth year when the reins of government came into his hands. To his stature he owed his surname, and to his looks a large amount of admiration.

In Sicily he was reached by the news of his father's death; but detained, by its unsettled state, in Guienne till August, 1274, when he and his wife were crowned at Westminster.

His peace was first disturbed by an irruption from Wales, led by prince Llewellyn, who was quickly forced to throw himself on Edward's mercy. Rigid terms were imposed but not nicely exacted. The king had conceived that his leniency would have conciliated good will. He did not know the incurable hatred of the ancient Briton. In 1282, Llewellyn's brother, David, initiated a general insurrection by surprising the castle of Hawarden. After much bravery, blood and hardship on both sides, this contest was brought to an issue on the banks of the Weye, in December, 1282, when Llewellyn was slain. The native chieftains hastened to submit; except David, who was afterwards seized, tried in London, and cruelly hanged as a traitor.

Edward passed a year in Wales, for the purpose of familiarizing the inhabitants with English manners, and grafting his law and polity. He very much piqued himself on his legislative abilities. Indeed he has been justly called *the English Justinian*, from the excellent code he caused to be passed by his first parliament. A pleasing event also gave him a happy opportunity of flattering Celtic vanity. During his stay his eldest son was born in the castle of Caernarvon, and he gave him the title of *Prince of Wales*, a distinction which has been continued to our day.

When Edward visited his Norman domains, he tarried so long that his English subjects compelled his return by the refusal of an aid. He now formed the project of annexing the crown of Scotland to that of England, by the marriage of the Prince of Wales to his first cousin, Margaret, the *Maid of Norway*, grand-daughter of Alexander III., king of Scotland. But this young lady died somewhat unexpectedly, making way for the pretensions of no less than thirteen claimants to her crown. She was the only child of Eric, king of Norway, by Margaret, great grand-daughter, and heiress of William the Lion. But his brother David had three daughters, all of whom had living representatives. John Baliol was the grandson of the eldest; and Robert Bruce the son of the second eldest. Edward was chosen umpire by these rivals, and Edward, as lord paramount, summoned the estates of Scotland to meet him at Norham. He decided in favour of Baliol, on the principles of primogeniture; and took good care to make the man of his choice do him homage. Baliol soon tasted the bitterness of vassalage. Macduff, son of Malcolm, earl of Fife, appealed to Edward, from a decison of the Scottish king concerning the possession of certain lands. Edward decreed against his vassal. The result was a war, which cost the latter his crown.

But this haughty prince had to undergo a mortification similar to Baliol's, at the hand of Philip. Between the seamen of France and England a quarrel broke out which attained such magnitude that their respective princes became involved. The French mariners having experienced a murderous defeat, Philip summoned Edward, as duke of Aquitaine, to appear and make reparation. The former affected moderation, saying that he would be satisfied with the surrender of Guienne for forty days, and promising to restore it at the end of that time. This engagement was not kept; and Edward prepared to punish the bad faith. An outbreak of the Welsh delayed him; and it took some time to repress it. Baliol also gave him trouble at this time, by forming an alliance with the king of France, and formally renouncing his vassalage to Edward. The Scot was defeated; compelled to admit Edward's superior rights; and after an almost nominal imprisonment in the Tower, suffered to disappear into France, where he died in 1305.

The discomfit of Baliol did not altogether extinguish the hopes of Scotland. It brought to light the ambition of some; the desperation of others, and the patriotism of thousands. Small bodies collected under bold leaders in several districts. The bishop of Glasgow and the steward of Scotland invited the chiefs to rally round them. Among the first to obey were Wallace, Douglas, Lindsay, Moray, and Lundy. Sir William Douglas was a captain of outlaws, who had received back his liberty and property from the generosity of Edward. Wallace was a refugee of the woods from the pursuit of justice, for a murder. Robert Bruce, the young earl of Carrick, although invested with the highest claims by Baliol's flight, joined rather tardily. In the absence of Edward, who was employed in the recovery of Guienne, out of which he had been cheated, his armies were commanded by Henry Lord Percy, Sir Robert Clifford, and earl Warrenne. In the furious struggle which now developed all the energies of both parties, Wallace defeated Warrenne at Stirling, September, 1297. This victory flushed every heart in Caledonia with expectation which was soon to ebb. The king took the command of his army, and by the overthrow of Wallace at Falkirk, where thirty thousand Scots fell, drove Wallace back to the woods a helpless outlaw.

In Baliol's name the bishop of St. Andrew's, the earl of Carrick, and John Comyn undertook the regency of the kingdom. They sent envoys to Rome. The Pontiff refreshed the minds of the disputants with his own rights, and left them to their own arbitrament. This neutrality is explained by the quarrel which then pended between the Pope and Philip. Hostilities were therefore resumed in 1303; but on Edward's crossing the border with an overwhelming force the regents submitted, and all resistance ceased with the siege of Stirling, where Sir William Oliphant held out for ninety days. Wallace was taken by surprise, and executed August 23, 1305. In his lifetime the victim was the idol of his countrymen. After his death he was revered as a martyr; and Scots are still proud and virtuous enough not to remember his failings.

Edward summoned a Scottish parliament at Perth; which appointed ten commissioners to confer with the king in London. The results were: the guardianship of Scotland was given to Edward's nephew, John of Bretagne; and the country divided into four districts for its better government.

The affairs of the Scottish succession had thus apparently come to repose. Previously to the circumstances which have been narrated, a constitutional struggle was carried on in England, of more importance than that which led to *Magna Charta*.

In the year 1297, Edward had gathered reinforcements for his army in Guienne, which Bohun, earl of Hereford, and Roger Bigod, earl of Norfolk, refused to lead. The former was constable, the latter, marshal of England; and they pleaded that their office bound them to personal service, only as regarded the king. He threatened them, appointed others to their offices, appealed to the people from a platform raised before Westminster; and conceived he had recovered all the power and popularity necessary to leave the kingdom with perfect safety to his interests. On his way to Flanders, he received a national remonstrance as he reached Winchester, in which his people declared they were not bound to serve in Flanders, that even if they were, oppressive taxation had disabled them; and that the expedition itself was imprudent. Under pretence of taking the advice of his council, the king proceeded on his way. Two days after he sailed, Bohun and Bigod visited the Exchequer, and forbad, in the name of the barons, the levying of the tax last imposed. From the Exchequer they went to Guildhall, where the city declared for them.

It was at this critical moment the Scots were victorious at

Stirling, and Edward paralyzed at Ghent, in presence of a superior French force. The prince and council in whose hands England was left, called a parliament, before which the crown was compelled to relinquish its pretension of levying taxes without the consent of the nation. An aid was now granted which enabled Edward to conclude a truce, and come home with the intention of revoking the engagements lately made in his name, by his administration. The splendid victory at Falkirk strengthened his hands; so that when pressed by Hereford and Norfolk to ratify the concessions; he inserted a clause reserving the rights of the crown, which was justly regarded as a denial of the promises. The earls withdrew with their adherents. The king proceeded to St. Paul's, hoping to bring over the citizens. Clause after clause of his confirmation of the charters, was vociferously applauded; but the reservation came at last, and was visited with a convincing burst of indignation. The obnoxious clause was withdrawn, and the king never again ventured to revive it. Thus were the true principles of taxation, first asserted and admitted. In the grave contest involving those principles, besides Bohun and Bigod, the name most conspicuous, is that of Winchelsea, archbishop of Canterbury. The most remarkable feature of it was the separation of the elements of the great council of the nation, or parliament, into two separate assemblies, which have been since known as the *lords and commons*. In the parliament held by Leicester, in 1265, representatives from boroughs sat for the first time, whom he had summoned to strengthen his party. In the parliament of 1295, these *burgesses* joined the *knights* of the shire, who were the deputies of the freeholders and less barons; and having formed themselves into a distinct body, traced the outlines and laid the foundations of that edifice which has become so famous as the British Constitution; and which notwithstanding its strong and ugly feudal features, has retained the admiration of centuries.

Edward had begun to feel the infirmities of age, when the state of Scotland again added to his vexations, as he approached his seventieth year. In 1306, the surviving claimants to the Scottish crown, deeming the time opportune, took council together. These were Robert Bruce, a young man of twenty-three, and grandson to the former claimant of that name, and John Comyn of Badenoch, nephew of Baliol, and acting as the guardian of Baliol's son Edward, who was prisoner in the Tower of London. Bruce and John Comyn held a conference in the church of Dumfries, at which a quarrel arose, and Comyn fell by the dagger of Bruce. The king vowed vengeance, and directed that his body should never be buried until it was fully taken. His son, Edward, swore he would not sleep two nights in the same place, till he had inflicted chastisement, for what was denounced as a murderous plot, but which yet remains behind an impenetrable veil.

However it may darken the suspicions which hung over Bruce, no hope of safety was now left him but in proclaiming himself king. He was crowned at Scone without any opposition, but was soon after defeated at Methuen, by the earl of Pembroke. He fled to the north of Ireland, where he lay concealed to the end of winter; when he sailed for Scotland, and was there joined by his vassals and adherents.

Edward, roused by some trifling advantages gained by Bruce, put himself at the head of his army, in July 1307. But he was overcome by the exertion. Within a few days after he set out on this expedition, he expired at Burgh-on-the-sands, in the thirty-fifth year of his reign.

He was twice married, first to Eleanor of Castile, by whom he had four sons and eleven daughters; and secondly, to Margaret of France, by whom he had two sons who survived him, and a daughter. One son his successor, and two daughters of Eleanor also outlived him. This queen died in 1290, at Grantham, near Lincoln. She was a beautiful and benevolent woman, as much beloved by her people as by her lord, who commemorated her virtues and his noble sentiments, by the erection of a beautiful cross wherever her funeral rested for a night, on its way to Westminster. Be this enough to redeem his failings, tinctured with the sternness of his age, and to make his name sweet to the lips of conjugal affection.

It was the parliament of 1297, that passed the statute, *De tallagio non Concedendo*, by which it was declared unlawful for the king to raise money without the consent of parliament.

10. EDWARD II. surnamed CAERNARVON.

After the interment of his father, Edward II. advanced to Dumfries, received the homage of the Scottish barons; and returned home. Then one of his first acts was the recall of his companion, Piers Gaveston a Gascon, whom the king had banished from the prince's company as a loose and worthless parasite. He made Gaveston earl of Cornwall, and lord chamberlain; gave him his niece in affiance, and appointed him regent during his intended absence in France; whither he went to wed the beautiful Isabella, daughter of the French king.

On his return the barons demanded the expulsion of Gaveston. He pretended to comply, but exasperated those formidable remonstrants by appointing his favourite to the lieutenancy of Ireland, where he won distinction without much difficulty.

But Edward was soon menaced by parliament for this trifling with grave complaints. When he solicited a supply, he was informed that it must be preceeded by a redress of grievances. He prorogued the parliament. Meanwhile he contrived to win over a majority of the barons, to obtain the money; and best of all, permission to recall Gaveston, who speedily exhausted his treasury.

To escape from his troublesome peers, Edward invaded Scotland. There his fortune did not smile. His strength was counterbalanced by the caution of his adversary, and he returned to London to meet his parliament with empty hands. This assembly was more exorbitant than ever. They not only demanded the perpetual banishment of the minion, and the abolition of the new taxes, but insisted that the king should neither levy war, nor leave the kingdom without their assent. Edward remonstrated, the barons persisted; and the ordinances received the royal signature. Nevertheless Gaveston within a short space met his master at York, by his command, as announced in a royal proclamation. But the king's cousin-german Thomas, earl of Lancaster, punished this temerity, at the head of the barons. He became their prisoner, and was beheaded, June 19, 1312, at Blacklow Hill, near Warwick.

The war in Scotland was renewed in 1314, but Edward, instead of retrieving his popularity, lost the great battle of Bannockburn, near Stirling, June 24. The Scots were commanded by Bruce, his brother Edward, Stewart, Douglas, and Randolf. Bruce in turn invaded Ireland, when his proposals for an accommodation were rejected. His brother landed at Carrickfergus with six thousand men. Having suffered some reverses he sent home for reinforcements; obtained several advantages, but none of any permanence; and was at last crowned to little purpose, near Dundalk.

At Ahenree (Athenry) the greatest army ever opposed to English power in Ireland, and led by the bravest of her princes, Phelim O'Connor, king of Connaught, was defeated by de Burgh and de Bermingham, a short time before; but on the arrival of

Robert Bruce, the whole country rallied afresh. The Scots, however, proceeded in the middle of a severe winter to the south, where they were destroyed with famine, disease, and hardship. Robert went home, and Edward returned back to Dundalk, where he reluctantly delivered battle and was slain.

Bruce's career in Scotland was prosperous to his heart's content, one strong place after another became his prey; and the distracted state of England made him slow to negociate.

The king's partiality for Hugh de Spencer, and his aged father, the earl of Winchester, again brought into play the machinations of Lancaster and his party, who ultimately compelled their patron to banish them. But an offence offered to the queen unexpectedly led to their recal. On her way to Canterbury, Isabella was refused a night's lodging in one of the royal castles by Lady Badelsmere. This affront was indignantly taken up by the country. The strength of Lancaster declined, while that of the royalists daily encreased. The Spencers were recalled, and several of their enemies severely treated. Lancaster proceeded to the north, to effect a junction with the Scots. On his way, his friend the earl of Hereford was killed; and he himself made prisoner March, 1322, at Borough-bridge. He was led to his own stronghold, Pomfret Castle, and there beheaded, by order of the king and a council of peers.

A truce for thirteen years, which had been proposed by the Scots, and in which Bruce waved his title of king, promised Edward some desirable repose. It was not decreed, however, that he should enjoy it. Roger, lord Mortimer, who had been twice convicted of treason, and owed his life to Edward's clemency, escaped from the Tower to France, and entered into communication with the discontented barons of Lancaster's party.

It soon became evident that her mission as a mediator between her husband and her brother Charles le Bel was a mere pretence in order to rejoin Mortimer. For when Edward had consented to conditions such as it was thought he would never have accepted, Charles, at the suggestion of his wicked sister, demanded that the possession of Guienne and Ponthieu should be transferred to the Prince of Wales, then but twelve years old, and that the new possessor should do homage for them in person. To this suspicious proposal the English sovereign also assented. Young Edward sailed with a splendid retinue, and performed his service without delay. He was instructed not to tarry, but he was detained by his mother; and the repeated commands of the king to return home were disregarded by both.

The Pope, having remonstrated with Charles for harbouring Isabella and her son, in opposition to king Edward's will, an asylum was prepared for her with William, count of Hainault; to whose court she was accompanied with her accomplice and adviser, Roger Mortimer. Here she affianced her son Edward to Philippa, the count's second daughter. On the other hand, count William furnished her with two thousand men at arms for the invasion of England. She landed at Orwell in Suffolk, September 24. She was recruited by all the Lancastrian faction, and the two half-brothers of the king. Her husband and his favourite fled to his estates in Wales, where they met little sympathy. The aged Winchester held Bristol and its castle, which he surrendered to the queen, and was immediately put to death by her followers. The younger Spencer and the king were captured after a brief pursuit in Wales; the former was arraigned before the queen at Hereford, condemned and executed; the latter was sent to Kennilworth castle.

The king was forthwith deposed by a parliament held at Westminster, and his sceptre formally transferred to his son, who was crowned, January 25, 1327, within a few days after a pretended or extorted abdication. Berkely castle was Edward's last prison, where he was in the keeping of Lord Berkely and Sir John Maltravers. He was put to death on the night of the 21st of September, 1327, while in charge of two officers, Gourney and Ogle. His shrieks were heard by the inmates; but when his corpse was shown next day, no external marks of violence were visible, except the horrid expression of agony remaining on the visage. It was interred in St. Peter's abbey, Gloucester.

11. EDWARD III., surnamed WINDSOR.

Tempted by the unsettled condition of England, Bruce prepared for an irruption. His intentions were anticipated by the appearance of Edward at Durham, at the head of a large army. The Scot refused to engage, eluded pursuit, and wearied with skilful manœuvres his powerful enemy. It was finally agreed that Edward's sister Jane should marry Bruce's son, afterwards David II., and that Edward himself should renounce all claim of superiority over the crown of Scotland, 1328.

The power usurped by Isabella and Mortimer, and their

wide spoliations, fomented much discontent and conspiracy. To secure themselves they followed up their crimes. They compelled the king's cousin and guardian, the Earl of Lancaster, president of the council, to enter into recognisances for his good behaviour. They arrested his uncle, the Earl of Kent, son of Margaret of France, in parliament; put him on his trial; and Isabella herself, it is said, witnessed his decapitation.

When Edward arrived at his eighteenth year, he knew his right to the reins of government, and the difficulty of seizing them from the foul hands which held them. He broke his mind to Lord Montacute, and Mortimer was surprised in Nottingham Castle, where he then abode with the queen and the young king, who lent his assistance. Mortimer was hanged at Tyburn, Nov. 29, 1330. Nor was justice yet satisfied. From this culprit descended many eminent wretches pursued by the bolts of unerring vengeance. It is a remarkable and instructive piece of history. This Roger's great-grandson, Edmund, was married to Philippa, daughter of Lionel, duke of Clarence, and consequently grand-daughter of Edward III.

Philippa's son Roger, earl of March, was slain in Ireland. Her grandson, Edmund, earl of March, was the lawful heir at the accession of Henry IV, but never recovered his rights.

Her daughter Elizabeth married Hotspur, who was slain in the battle of Shrewsbury.

Her granddaughter Anna was grandmother of that Richard, duke of York, who was killed in the battle of Wakefield.

From this Richard sprung a luckless race. His grandsons, Edward V. and Richard, duke of York, were murdered in the Tower, by their uncle Richard.

His son Richard III. perished in the battle of Bosworth.

His son George, duke of Clarence, was condemned by Edward IV., his elder brother, to be smothered.

The children and descendants of George, duke of Clarence, were very unfortunate. His son, Edward, earl of Warwick, was brought to the block by Henry VII.; and his daughter Margaret, countess of Salisbury, by Henry VIII.; Margaret's son, Henry lord Montagu, was beheaded a little before herself, by order of the same tyrant.

This list of calamities and judgments could be extended, but it has occupied us too long.

It was not thought becoming to lay open the queen's guilt

before the public. She was condemned to an obscure but safe life in Risings castle, where she lasted for twenty-seven years.

On the death of Bruce, Edward Baliol, the son of John, was prompted to revive his claims to the Scottish crown. By again compromising its independence he secured the friendship of Edward, by whose aid he gained the battle of Halidon Hill, in which Sir Archibald Douglas, the guardian of David, fell. Baliol ascended the throne from which the boy fled into France, where he resided for many years. The outbreak of the war with France and Baliol's incapacity and unpopular conduct led to David's restoration in 1341.

The *Salic Law*, which excluded females from the inheritance of the crown, was certainly an ancient French institution. On the accession of Philip V. the elder branches of his house were without male representatives. The claims of Philip of Valois were therefore evident. But to strengthen the Salic law which had been for a long time little better than a tradition, Philip V., his brother Charles le Bel, their heiresses, and other members of their house, entered into a family compact, relinquishing and invalidating any right inconsistent with the ancient law. At the death of Charles, had not the Salic law force, Edward III. would have been hair, by virtue of primogeniture. But that this law did exist, about which matter some have had doubts, is manifest, from the very style in which Edward put forth his claim. He insisted that as he was born in the lifetime of Isabella's father, Philip le Bel, he was heir to his grandfather's rights, but not to his mother's disqualification. This is as plain an acknowledgment of the existence of the Salic law, as it is a whimsical plea to defeat it. But the acknowledging it deprived him of all ground of pretension, independently of the family arrangement referred to. Yet such was the pretence that led to such waste of money and of blood; to that destruction of life, which folly calls glory, and reason murder.

Nevertheless when summoned by Philip to do homage for Guienne, Edward thought prudent to obey, till ready to resist. But presently he began to form alliances with the revolted Flemish cities, with Jacob the brewer of Ghent, and the Emperor Lewis of Bavaria. Those showy alliances, however, produced little fruit. The king had to go home to improve his finances. To intercept his return, Philip had assembled a large fleet at Sluys. The English defeated it; and Edward marched at the head of two hundred thousand men to besiege Tournay and St. Omer. But these mighty preparations also ending in nothing, he again went home; and arriving unexpectedly imprisoned most of the officers of state, whom he suspected of pilfering from his exchequer. Having replenished his purse, he resumed the campaign in France, and won the famous victory of Creci, August 25, 1346, in which his son, called the *Black Prince*, from the colour of his armour, first distinguished himself, being then in his fifteenth year. The French lost thirty thousand; among them were the count D'Alençon, brother of Philip, the count of Flanders, the duke of Lorraine, and John of Luxemburgh, king of Bohemia, whose device, "Ich dien," (I serve,) the Prince of Wales adopted as motto.

News from Scotland greatly influenced the joy diffused by this success. Two months were not elapsed since it had been achieved, and Edward's strength was drawn round Calais, when the defeat of the Scots at Neville's cross, by queen Philippa, was announced, and the capture of David II., to be a tenant of the tower for eleven years.

Twelve months had been consumed before Calais, which was not assaulted, but reduced by blockade and famine. Edward, exasperated at their obstinacy, would not grant the garrison capitulation when they begged it. To avert the dread consequences apprehended from an unconditional surrender, Eustace St. Pierre and five other burgesses offered themselves as a sacrifice to appease the victor's wrath. Before him they presented themselves, bare as to their feet and heads, with halters in their hands; accompanied by fifteen knights, their swords inverted; and led by the governor of the town. This sad and submissive spectacle moved not the severe king. Their prayers touched him not, though they softened his flinty barons, who mixed their entreaties with the pleas of misfortune and the broken eloquence of despair. Edward listened, still inexorable. He was bent on punishing men by whose piracies at sea he had suffered much; and by whose obstinacy he had lost many men and months of valuable time. His stern refusal of the expiation offered him was pronounced, and the scene about to change from prayer to punishment; when Philippa, a tender spectator, who had been herself the herald from Neville's Cross, interposed. To her advocacy and tears the fierce warrior gave way, and turned aside to enjoy perhaps the happiest moment of his life. The devoted embassy were left at the queen's disposal, who entertained them kindly, and sent them back to their anxious townsmen laden with benefactions and joyful tidings.

Edward had attained a lofty position, which enabled him to listen to the dictates of prudence without any hurt to his pride. He proposed to exchange his claims to the French crown for the acknowledgment of his sovereignty over those provinces he held as vassal; but Philip scornfully rejected his terms. John, his son and successor, seemed willing to accept them, but found his inclinations thwarted by those of his people; and the war was opened by Edward with sixty thousand men in the year 1355. With these he laid waste in seven weeks not less, it is related, than five hundred cities, towns, and villages. Yet the great object was baffled by John, who prudently avoided coming to a decisive engagement. The want of provisions began to be felt; and the English army was thereby obliged hastily to fall back on Calais. There, while John was amusing him with proposals for a general engagement, by the issue of which the combatants were finally to abide, the news from Scotland alarmed Edward, and summoned his presence there. There, however, his chagrin was short. After retaking Berwick, he bought from Baliol all his rights to the throne of Scotland, together with his patrimony in Galloway.

During his absence his gallant son, the Black Prince, prosecuted hostilities in France, with a temerity natural to youth and success. With a small army, 12,000 strong, he left Bordeaux, ascended the Garonne, and spread pillage and devastation over the fertile provinces of Querci, Limousin, Auvergne, and Berri. Fears for his critical position reached him late in the very heart of France. No sooner did he make a motion for retreat than John, a captain of unquestionable courage and capacity, planned to intercept him. The prince directed his march towards Poitiers, and within five miles of it, his van unexpectedly came up with the rear of the enemy. Next morning the terrible array was drawn out on either side. The French were five times more numerous than the English. The cardinal legate, Talleyrand, made several efforts to prevent this unequal combat. The prince offered fair terms— the giving up of his conquests, spoils, and captives; and not to bear arms against France for seven years. John, confident of his superiority, demanded the surrender of the prince, and a hundred knights as hostages. Next day was fought the battle of Poitiers, in which the flower of the French chivalry

DEATH OF THE BLACK PRINCE.

was destroyed, and king John with Philip, his son, fell into the hands of their enemy. The unhappy monarch was received in England with becoming respect, and conducted through the city by the prince in quality of an attendant, and serving with the spirit of a generous humility. A magnificent banquet awaited him at the Westminster Hall; where, as he made his appearance before the peers and prelates of England, king Edward rose from his throne and embraced him. He was lodged in the palace of the Savoy, and subsequently at Windsor.

At this triumphant moment it was easy to procure king David's release on ransom. He did not long survive his liberation; nor was it paid for some time after. "The Great Truce" for twenty-five years was made June, 1365.

The terms submitted by Edward, in reference to king John's release, were not acceptable to the French. Edward again swept over France, and planted his banners before the gates of Paris. Weary of the victories, the expenses, and perhaps mindful of the fickleness of fortune—Edward dictated the *great peace* of Bretigni, 1360, on more moderate conditions than could have been expected. He relinquished all his possessions and pretensions for the full sovereignty of Poitou, Guienne, Ponthieu, Calais, and Guisnes, a ranson of three million crowns of gold for king John, and hostages for its payment within six years.

This compact did not secure peace. Edward having formed all his dominions between the Loire and Pyrenees into one principality, under the name of Aquitaine, he bestowed it on the Black Prince. In 1364, John died in London, and was succeeded by the dauphin, Charles V. (*the Wise.*) In 1369 a dispute arose between Charles and the Prince of Aquitaine. The former, in breach of the late treaty, pronounced a judicial decree of annexation against Aquitaine. For six years victory followed the French standards. The prince lay in the castle of Angoulême, a prey to disease and vexation; but reinforcements having come from his father, he unfolded his standard at Cognac. The noise of his name stopt the career of conquest and exultation. The French dukes retired to their garrisons. The English prince closed and disgraced his career by the retaking of Limoges, 1370. He followed up his success by an indiscriminate massacre of the inhabitants. Shortly after he was ordered to England, where his stout constitution held out for six years against the continued assaults of disease. It is five hundred years since he died, and yet his laurels are green. And he owes nothing to the bard of the heroic ballad.

The king survived his son but one year. He died at Sheen, now Richmond, June 21, 1377, in the sixty-fifth year of his age. Of his twelve children only four survived him, three sons and a daughter.

In this reign John Wycliffe, rector of Lutterworth, whose followers were afterwards called *Lollards* (singers), created much public excitement by his invectives against the clergy, especially the friars. His violent discourses were countenanced by John of Gaunt and Percy, earl marshal. Having been summoned before the Primate and the Bishop of London, he made an apology; was dismissed with a reprimand, and ordered to hold his peace for the future. He died at his rectory, 1385, where his pulpit is yet to be seen.

12. RICHARD II., surnamed BORDEAUX.

The son of the Black Prince was in the eleventh year of his age, when he was crowned at Westminster, July 16, 1377, and a council of regency appointed to conduct the administration.

The war with France revived for a while, but subsided in a peace effected with a regency which acted for another minor Charles VI. A great deal of discontent prevailed amongst the *villeins* or bondsmen. The infection gradually spread upward amongst a better class, and found sympathisers and expounders. Grievances became opinions, and opinions began to question systems. If in the development there was much extravagance, in the germ there was much truth. The population had increased, but employment had not increased with it! Feudal lords do not discover employment, nor even dream of it. The demands of the royal exchequer had grown more frequent and more burthensome, but the supplies of the royal mint did not keep pace with them. Taxes and tallages had enormously multiplied; not so the groats and shillings; for the barons were not coiners; they earned no groats and made no shillings. There were exactions which could not be paid; oppressions which could not be legally resisted; and misery which could not be referred to idleness, drunkenness, or crime. Popular distress is a warm soil for the sowing of levelling doctrines. Some of Wycliffe's were of this character very decidedly: one was that every man living in sin may be justly deprived of his property. The aristocracy candidly admitted that such a proposition was nothing less than a bill of confiscation against two-thirds of their class; and their hostility was in proportion to their fears.

Where the new theory failed to persuade, it was necessary to carry intimidation. The peasants rose against their lords, and set the laws at defiance. The revolt began in Essex, under the guidance of a priest, who was popularly called Jack Straw. The kindling of the insurrection in Kent is attributed to an accident. A tyler of Dartford slew a tax-gatherer for insulting a young girl, his daughter, when levying a poll-tax. Wat Tyler became a hero, and was immediately chosen leader of the commons of Kent. In a brief space the insurgents mustered on Blackheath one hundred thousand men, to whom their chaplain, John Ball, preached from such a fascinating text as this;—
"When Adam delved, and Eve span,
Who was then a gentleman?"

The multitude marched on London, where they committed many excesses, but rigidly abstained from private plunder. The council had no safety but in promises and civility. To the crowds on Tower Hill, a herald proclaimed that the king wished his people to meet him at Mile-end, where he would listen to all their demands. These were but four; the abolition of slavery, the reduction of the rent of land to four-pence the acre, the free liberty of buying and selling in all fairs and markets, and a general pardon. These were granted by charter. Tyler and Straw, however, gave way to some excesses, the motives for which are not known, and cannot now be easily imagined. They burst into the Tower, liberated the prisoners, and murdered Sudbury, Archbishop of Canterbury, and Chancellor. Next morning, as Richard rode through Smithfield, with sixty horsemen, he met Tyler with his multitudes. A parley ensued, which seemed to be growing warm. Tyler was noticed by Walworth, the mayor, to be playing with his dagger. The demagogue proceeded to lay hold of the king's bridle. Walworth, who was on the alert, thrust his sword through the assailant's throat, whom Standish, one of the royal esquires, instantly despatched. The king, with great presence of mind, rode boldly to the crowd, offered himself as their leader, and thus escaped those bows which were already drawn to avenge the death of their hero. He led the malcontents to Islington, where a force sufficient to protect him speedily followed. Shortly after, the confederacy fell to pieces, and Richard revoked the charter, the points of which appear equitable and temperate. But this the first Revolution in England was not without a beneficial consequence. It caused the king to propose to Parliament to take into consideration the expediency of abolishing bondage altogether. But the barons were not prepared for such an advancement towards humanity; the suggestion of the king and his council, was answered with a refusal; which, considering the intelligence of the times, may have been beneficial to both parties.

In 1382 a Carmelite friar had given information respecting a disloyal intention of John, duke of Lancaster, towards the king. The duke demanded trial by battle, to prove his innocence. The friar was given up to the care of Sir John Holland, half-brother to the king, and was strangled by the hands of his keeper. Richard was wise enough to suspect an understanding between the Hollands and Lancaster; and gave directions for the arrest of the latter; but Lancaster shut himself up in Pontefract Castle. But Jane of Kent, mother of Holland and Richard, procured a reconciliation between all parties. The king in this year married Anne of Bohemia, who gave character to a throne.

The old Scottish war was revived with the aid of France. The devastations on both sides were counted, and nearly balanced. The king rewarded his captains with an increase of title. He created his uncles Edmund and Thomas, dukes respectively of York and Gloucester; Henry of Bolingbroke, he made earl of Derby; and Edward Plantagenet, duke of Rutland. To cut off the ambitious hopes of his uncle Lancaster, he declared Roger earl of March, heir presumptive, as he had no offspring himself.

The absolute incapacity of the king for the administration of public affairs subjected the nation to the havoc of parties contending for power. On one side was Lancaster; on the other Gloucester; and between them the people, victims of a selfish and vulgar ambition. The king lamented the absence of Lancaster; but Gloucester and his party soothed his sorrows by threatening his safety. They compelled him to assent to a commission to enquire into abuses, and left him stript of all power.

In 1387 he assembled a council at Nottingham, who declared that the conduct of the Commissioners was illegal; but

Fulthorpe, Kent, and Gloucester discovered these proceedings, and took the necessary precautions.

In these quarrels, parties and principles are not always discernible. Gloucester, Arundel, Derby, Nottingham, and Warwick appeared for the people, and impeached their rivals, and accused five of the king's favourites of treason. These obnoxious parties had to provide for their safety by flight or concealment, for the royal protection was powerless.

Gloucester and Derby took the keys of the city, and demanded an audience; in which Richard assented to the arrest of his friends. Gloucester ruled arbitrarily for a long time; but ambitious men, without definite objects, are sure of a check; and shortly after Gloucester was challenged by the king as to his years and regnant powers. When Richard was fairly invested with royal authority, petty quarrels still existed; nor was any constitutional power existing to interfere. This is a dark period. There was not people, nor king, nor parliament; and history must leave the student to guess how a nation may fall a prey to civil dissension directed by private views. From parliament all the bishops and abbots retired; yet the lords proceeded against Tresilian and Brembre, and had them executed. Gloucester was triumphant; and no tyranny was ever more complete; but it was not to last long. York and Derby came quietly forward; undertook the patronage of the royal authority; and presuming greatly on the rights of the people brought Gloucester to a decent submission. He was recalled to the council on the return of Lancaster from Guienne.

Pending those troubles in England, it is necessary to turn the reader's eye towards Ireland, the island of history. After the death of queen Anne, Richard visited Ireland. That country had produced a revenue of thirty thousand pounds; now the receipts were nothing. The English pale had been gradually tightened; and the gentlemen of the north sternly kept Ulster in their own hands. But excessively irritating statutes were passed in the parliament of Kilkenny. The lords of the pale sought Irish nurses for their babes; and this was declared, statutably, treason.

The statute of treasons, revised and published in the late reign, referred exclusively to compassing the king's life or authority, with overt act. The parliament of Kilkenny made the nursing of a child of English parentage by an Irish woman High Treason. Poor Richard went to Ireland to witness such a ruinous civil code, among people then in the same Christian faith.

To restore tranquillity, Richard, in the ninth year of his reign created Oxford, marquis of Dublin; bestowed the government of Ireland for life; and gave him grant of all lands he should conquer from the natives, excepting what had already been conferred upon previous adventurers. To facilitate this simple plan of a confiscation, new to history and morals, the parliament granted thirty thousand marks; and all this was done by mere will of a boy. With four thousand men at arms and thirty thousand archers, Richard landed at Waterford. The duke of Gloucester and the earls of Rutland and Nottingham aided him with their advice, and though the state of the country, intersected with lakes, morasses, and forests, impeded his progress; though the enemy, by retiring into inaccessible fastnesses, shunned his approach; yet, in a short time, the idea of resistance was abandoned. The Irish chieftains were entertained at the king's table; accepted knightly robes; and were adorned with English titles.

While the king was thus establishing his power in Ireland, he was recalled home by Lollardism. Its disciples drew up a very inflammatory petition to the Commons, which no one had the courage to present. The teachers of the new ideas were expelled from the University of Oxford.

On the death of his queen, Richard solicited the hand of Isabella, daughter of Charles VI., a princess in her eighth year. The truce between the two crowns was extended to twenty eight years. The marriage ceremony was performed by the archbishop of Canterbury, and the little queen was crowned afterwards at Westminster.

Nottingham now found the alliance with France useful in his projects against Gloucester. When the latter fell into his hands as earl Marshal, he was demitted to Calais, and there is no further knowledge of his fate than that he disappeared.

The crown had at this time not one honest man in England to defend it. The proud, aspiring, barons saw the sceptre in the hands of a weak boy. Instead of wise council they gave him such advice as led him gradually from the hands of one rogue to those of another. And, therefore, it appears on the face of history that the peerage of England for personal purposes absolutely made vile the sovereign's life.

It was this heartless rivalry which led to the king's deposition. Mowbray, the earl-marshal, who had been raised to the duchy of Norfolk, suspected the king's sincerity and imparted his doubts to his kinsman, Henry, son of John of Gaunt. This Henry conferred with Richard; and the result was the challenge of battle. Richard condemned Norfolk to banishment for life; and Hereford for ten years. On the death of Hereford's father, he became duke of Lancaster. He returned immediately; and the king was almost instantly deposed.

CHAP. V.—HOUSES OF LANCASTER AND YORK.

13. HENRY IV., surnamed BOLINGBROKE.

The new king assumed the name of Henry IV., and was crowned within a fortnight after the deposition of Richard. The attainders of the earls of Arundel and Warwick were reversed. Henry's eldest son was created prince of Wales, duke of Guienne, Lancaster, and Cornwall, and heir apparent.

Several statutes were passed conferring more security on the person. Treason was again limited to the acts enumerated in the famous decree of Edward III. The appeals in parliament were reserved for the ordinary courts, and liveries to retainers were made a royal privilege. Henry soon learned that it was more easy to win the crown than to retain it. Foreign princes treated him as an usurper. He could not trust the fidelity of his own subjects. For nine years he was kept in fear of his liberty by the conspiracies of malcontents. The first attempt against him was made by five of the lords appellants who had so narrowly escaped in the last parliament. The new king resolved to signalize his advent to the throne by a Scotch expedition. He summoned all persons possessed of fees or annuities granted by the three preceding kings to meet him at York, under penalty of forfeiture. He despatched heralds to the barons of Scotland and king Robert to appear at Edinburgh, on the 23rd day of August, and do homage. But the Scots did not answer this invitation, and Henry had to retire within his own borders.

His attention was now turned towards Wales, where Owen Glendower had raised the standard of independence. It happened that a powerful neighbour, Grey of Ruthyn, seized some of Owen's patrimony. Glendower petitioned the king, and was offended by a scornful refusal, which drove him to arms. Henry invaded Wales from three different quarters; and returned with disgrace to England. The weather favoured the

F

Welsh prince, and this campaign was an error and a disappointment.

Glendower had Grey and Sir Edward Mortimer prisoners. Grey purchased his liberty with permission of Henry; but Mortimer was refused the royal sanction. Mortimer was the natural guardian of the young earl of March, the heir to the throne; and this fact explains the conduct of Henry, a known usurper. Henry Percy was Mortimer's brother-in-law; and the friendship between the Northumberland house and the king had been long on the wane. To free himself from his fetters Mortimer married the daughter of Glendower. Hotspur hastened into North Wales; and the men of Cheshire joined him, declaring for Richard if yet alive. The rival parties met at Shrewsbury, where the fall of Hotspur brought the dispute to an end, and left Bolingbroke without a party able to give him any opposition.

The attempt instigated by lord Bardolf in Yorkshire, in 1408, was still weaker, though promoted by Archbishop Scrope and the earl-marshal. Here it was that Gascoigne, chief justice of England, declared his incompetency to issue sentence against those high personages on the mere demand of the crown. But the unbending integrity of Gascoigne did not save the enemies of Henry. He procured an obsequious agent, named Fulthorpe, to pronounce sentence against them, and they were beheaded. The attempt finally closed by the fall of Northumberland in battle, and the death of Bardolf from his wounds. Glendower maintained his struggle in his native hills till the beginning of the next reign.

Henry secured succession to his four sons by Mary de Bohun, daughter of the earl of Hereford. Of these the eldest had already won popular favour by his valour on the field of Shrewsbury, and was subsequently crowned king of France.

It is thought this usurper perished of a guilty conscience, for he died in his forty-ninth year; and having defeated all adversaries, never enjoyed one minute's happiness. On his death-bed he could leave his son no better title than his sword. He lived without regard to any principle which did not benefit his immediate exigency; and to the last the thought of an earthly crown appeared much too precious in his estimation. Religion would have shown him a brighter vista, and softened the last pang. Human glory occupied, it is to be feared, his departing moments. He left no issue by his second wife, Jane of Navarre.

14. Henry V., surnamed of Monmouth.

Henry set at liberty the earl of March at his accession. It was an act of grace and justice, which served him much. Oldcastle had been his friend; and Henry desired to befriend him; but Oldcastle on his trial rejected all proposals. Henry set free the earl of March, and never after allowed his life or liberty to be threatened.

The French ministers now sent ambassadors to Henry at Winchester; Canterbury next day sent word that the king of England could take nothing less than the restoration of all his provinces in France. Every preparation was now complete. Henry tried his enemies and had them executed. Then he marched into France, and on the 24th of October, 1415, won the battle of Azincourt. The result was, Catharine of France was given to the victor; and this lady when a widow, became wife of Owen Tudor. After the marriage of Henry of Monmouth with the daughter of Charles Le Bien-aimé no event attracts notice. At Azincourt Henry and Alençon, the kindest and bravest captains of the age, shook hands.

It was in 1417 that Henry invaded France, with pretensions not justified by any right of descent. But he advanced at the head of a vast army; and all the French towns bent before him, Touques, Auvillers, Villers, Caen, Bayeux, dropt into his hands. Rouen held out for four months, but at last surrendered. The murder of the duke of Burgundy caused fresh dissensions among the French. Henry was sought by the friends of Burgundy, and was married to Catharine, May 21, 1422. The king was seized with a slow malady, of which we have no account. He left a memorable name. As a hero he is nearly equal to Alexander, so in youth, so in glory.

The remains of the great prince were vastly honoured by the piety and bravery of his time. The barons, the bishops, the people, deplored the husband of Catharine of France, the boy of Shrewsbury, and the victor of Azincourt.

He met his fate with composure, and divided the short remnant of his time between the concerns of his soul and those of his family. On the day of his death he called to his presence, Bedford, Warwick, and four others. He appointed Warwick tutor to the prince, and Gloucester guardian to the kingdom. He died, amidst much consolation of friends and clergy, on the last day of August, 1422.

By military men he was beloved and admired. The body of the king was conveyed to Paris and Rouen, where it lay in state; and from Rouen by short journeys to Calais, where a fleet was in waiting to transport it to England. As the procession approached London, the dignitaries received the body of Henry V. with all expression of public respect.

In Dec., 1417, Sir John Oldcastle, a leader of the Lollards, was hanged by the waist over a slow fire, for treason and heresy. He had some time before failed in an outbreak of that party.

15. HENRY VI., surnamed WINDSOR.

The French throne was saved by the premature death of Henry V. The new king, the son of Henry and Catharine of France, was scarcely nine months old. On the first advice of his father's decease, several peers assembled at Westminster; issued commissions in the king's name to the judges, sheriffs, and other officers; and summoned a parliament to meet in November. Gloucester was named president of the council of state, and Bedford regent for France. Two sisters of the duke of Burgundy were married by Bedford and Bretagne; and these alliances were used against the French monarchy. After some years it was determined to cross the Loire, and attack Charles in the provinces that had always been true to his cause. The first proposal was to reduce Orleans, which was saved by one of the most remarkable events in history. Joan, the daughter of a poor innkeeper of Domreny, a village between Vaucoleurs and Neufchateau, was seized by an inspiration that in the hands of God she may be an instrument to save her country. She presented herself before the king and his court. Affairs were in despair. A moment of enthusiasm had arrived. The leadership of a woman, a girl, roused the spirit of the whole nation. Wise men took advantage of the simple girl's courage. She was of blameless life; of true patriotism; and had no motive but to sacrifice herself for the nation. The first to whom she presented herself was General Baudricourt. To prove her mission she is said to have discerned the king amongst his courtiers. "In the name of God," she exclaimed, "it is you are the king. Most noble dauphin, I am the maid Joan, sent on the part of God to aid you and the kingdom, and by his order I announce that you will be crowned in Rheims." On the following day she appeared in arms, on horseback, and assumed the lead of French chivalry

THE MAID OF ORLEANS.

in her seventeenth year. Dunois, governer of Orleans, led her secretly into the city, which was besieged by Suffolk, a commander of great resolution, who thought it right to raise his siege. This was the first triumph of the maid of Orleans. Her next was at Rheims. The Burgundian garrison had possession of the city in the English interest, but the citizens rose, drove them out, and received their king to crown him as the girl had promised. She subsequently fell into the hands of the duke of Burgundy at Compeigne. An accusation of heresy was raised against her. Her trial occupied the court for sixteen days; and she was induced by terror to subscribe a declaration of guilt of which she could not have been conscious. About twelve months after her capture, May 30, 1431, flames were kindled round the maid of Orleans in the city of Rouen, midst an immense concourse of spectators.

His partisans crowned the English monarch king of France, December 17, 1430, but the desirable place was Rheims, where the enthusiasm and courage of a pious girl had prevented this intention.

The deaths, in 1447, of the duke of Gloucester and Cardinal Beaufort removed the two firmest supports of the house of Lancaster, and revived those of Richard duke of York; descended from Edward Langley, son of Edward III., and who united in himself the claims of two branches. The claims of Richard were the origin of the "War of the Roses;" the Yorkists being distinguished by a white rose and the Lancastrians by a red. For thirty years the people were torn by this internecine contest. Party alone was concerned. The rights of succession were not canvassed. The nobles sought their immediate interests. The people were forgotten. The law was employed as an instrument of death. The fields that should have been tilled were stained with the blood of husbandmen, dragged from the plough to serve Richard or Henry.

The representative of the Mortimers now appeared in Richard, who left his command in Ireland to attack the Duke of Somerset. He was made protector, March, 1454. The party opposed to him contracted with Réné of Sicily, nominal duke of Anjou, a marriage with Henry for his daughter Margaret. This union disturbed the minds of the people. Nobles of England had grants of land in Anjou, Guienne, and Maine, and it was plain to all that these possessions were surrendered to Margaret's father.

Every tongue was employed to bewail the decay of England's glory, and request punishment on Suffolk. He was condemned to five years' imprisonment, and the sentence was improved by banishment. He was arrested at sea with the ominous salutation, "Welcome Traitor." Suffolk was executed next morning on board the pinnace.

Jack Cade, an Irishman, now assumed the pretensions of Mortimer, cousin to the duke of York. At the head of twenty thousand men he appeared at Blackheath. Cade demanded that York, Exeter, and Buckingham should be entrusted with the government and the keeping of the king's person. At Sevenoaks Cade turned on his pursuers. He took possession of London. Henry's friends rallied, and Cade was judicially condemned and beheaded.

Henry about this time sank into a state of mental weakness. York was recalled to the cabinet, and Somerset sent to the Tower. When the king recovered his health he liberated Somerset. But York placed himself immediately at the head of that party which succeeded in putting Edward IV. on the throne. At Ludlow the king, at the head of 60,000 men, defeated all opponents. Richard fled to Ireland, and his son Edward to Calais. In the battle of Northampton duke Richard and the earl his son made the king prisoner, July 1460. A parliament was called, at which it was decided that Richard should succeed. Margaret would not assent. She appeared in the north, where all the adherents of Lancaster rose. York and Salisbury fell at Wakefield, December, 1460. Salisbury was led to Pomfret and beheaded. Young Edward won the battle of Mortimer's Cross, near Wigmore, February 2, 1461, and was proclaimed in London, in March of the same year.

16. EDWARD IV. surnamed York.

At Towton, March 29th, 1461, the contest between York and Lancaster was decided in favour of the former house. The red rose had scarcely any support except in the exertions of Margaret on the continent. Henry sought an asylum in Lancashire; where the fidelity of the people protected him for a year. He was betrayed to Warwick, and conveyed to the Tower. Edward turned his attention to the interests with foreign states. He contracted marriage with the widow of Sir John Grey of Lancaster, and procured a parliament to declare her queen. But in 1469 an insurrection burst forth. On the first intelligence of this rising, Edward called his retainers

BATTLE OF TEWKESBURY.

to meet him at Newark. He was deserted. His enemies beat him at Edgcoat. In a few days he found himself captive to his brother and the two Nevilles, at Olney, plunged in the deepest distress. They removed him to Middleham, in Yorkshire. Two kings were now prisoners, in possession of parties who thought only of their own concerns. Warwick proclaimed Henry VI. Along with Clarence he marched into London. Edward's friends were all attainted and Warwick was called the king-maker. In the battle of Barnet, on Easter-day, 1471, Warwick and Montague were slain. On that day Margaret and her son landed at Weymouth. The contest was renewed, but the Lancastrians lost their whole hopes at Tewkesbury. The queen was imprisoned; ransomed in 1475, and died in 1482. She has left a heroic name, fighting battles to which she had manifest pretensions; but Edward, through his mother, had better claims.

Prince Edward was made prisoner in the battle of Tewkesbury, brought immediately before the three Yorkist brothers, and despatched, either by them or their attendants. A week after, Edward IV. triumphantly entered London; next day the dead body of Henry VI. was publicly exposed.

The duke of Clarence, the king's brother, was convicted of treason, and suffered in the Tower. Buckingham was summoned as steward, and pronounced sentence of death.

In the same year war was declared between England and Scotland, which, as usual, ended in nothing. Edward was much disappointed respecting the projected marriage of his daughter Elizabeth with the dauphin of France. When she had completed her twelfth year, it was hoped that Louis would have sent for the princess. Louis sent for Margarita of Austria. It is thought the vexation of Edward preyed so on his mind, in respect to this family affair, that he took sick, and died of mental anguish. Preceding his death he manifested serious moments of compunction and penitence; and perhaps not too late. On April 29, 1483, in the twenty-third of his reign, he appeared before the Great Judge.

17. EDWARD V.

On the death of the king, the young prince was proclaimed, and left in charge of Richard his uncle. Gloucester and Rivers were most interested in the safety of Edward's children; but Richard sought the throne, and the children were put to death in the Tower. To meet the usurpation of the tyrant Richard, Gloucester aimed at the crown. On the 24th June, 1483, the duke of Buckingham proposed Richard for king, and the citizens accepted him. Richard hesitated, but expressed a duty to comply with the will of the people. The farce was finished. Next day, June 26, 1483, Richard proceeded to Westminster, put himself in the marble seat, and forgave all pretended offences. The deposed children were destroyed by Forest and Dighton, while Sir John Tyrrel watched without the Tower.

18. RICHARD III. surnamed CROUCHBACK.

This prince reached a throne by artifice. He did not enjoy it long. His career is an example of a corrupt ambition, which was speedily punished and never admired. He opened his reign by a declaration of general forgiveness. But the announcement of the death of the princes struck the nation with horror. The 18th of October, 1483, was fixed by the bishop of Ely, for a general rising. All the virtue of England answered the venerable man. Henry of Richmond could advance no right; but he swore to marry the eldest daughter of York, and thus secured much of the support of that party.

Yet on the 21st August, Richard departed from Leicester, and encamped about two miles from Bosworth. Northumberland remained inactive, and Stanley took the field against him.

Richard's body was recovered from the field of battle, conducted to Leicester, exposed for two days, and buried in the church of the Grey Friars.

CHAP. VI.—HOUSE OF TUDOR.
19. HENRY VII., surnamed TUDOR.

The victory at Bosworth left Henry master of the throne. But a pretender named Simnel was sent forth by the duchess of Burgundy. Henry made this pretender a scullion in his kitchen.

The act was now passed against wearing the badge, against maintenance, support and protection of barony. This contributed much to popular privileges. But the increasing power of France had begun to alarm Europe. Henry went to France and returned a stipendiary by the treaty of Estaples, November 1492.

One Warbeck also received the patronage of the duchess of

Burgundy. James IV. of Scotland gave him his niece, the lady Catharine Gordon. Perkin Warbeck visited Cork, returned to Cornwall, and mustered about 6,000 followers as he approached Taunton. Warbeck surrendered on promise of pardon, Nov., 1497.

He was confined with Warwick in the tower; both were executed for attempting to escape.

A few years afterwards Henry lost his eldest son, who was married to Catharine of Arragon. Arthur's widow was affianced to his next son to save the return of the dower.

Henry's daughter Margaret was married to James IV. of Scotland, and thus introduced afterwards the House of Stuart.

Henry sought foreign alliances to support his throne; and spared the revenues to protect himself against the barons. Dudley and Empson were employed to enrich his exchequer, and these instruments were punished by his son. He had long suffered under bodily disease, and died 21st April, 1509. He left three children; Henry who succeeded him, Margaret queen of Scotland, and Mary the queen of Louis XII. of France. By his economy he lived without much dependence on his parliament. His charities were many and profuse.

The chapel bearing his name in Westminster is a lasting evidence of his taste, and he intended it as a memorial of penitence.

Henry was a man of large intelligence, and a benefactor of his fellow men. He paid and equipped the vessel that sailed from Bristol, under the command of John Cabot, the Venetian, who first explored Newfoundland.

20. Henry VIII.

The late king had forfeited, long before his death, the affections of his people; and the accession of his son, of the same name, was hailed as the commencement of a new era. The young Henry had almost completed his eighteenth year. He was handsome in person, apparently generous in disposition, and adroit in every martial and fashionable exercise.

With the unanimous assent of the council, he was now publicly married to the Spanish princess by the archbishop of Canterbury; their coronation followed, and these two events were celebrated with rejoicings, which occupied the court during the remaining part of the year.

Peace abroad and tranquillity at home, allowed the young monarch to indulge his natural taste for amusements. It was not long, however, before a quarrel between Julius, the Roman Pontiff, and Louis XII., king of France, caused Henry to engage in war. Henry took part with the Pope, and invaded France.

The memorable battle of Flodden was fought at this period. James IV. of Scotland had married Margaret, the sister of Henry. This new connexion did not, however, extinguish the hereditary partiality of the Scottish prince for the ancient alliance with France; and his jealousy of his English brother was repeatedly irritated by a succession of real or supposed injuries. James renewed the ancient alliance between Scotland and France, with an additional clause reciprocally binding each prince to aid his ally against all men whomsoever. Henry was already in France; and James despatched his fleet with a body of three thousand men to the assistance of Louis. At the same time a Scottsh herald sailed to France, the bearer of a letter from James to Henry, requiring the retreat of the English army out of that country; to which demand Henry refused to accede. James, at the head of one of the most numerous armies that had ever been raised in Scotland, passed the Tweed, and turning to the north, took numerous strong places. The earl of Surrey challenged James to battle, and the Scottish king, leading his army across the river, encamped on the hill of Flodden, the last of the Cheviot mountains, which border on the vale of Tweed. The memorable engagement of "Flodden Field" took place on the 9th September, 1513. James fought on foot, surrounded by some thousands of chosen warriors, who were cased in armour, and on that account less exposed to the destructive aim of the English archers. James was slain by an unknown hand, and fell about a spear's length from the feet of Surrey.

When the news of this important victory reached the king of England, he was besieging Tournay. This city contained a population of eighty thousand souls, and though situate within the territory of another power, had long been distinguished by its attachments to the French crown. To the summons sent by Henry, the inhabitants turned a bold and chivalrous defiance; but their resolution evaporated amid the fatigues and dangers of a siege, and on the eighth day they submitted.

Henry soon returned to England, proud of his victory, and

spent the winter in preparations for new conquests which he contemplated. But Louis, humbled by a long series of disasters, preferred negociation to war. Louis soon died, and his successor, Francis I., renewed all the engagements of his predecessor to the satisfaction of the English monarch.

Among the inferior dependents of Henry, there now appeared one whose aspiring views and superior talents rapidly enabled him to supplant every competitor. Thomas Wolsey, a native of Ipswich, and a clergyman, had been appointed in the last reign to one of the royal chaplains. After the death of his patron, he attached himself to the service of the bishop of Winchester, at whose recommendation he was intrusted with a secret and delicate negociation at the imperial court; and the expedition and address with which he executed his commission, not only justified the discernment of his friend, but also raised the agent in the estimation of his sovereign.

The affairs of Scotland presented for some time a melancholy scene of confusion. By degrees the Scottish spirit recovered. The queen had been permitted, in conformity with the will of her husband, to assume the regency as guardian to her son James V. Seven months had not elapsed from the death of her husband, when she was safely delivered of a second son, Alexander, duke of Ross; but in less than three months afterwards, she displeased both the nation and her brother, by marrying the young earl of Angus. A national deputation invited the duke of Albany to assume the government of the kingdom. He consented, and compelled the queen to surrender the two princes, whom he placed under the custody of three lords appointed by parliament.

The French monarch, Francis, whose youth and accomplishments made him the idol of his people, had already formed the most gigantic projects of conquest and aggrandizement. His real object was soon manifest. The Italian princes, whose jealousy had guarded to no purpose the accustomed roads over the Alps, were filled with consternation; in a consistory at Rome, it was proposed to solicit the aid of Henry; and a few days later Leo, to secure the mediation of Wolsey, named that minister cardinal priest of St. Cicely beyond the Tiber.

Henry directed his attention to a matter which more nearly concerned his own interests, the conduct of the duke of Albany in Scotland. Against the regency of that prince he had remonstrated. The Scottish parliament returned a firm, though respectful answer; but Francis, who still dreaded the hostility of the king of England, advised the Scots to conclude a perpetual peace with Henry, and even required the regent, in quality of his subject, to return to France. Albany obeyed, but before his departure provision was made for the return of queen Margaret, who had sought an asylum in England; and a temporary council was appointed, in which the numbers of the two parties were nearly balanced, and under the nominal government of which, Scotland passed four years of dissension and anarchy.

Wolsey still retained the first place in the royal favour. He was made chancellor and papal legate. The consequence was, that as long as Wolsey presided in the council, the minister was feared and courted by princes and pontiffs, and the king held the distinguished station of arbiter of Europe.

When Charles V. of Spain was elected emperor of Germany, Francis and Henry, who had also been candidates for the imperial throne, became closer allies. Francis invited Henry to France; and the English monarch, with a numerous and splendid retinue leaving Greenwich, proceeded by slow stages to Canterbury, where, to the surprise of all who had not been admitted into the secret, advice was received that Charles with a squadron of Spanish ships had cast anchor in the harbour of Hythe. This apparently accidental meeting was celebrated at Canterbury with feasts and rejoicings; the young emperor, by his flattery and attentions, rooted himself in the affections of Henry, and by promises and presents secured the friendship of Wolsey. On the fourth day after he sailed from Sandwich, the king, with his court, crossed the strait from Dover to Calais. Henry and Francis met near the town of Ardres, in a field called "The Field of the Cloth of Gold," on account of the splendour of the preparations. As soon as the kings had reached their respective residences, the cardinal paid a visit to Francis, and remained with him two days. The result was an additional treaty, the terms of which proved the extreme anxiety of that monarch to secure the friendship, or at least the forbearance of the English king. After these preliminaries, the monarchs rode from their several residences, alighted from their horses, embraced each other, and walked arm-in-arm into a pavilion, which had been prepared for their reception. The next fortnight was consumed in feats of arms and in banquets. The queens of England and France, with their ladies and officers, beheld the combatants from the galleries; and the heralds daily registered the names, the arms, and the feats of the knights. On every occasion the two kings appeared with equal splendour, and acquitted themselves with equal applause; their bravest antagonists deemed it no disgrace to yield to royal prowess; and Henry and Francis, though they fought five battles each day, overcame every opponent.

Ever since Henry had failed in his attempt to procure the imperial dignity, he had turned his thoughts and ambition towards the crown of France. This subject had been secretly discussed by Henry and Charles, and had led to the proposal of a stricter union between the crowns by the marriage of the emperor with the daughter of Henry. The flames of war were unexpectedly rekindled in 1521, between Francis and Charles, in Spain, Italy, and the Netherlands. The contending parties immediately appealed to Henry, and each claimed his aid in virtue of treaty. He exhorted each monarch to conclude a peace, and then proposed, that before he should make his election between them, they should appoint commissioners to plead before him or his deputy. Charles instantly signified his assent. Francis wavered, but, at length, condescended to accept the proffered mediation.

Henry conferred the high dignity of arbitrator on Wolsey, who proceeded to Calais in great state, as the representative of his sovereign. The mediation failed, and Wolsey declared that Francis had been the aggressor in the war, and that Henry was bound by treaty to aid his imperial ally.

Francis, having fruitlessly attempted to recover the friendship of the king of England, at length laid an embargo on the English shipping in his ports, and seized all the property of the English merchants. In retaliation, Henry confined the French ambassador to his house, ordered all Frenchmen in London to be taken into custody, and at length sent a defiance to Francis. The emperor, Charles V., landed at Dover, and was accompanied by the king through Canterbury, London, and Winchester, to Southampton. It was agreed between them that each power should make war on Francis, with forty thousand men. At Southampton, the emperor took leave of the king, and embarked on board his fleet. The money, necessary for the support of the army destined to invade France was yet to be raised: and to supply the deficiency, required all the art of Wolsey, aided by the despotic authority of the king.

At length, the earl of Surrey, who had been named to the command, mustered his army under the walls of Calais. He marched towards Amiens, carefully avoiding the fortified towns, and devoting to the flames every house and village which fell in his way; while the French, who had been forbidden to risk an engagement, hovered in small bodies round the invaders.

The duke of Albany, after his base negociation with Lord Dacre, had left Scotland; but the principal lords remained constant in their attachment to France, and impatiently expected his return with supplies of men and money. Henry sought a reconciliation with his sister, Queen Margaret, that he might set her up in opposition to Albany; and gave the chief command in the north to the earl of Surrey, son to the victor of Flodden Field, with instructions to purchase the services of the Scottish lords with money, and to invade and lay waste the Scottish borders. Margaret gladly accepted the overture, and consented to conduct her son, now in his twelfth year, to Edinburgh, and to announce by proclamation that he had assumed the government, provided the English general would march a strong force to her support. Surrey repeatedly entered the marches, spread around the devastation of war, and at last reduced to ashes the large town of Jedburgh. But on that very day Albany landed at Dumbarton with two thousand soldiers, and a great quantity of stores and ammunition. The projects of Margaret were instantly crushed; at the call of the parliament the whole nation rose in arms! and Albany saw above sixty thousand men arrayed round his standard. Surrey, however, received reinforcements, and Albany, after an ineffectual attempt to retain the regency, sailed for France, never more to set foot in Scotland.

Among the different projects which occupied the restless mind of Julius II., was that of erecting a temple worthy of the capital of the Christian world, of enormous dimensions and unrivalled magnificence. To raise money for this purpose, he had published an indulgence in Poland and France; which his successor, Leo X., had with the same view extended to the northern provinces of Germany. The papal commission was directed to Albert, elector of Mentz, and archbishop of Magdeburg; and that prelate employed as his delegate Tetzel, a Dominican friar, whose brethren rapidly spread themselves over Saxony.

The origin of the revolution which followed may, with probability, be attributed to the counsels of Staupitz, vicar of the friars of St. Augustine. It has been generally supposed that he was actuated by a spirit of opposition to the Dominicans.

About this time Leo published a bull declaratory of the doctrine of the Roman Church respecting indulgences, the original subject of the controversy. Though it does not mention Luther by name, it is evidently pointed against his assertions. It teaches that the pope, as successor of St. Peter, and the vicar of Christ upon earth, possesses the power of granting, for reasonable causes, certain indulgences in favour of such of the faithful as are in a state of grace, whether they be alive or dead, for the remission of the temporal punishment due on account of actual sin. This bull probed the sincerity of Luther to the quick.

There existed in Germany a very prevalent feeling of disaffection to the see of Rome. The violent contest between the popes and the emperors in former times had left a germ of discontent, which required but little aid to shoot into open hostility.

The politicians at Rome blamed the tardiness and irresolution of Leo himself, who for two years had suffered the innovator to brave the papal authority. The Pope thought that the storm might be allayed by gentleness, and commissioned Miltitz, a Saxon nobleman, to bring Luther back to his duty by persuasion and promises. Miltitz exhorted and advised, but without success. Leo soon published a bull in which he stigmatised Luther's propositions as false, scandalous, and heretical; allowed him sixty days to retract his errors; and pronounced him excommunicated if he continued obstinate after the expiration of that term. But success and impunity had taught Luther to deride the authority before which he had formerly trembled. He appealed to the decision of a general council; and having called an assembly of the inhabitants of Wittemberg, led them to a funeral pile, erected without the walls, and cast into the flames the books of the canon law, and the bull of Pope Leo against himself.

Accounts of all these transactions had been transmitted to England by the royal agents. Wolsey, by his office of legate, was bound to oppose the new doctrines. By a letter to Charles V. he had evinced his hostility to innovations in doctrine; but it was deemed prudent to abstain from any public declaration till the decision of the diet.

Henry himself was anxious to enter the lists against the German; nor did Wolsey discourage the attempt, under the idea that pride no less than conviction would afterwards bind the royal polemic to the support of the ancient creed. That the treatise

Defensio Septem Sacramentorum, which the king published as his own composition, was planned, revised, and improved by the superior judgment of the cardinal and the bishop of Rochester, was the opinion of the public. The dean of Windsor carried the royal production to Rome, and in a full consistory submitted it to the inspection and approbation of the pontiff. Clement accepted the present with many expressions of admiration and gratitude, and conferred on the English monarch the title of "Defender of the Faith."

Henry fell in love with Anne Boleyn, one of the queen's maids of honour, and, in order that he might marry her, he, to obtain a divorce, affected scruples of conscience concerning marriage with his brother's widow. The royal wish was no sooner communicated to Wolsey, than he offered his aid, and ventured to promise complete success.

Hitherto the king had concealed his thoughts respecting a divorce from the knowledge of the queen; but Catherine's eyes had witnessed his partiality for her maid, and her jealousy at last discovered the whole intrigue. In a fit of passion she reproached him to his face with the baseness of his conduct. Henry, however, appeased her by appealing to her piety, and protesting that his only object was to search out the truth, and to tranquillize his own conscience.

A commission was obtained from the pope authorizing Wolsey, with the aid of any one of the other English prelates, to inquire summarily, and without judicial forms, into the validity of the dispensation which had been granted by Julius, and of the marriage between Henry and Catherine; to pronounce, in defiance of exception or appeal, the dispensation sufficient or surreptitious, the marriage valid or invalid, according to the conviction of his conscience; and to divorce the parties, if it were invalid, but at the same time to legitimate their issue, if such legitimation were desired.

Wolsey now began to hesitate; and took the opportunity of declaring to the king at one of the consultations, that his gratitude did not destroy his duty towards God.

The court, for the trial of the validity of the marriage, met at the Blackfriars, and summoned the king and queen to appear on the eighteenth of June, 1529. The latter obeyed, but appealed to the pope. At the next session Henry sat in state on the right of the cardinals, and answered in due form to his name. Catherine was on their left; and, as soon as she was called, rising from her chair, entered a protest. On the refusal of the cardinals to admit her appeal, she rose a second time, crossed before them, and, accompanied by her maids, threw herself at the king's feet. "Sir," said she, "I beseech you to pity me, a woman and a stranger, without an assured friend, and without an indifferent counsellor."

Notwithstanding the queen's appeal, the cause proceeded, and on her refusal to appear in person or by her attorney, she was pronounced contumacious.

The legates had prolonged the trial by repeated adjournments. On the twenty-third of July, 1529, they held the last session; the king attended in a neighbouring room, from which he could see and hear the proceedings; and his counsel in lofty terms called for the judgment of the court. But Campeggio replied, that judgment must be deferred till the whole of the proceedings had been laid before the pontiff. He was too old, and weak, and sickly to seek the favour, or fear the resentment of any man. The defendant had challenged him and his colleague as judges, because they were the subjects of her opponent. To avoid error, they had therefore determined to consult Rome, and adjourned the court to the next term.

Henry seemed to bear the disappointment with a composure of mind which was unusual to him. But he had not been unprepared for the event. By the advice of Wolsey he resolved to conceal his real feelings, to procure the opinions of learned men in his favour, to effect the divorce by ecclesiastical authority within the realm, and then to confirm it by act of parliament.

Wolsey's good fortune now began to abandon him. At this moment, while Henry was still smarting under his recent disappointment, an instrument arrived from Rome, forbidding him to pursue his cause before the legates, and citing him to appear by attorney in the papal court under a heavy penalty. The whole process was one of mere form; but it revived the irritation of the king; he deemed it a personal insult, and completed the cardinal's folly. Hales, the attorney-general, soon afterwards, filed two bills against him in the King's Bench, charging him with having, as legate, transgressed the Statute of *Premunire*. This stroke, though it was not unexpected, plunged Wolsey into despair. His enemies laboured doubly to keep alive the royal displeasure against him. They represented him as an ungrateful favourite, who had sought nothing but his own interest and gratification. Still the king's partiality for his former favourite seemed to be proof against all the representations of the council. He continued to send to the cardinal from time to time consoling messages and tokens of affection, though it was generally by stealth, and sometimes during the night. When the court pronounced judgment against him, he took him under the royal protection; and when articles of impeachment had been introduced into the house of lords, and passed from it to the house of commons, he procured them to be thrown out by the agency of Cromwell, who from the service of the cardinal had risen to that of the king. Wolsey, however, sank in health and spirits. The anguish of his mind rapidly consumed the vigour of his constitution. About Christmas, 1529, he fell into a fever, which obstinately defied the powers of medicine. When Henry heard of his danger, he exclaimed, "God forbid that he should die. I would not lose him for twenty thousand pounds." He immediately ordered three physicians to hasten to Esher, where Wolsey lived, and repeatedly assured the cardinal of his unabated attachment.

As the agitation of Wolsey's mind subsided, the health of his body was restored; but his enemies had prepared for him a new conflict, and required of him additional sacrifices. It was ultimately agreed that Wolsey should retain the administration, temporal as well as spiritual, of the archiepiscopal see of York, but, in consideration of a general pardon, make over to the crown all his other ecclesiastical revenues.

On the 4th of November, 1530, Wolsey was unexpectedly arrested on a charge of high treason. He betrayed no symptoms of guilt; the king had not, he maintained, a more loyal subject than himself; there lived not on earth the man who could look him in the face and charge him with untruth; nor did he seek any other favour than to be confronted with his accusers.

His health (he suffered much from dropsy) would not allow him to travel with expedition; and at Sheffield Park, a seat of the earl of Shrewsbury, he was seized with a dysentery which confined him a fortnight. As soon as he was able to mount his mule he resumed his journey; but feeling his strength rapidly decline, he said to the abbot of Leicester, as he entered the gate of the monastery, "Father abbot, I am come to lay my bones among you." He was immediately carried to his bed; and the second day, seeing Kyngston, the lieutenant of the Tower, in his chamber, he addressed him in these well-known words: "Master Kyngston, I pray you have me commended to his majesty; had I but served God as diligently as I have served him, he would not have given me over in my grey hairs. But this is my just reward for my pains and study, not regarding my service to God, but only my duty to my prince." Having received the last consolations of religion, he expired the next morning, in the sixtieth year of his age.

To appoint a successor to Wolsey, in the Chancery, was an object of great importance; and the office was at length given to Sir Thomas More, the treasurer of the household, and chancellor of the duchy of Lancaster. The merit of More was universally acknowledged, and even Wolsey declared that he knew no one more worthy to be his successor.

About this time, Thomas Cromwell appears in history. His father was a fuller in the neighbourhood of the capital. The son in his early youth served as a trooper in the wars of Italy; from the army he passed to the service of a Venetian merchant, and, after some time, returning to England, exchanged the counter for the study of the law. Wolsey had employed him to dissolve the monasteries which had been granted for the establishment of his colleges, a trust which he discharged to the satisfaction of his patron, at the same time that he enriched himself. His principles however were flagitious.

When Henry, despairing of obtaining the pope's consent to the divorce, declared that he would abandon the idea, Cromwell urged him to imitate the princes of Germany, who had thrown off the yoke of Rome; and, with the authority of parliament, to declare himself the head of the Church within his own realm. Henry listened with surprise and pleasure to a discourse which flattered not only his passion for Anne Boleyn, but his thirst of wealth and greediness of power. He thanked Cromwell, and ordered him to be sworn of his privy council.

The bishoprics of York and Winchester, two of the most wealthy preferments in the English church, had remained vacant since the death of Wolsey, through the desire of Henry to bestow one of them on his kinsman, Reginald Pole. He was told that the king had marked him out for the first dignities in the English church, but previously expected from him a faithful explanation of his opinion concerning the divorce. Pole frankly owned that he was against it, but requested the respite of a month, that he might have leisure to study the question. He condemned the divorce, and the vacant sees were given to others.

Five years had now rolled away since Henry first solicited a divorce, and still he appeared to have made but little progress towards the attainment of his object. Anne Boleyn, in 1532, proved to be in a condition to promise him an heir; and the necessity of placing beyond cavil the legitimacy of the child induced him to violate a pledge which he had solemnly given to the king of France, that he would not marry Anne without the consent of the church, and he was privately married to her in January, 1533; but the marriage was not publicly avowed till the following Easter.

The next step was to obtain some ecclesiastical decision in favor of the divorce. With this view, Thomas Cranmer, who was in Henry's interest, was appointed archbishop of York. He held a court to which Catherine was summoned, but she did not appear, and Cranmer, in May, 1533, pronounced his judgment, that the marriage between her and Henry was null and invalid, and without force from the very beginning.

As soon as Cranmer had pronounced judgment, Catherine received a command from the king to be content with the style of dowager princess of Wales; and those among her dependents who gave her the title of queen were ordered to be irrevocably dismissed from her service. In foreign nations her lot became the object of universal commiseration; even in England, the general feeling was in her favour. At Rome, Clement was daily importuned by Charles V. and Ferdinand to do justice to their aunt, and he annulled the sentence given by Cranmer, as the cause was at the very time pending before himself, and excommunicated Henry and Anne, unless they should separate before the end of September.

But, in reality, it mattered little to Henry whether Clement had pronounced for or against him. The die was already cast; violent councils began to prevail in the English cabinet; and a resolution was taken to erect a separate and independent church within the realm. Act after act contradictory to the papal claims, was debated and passed in parliament; and the kingdom was severed by legislative authority from the communion of Rome, in 1534. Appeals to Rome were prohibited in all cases whatsoever; and in lieu of the right thus abolished, suitors were allowed to appeal from the court of the archbishop to the king in Chancery. It was enacted that bishops should no longer be presented to the pope for confirmation, nor sue out bulls in his court; but that, on the vacancy of any cathedral church, the king should grant to the dean and chapter, or to the prior and monks, permission to elect the person whose name was mentioned in his letters missive. It was also enacted, that since the clergy had recognised the king for the supreme head of the church of England, every kind of payment made to Rome, and every species of licence, dispensation, and grant, usually obtained from Rome, should forthwith cease; that hereafter all such graces and indulgences should be sought of the archbishop of Canterbury.

By another act, the marriage between Henry and Catharine was pronounced unlawful and null, that between him and Anne Boleyn lawful and valid; the king's issue by the first marriage was of course excluded from the succession, that by the second was declared entitled to inherit the crown.

The king had now accomplished his two great objects: he had bestowed on Anne the rights of a lawful wife, and had invested himself with the supremacy of the church. But the opposition which he had experienced strengthened his passions and steeled his heart against the common feelings of humanity; and each succeeding year of his reign was stained with the blood of many, often of noble and innocent, victims. Fisher, bishop of Rochester, and Sir Thomas More, lately lord chancellor, were sacrificed to Henry's anger, in 1534. More opposition to the divorce gradually effaced the recollection of his merit and services. He was accused of misprision of treason; attainted with others, and compounded with the crown for his freedom and personalties in the sum of three hundred pounds.

Sir Thomas More had ceased at this time to fill the office of chancellor. He opposed the divorce; and as, in the execution of his office, he had found himself unavoidably engaged in matters which he could not reconcile with his conscience, he tendered his resignation, and avoiding all interference in politics, devoted his whole time to study and prayer.

Fisher and More were summoned before the council at Lambeth, and were asked whether they would consent to take the new oath of succession. They offered to take the oath of succession if some matters were expunged which they considered wrong in theology. Both were remanded that they might have more time for consideration. The oath was tendered to them a second time; and both, on their refusal to take it, were committed to the Tower.

Fisher was soon afterwards tried for denying the king's ecclesiastical supremacy, found guilty, and beheaded.

More was soon afterwards tried for the same cause of offence, and was of course convicted. He met his fate with constancy, even with cheerfulness, declaring that he died a faithful subject to the king, and a true Catholic before God. His head was fixed on London Bridge. A bull was at this time signed by the pope against Henry and his abettors, but on account of the state of Europe, it was not thought prudent to promulgate the instrument.

Although Henry had now obtained the great object of his ambition, the extent of his ecclesiastical pretensions remained subject to doubt and discussion. Henry himself did not clearly explain, perhaps knew not how to explain, his own sentiments. Cromwell had long ago promised that the assumption of the supremacy would place the wealth of the clerical and monastic bodies at the mercy of the crown. Hence that minister, encouraged by the success of his former counsels, ventured to propose the dissolution of the monasteries; and the motion was received with welcome by the king and by archbishop Cranmer, whose approbation of the new doctrines taught him to seek the ruin of those establishments which proved the firmest supports of the ancient faith. A general visitation of the monasteries was therefore enjoined. The instructions which the visitors received breathed a spirit of piety and reformation, and were formed on the model of those formerly used in episcopal and legatine visitations; so that to men not intrusted with the secret, the object of Henry appeared, not the abolition, but the support and improvement of the monastic institute. A statement was compiled and laid before parliament, which, while it allotted the praise of regularity to the greater monasteries, described the less opulent as abandoned to sloth and immorality. A bill was introduced and hurried, though not without opposition, through the two houses, giving to the king and his heirs all monastic establishments, the clear yearly value of which did not exceed two hundred pounds. By this act about 380 communities were dissolved; and an addition of £32,000 made to the yearly revenue of the crown, besides the present receipt of £100,000 in money, plate, and jewels.

Henry had the cruelty to refuse an interview with her child Mary, to Catherine, who from her death-bed dictated a short letter to him, in which she conjured him to think of his salvation; forgave him all the wrongs which he had done her; and recommended their daughter Mary to his paternal protection. As he perused the letter, the stern heart of Henry was softened; he even shed a tear, and desired the ambassador to bear to her a kind and consoling message; but she died January 8, 1536, before his arrival; and was buried by the king's direction, with all becoming pomp, in the abbey church of Peterborough.

Four months did not elapse before Catherine was followed to the grave by Anne Boleyn. Henry's passion for her gradually subsided into coldness and neglect; and the indulgent lover became at last a suspicious and unfeeling master. At the death of Catherine she made no secret of her joy. Out of respect for the Spanish princess, the king had ordered his servants to wear mourning on the day of her burial; but Anne dressed herself in robes of yellow silk, and openly declared that she was now indeed a queen, since she had no longer a competitor. In this, however, she was fatally deceived. Among her maids was one named Jane Seymour, the daughter of a knight of Wiltshire, who, to equal or superior elegance of person, added a gentle and playful disposition. The queen discovered that an intimacy existed between Jane and Henry, and was so much affected thereby, that she prematurely gave birth to a dead male child, which was a bitter disappointment to Henry. Reports injurious to Anne's honour, had been circulated at court; they had reached the ear of Henry, and some notice of them had been whispered to Anne herself. The king, eager to rid himself of a woman whom he no longer loved, referred these reports to the council; and a committee was appointed to inquire into the charges against the queen, who reported that sufficient proof had been discovered to convict her. On 1st May, 1536, the lord Rochford appeared as principal challenger in a tilting match at Greenwich; and was opposed by Sir Henry Norris, one of those with whom Anne was suspected of being too familiar, as principal defendant. The king and Anne were both present; and it is said that, in one of the intervals between the courses, the queen, through accident or design, dropped her handkerchief from the balcony; that Norris, at whose feet it fell, took it up and wiped his face with it; and that Henry instantly changed colour, started from his seat, and retired. The next day Anne was sent to the Tower. Anne was soon tried and convicted. By the result of this trial her life was forfeited to the law; but the vengeance of Henry had prepared for her an additional punishment in the degradation of herself and her daughter Elizabeth. He ordered Cranmer to declare that the marriage with Anne had been invalid. To hesitate would have cost the archbishop his head. Never, perhaps, was there a more solemn mockery of the forms of justice than in the pretended trial of this extraordinary cause. Cranmer pronounced definitively that the marriage formerly contracted between Henry and Anne Boleyn was, and always had been, null and void. About noon, 19th May, 1536, Anne was led to the scaffold, dressed in a robe of black damask, and attended by her four maids. With the permission of the lieutenant, she addressed the spectators, but neither confessed guilt nor—as at her trial—protested innocence. She then knelt down; one of her attendants tied a bandage over her eyes, and, as she exclaimed, "O Lord God, have mercy upon my soul," the executioner, with one blow of his sword, severed her head from the body. Her remains were immediately afterwards buried within the chapel of the Tower. Thus fell this unfortunate queen within four months after the death of Catherine. Henry had wept at the death of Catherine; but, as if he sought to display his contempt for the memory of Anne, he dressed himself in white on the day of her execution, and was married to Jane Seymour the next morning.

An insurrection took place, in the autumn of 1536, in the northern counties, where the people retained a strong attachment to the ancient doctrines; and the clergy, further removed from the influence of the court, were less disposed to abjure their opinions at the nod of the sovereign. When they saw the ruin of the establishments which they had revered from their childhood; the monks driven from their homes, and in many instances compelled to beg their bread; and the poor, who had formerly been fed at the doors of the convents, now abandoned without relief; they demanded the redress of their grievances. Nor was the insurrection long confined to the common people. The nobility and gentry joined the insurgents, either through compulsion, as they afterwards pretended, or through inclination, as was generally believed. The enterprise was termed the "pilgrimage of grace;" on the banners were painted the crucifixion; and wherever the pilgrims appeared, the ejected monks were replaced in the monasteries, and the inhabitants were compelled to take the oath, and to join the army. The insurgents appointed delegates to lay their demands before Henry. After some delays, the king offered, and the insurgents accepted, an unlimited pardon, with an understanding that their grievances should be shortly and patiently discussed in a parliament to be assembled at York. But the king, freed from his apprehensions, neglected to redeem his promise; and within two months the "pilgrims" were again under arms. They failed, however, in two attempts to surprise Hull and Carlisle. Most of the leaders were taken and executed, and tranquillity was restored by a general pardon; but not until many had been put to death.

The northern insurrection, instead of securing the stability, accelerated the ruin of the remaining monasteries. They were visited under pretext of the late rebellion; and by one expedient or other were successively wrested from the possessors, and transferred to the crown. Many superiors, deemed it prudent to obey the royal pleasure: some resigned their situations, and were replaced by successors of more easy and accommodating loyalty; and the obstinacy of the refractory monks and abbots was punished with imprisonment during the king's pleasure. Some of them, like the Carthusians, confined in Newgate, were left to perish through hunger, disease and neglect; others, like the abbots of Colchester, Reading, and Glastonbury, were executed as felons or traitors. A bill was next brought into parliament vesting in the crown all the property of the monastic establishments. The suppression of the religious houses failed to produce the benefits foretold. Pauperism increased; the monastic property was squandered among the parasites of the court; and the king, instead of lightening the national burthens, demanded compensation for the expense which he had incurred in the reformation of religion. By the spring of the year, 1540, all the monastic establishments in the kingdom had been torn from the possession of the real owners by forced and illegal surrenders. To soften the odium of the measure, much has been said of the immorality practised, or supposed to be practised, within the monasteries. It is not in human nature that in numerous societies of men, all should be equally virtuous. The monks of different descriptions amounted to many thousands; and in such a multitude there must have existed individuals whose conduct was a disgrace to their profession. But when this has been conceded on the one hand, it ought to be admitted on the other, that the charges against them are entitled to very little credit.

In 1535, Henry sent to the German Protestant princes an embassy to represent to them that, as both he and they had defied the authority of the pontiff, it might be for their mutual interest to join in one common confederacy. But as the Germans, assuming a lofty tone, required that he should subscribe to their confession of faith, and should advance, partly as a loan, partly as a present, a large sum of money, the negociations were broken off. Henry, with the aid of his theologians, compiled a book of "Articles," which was presented to the convocation by Cromwell, and subscribed by him and the other members. It may be divided into three parts. The first declares that the belief of the Apostles' Creed, the Nicene Creed, and the Athanasian Creed, is necessary for salvation: the second explains the three great sacraments of baptism, penance, and the altar, and pronounces them the ordinary means of justification; the third teaches that, though the use of images, the honouring of the saints, the soliciting of their intercession, and the usual ceremonies in the service, have not in themselves the power to remit sin, or justify the soul, yet they are highly profitable, and ought to be retained. A work entitled "The godly and pious Institution of a Christian Man" was soon afterwards published, subscribed by the archbishops, bishops, archdeacons, and certain doctors of canon and civil law, and pronounced by them to accord "in all things with the very true meaning of Scripture." It explains in succession the creed, the seven sacraments, the ten commandments, the Pater Noster and Ave Maria, justification, and purgatory.

In 1537, a new edition of the Bible was published in the English language, and injunctions were issued, that a copy of this edition should be placed in every church at the joint expense of the incumbent and the parishioners.

For many years persecution raged against those who differed from Henry's opinions; and the prelates of the new doctrines were not less eager than those of the old to light the faggot for the punishment of heresy. The first victims were John Frith, and Hewet, a tailor, who maintained that it was not necessary to believe or deny the doctrine of the real presence. When, in 1535, a colony of German Anabaptists landed in England, they were instantly apprehended; and fourteen, who refused to recant, were condemned to the flames.

In 1538, a truce of ten years was concluded between Charles V. and Francis I., and the pontiff embraced the favourable opportunity to sound the disposition of the two monarchs relatively to the conduct of Henry. From both he received the same answer, that if *he* would publish the bull, *they* would send ambassadors to England to protest against the schism, and would strictly forbid all commercial intercourse between their subjects and the English merchants. The substance of these negociations was soon conveyed to Henry, who ordered his navy to be equipped, the harbours to be put in a state of defence, and the whole population to be called under arms.

The pontiff, encouraged by the promises of Charles and Francis, soon ordered the publication of the bull. At the same time Cardinal Pole, many of whose relatives in England had been put to death on account of his acts, was despatched on a secret mission to the Spanish and French Courts; but his arrival had been anticipated by the English agents: neither Charles nor Francis would incur the hostility of Henry by being the first to declare himself,; and both equally prohibited the publication of the bull within their dominions. The pontiff, who saw that he was deluded by the insincerity of the two monarchs, recalled Pole to Rome; and the papal court, abandoning all hope of succeeding by intimidation, submitted to watch in silence the course of political events.

For some time Cromwell and Cranmer had reigned without control in the council. But the general understanding between the pontiff and the Catholic sovereigns, and the mission of Pole to the emperor and the king of France, had awakened serious apprehensions and new projects in the mind of Henry. He determined to prove to the world that he was the decided advocate of the ancient doctrines, and therefore caused an act to be passed, known as the "Six Articles." Before his promotion to the archiepiscopal dignity, Cranmer had married in Germany. Some time after his wife followed him to England, where she bore him several children. He was too prudent to acknowledge her publicly: but the secret quickly transpired, and many priests imitated his example. When the celibacy of th· priesthood was made one of the six articles, Cranmer saw with dismay that his marriage was reputed void in law, and he sent off his children with their mother to her friends in Germany.

Henry had been a widower more than two years. In 1537, Jane Seymour, his third queen, had borne him a male child, afterwards Edward VI., and in less than a fortnight expired. Cromwell proposed to him to marry Anne, sister of William, the reigning duke of Cleves, and one of the Protestant princes of Germany. The English envoys reported to the king that Anne was both tall and portly; but when she arrived Henry's disappointment was evident. She was indeed tall and large as his heart could wish: but her features, though regular, were coarse, her manners ungraceful, her figure ill-proportioned. Cromwell received orders to devise some expedient to interrupt the marriage. Two days passed in fruitless consultation; and the king at length, unprovided with any reasonable excuse, and afraid of adding the German princes to his other enemies, was persuaded by Cromwell to submit to the ceremony.

This unfortunate marriage had already shaken the credit of Cromwell; his fall was hastened by a theological quarrel between Dr. Barnes, one of his dependents, and Gardiner, bishop of Winchester. The king summoned the former before himself and a commission of divines, and discussed with him several points of controverted doctrine. Barnes affected to recant, but in his next sermon maintained in still stronger terms the very doctrine which he had recanted. Irritated by this insult, the king committed him to the Tower. Henry ascertained that Barnes was the confidential agent of Cromwell; that he had been employed in secret missions to Germany; and that he had been the real negociator of the late marriage with Anne of Cleves. Cromwell was arrested on a charge of high treason. He was confronted, at his request, with his accusers in presence of the royal commissioners, but was refused the benefit of a public trial before his peers. He was beheaded July 28, 1540; the same day, Henry married Catherine Howard.

The disgrace of Cromwell was quickly followed by the divorce of the queen, upon the ground of alleged misrepresentation having been made to him as to her person, and the want of consent on his part both at the celebration, and ever since the celebration of the marriage. Henry and Anne now called each other brother and sister, and a yearly income of three thousand pounds, with the palace of Richmond for her residence, amply indemnified the degraded queen for the loss of a capricious and tyrannical husband.

Henry did not long remain a widower, after his divorce from Anne of Cleves. Within a month Catherine, daughter to the late Lord Edmund Howard, and neice to the duke of Norfolk, appeared at court with the title of queen. She was, however, accused of misconduct, and found guilty; and in six months after her marriage she was executed.

In 1536, it was enacted that the whole of Wales should be

united with the realm of England; that all the natives should enjoy the same rights, liberties, and laws, which were enjoyed and inherited by others the king's subjects.

When Henry ascended the throne, the exercise of the royal authority in Ireland was circumscribed within very narrow limits, comprising only the principal seaports, with one-half of the five counties of Louth, Westmeath, Dublin, Kildare, and Wexford. Henry's innovations in religion were viewed with equal abhorrence by the native Irish and the descendants of the English colonists. The Geraldines, aware of this circumstance, had proclaimed themselves the champions of the ancient faith. On the other hand, the cause of the king was supported by a courtly prelate, Dr. Brown, who, from the office of provincial of the Augustinian friars in England, had been raised to the archiepiscopal see of Dublin, in reward of his subserviency to the politics of Cromwell. But Henry determined to enforce submission. A parliament was summoned by which statutes were passed which were copied from the proceedings in England. The papal authority was abolished; Henry was declared head of the Irish church; and the first-fruits of all ecclesiastical livings were given to the king.

Several causes contributed to produce a rupture between Henry and his nephew the king of Scotland. The king of Scots, satisfied with his own creed, refused to engage in theological disputes; and the pontiff, to rivet him more closely to the communion of the Apostolic See, bestowed a cardinal's cap on the most able and most favoured of his counsellors, David Beaton, afterwards archbishop of St. Andrews. When Paul determined to publish the sentence of deprivation against Henry, James signified his assent, and promised to join with Charles and Francis in their endeavours to convert or punish the apostate monarch.

As, however, neither Charles nor Francis attempted to enforce the papal bull, their inactivity induced the king of Scots to preserve the relations of amity with his uncle. But Henry continued to grow more jealous both of the religious opinions of James, and of his connexion with the French court. The Scottish parliament, as if it meant to stigmatize the proceedings of that of England, passed several laws in support of the ancient doctrines and of the papal supremacy. In 1542, forays were reciprocally made across the borders; and each nation charged the other with the first aggression; but the Scots had the advantage, who at Haldenrig defeated three thousand cavalry, and made most of the captains prisoners. Enraged at this loss Henry published a declaration of war, in which he claimed the superiority over the Scottish crown, and ordered the duke of Norfolk to assemble an army at York. Norfolk defeated the Scots at Solway Moss, November 24th; and the Scottish king died through grief. A week before his death, his queen was delivered of a female child, who, under the name of Mary, was proclaimed successor to the Scottish throne. These events opened a new scene to the ambition of Henry, who determined to marry his son Edward to the infant Queen of Scotland; and in consequence of that marriage, to demand, as natural tutor of the young princess, the government of the kingdom.

In Edinburgh, soon after the death of the king, Cardinal Beaton had published a will of the deceased monarch, by which the regency was vested in himself and three other noblemen; but this instrument was disregarded by the lords assembled in the city. James Hamilton, earl of Arran, and presumptive heir to the throne, was declared governor during the minority of the queen; and the cardinal appeared to acquiesce in an arrangement which he had not the power to disturb. Seeming tranquillity soon vanished and war raged for some years. At length the Scots were comprehended in the treaty of peace between England and France; and though the conditions of that comprehension became the subject of dispute, the latter part of Henry's reign was not disturbed by open hostilities.

Respecting France the reader will recollect, that the king of that country complained of Henry's marriage with Anne Boleyn, as of a violation of his promise. This dissension, though it might weaken, did not dissolve, the friendship which had so long subsisted between them; but fresh bickerings ensued; the tempers of the princes became reciprocally soured; each wishing to chastise what he deemed the caprice, the ingratitude, and the perfidy of the other. The military transactions which this hostile feeling caused belong rather to the history of France than of England. Peace was concluded in 1546.

Henry's sixth queen was Catharine Parr, relict of the late Lord Latimer, who with her brother, the earl of Essex, and her uncle, created Lord Parr of Horton, zealously promoted the new doctrines. But her zeal transgressed the bounds of prudence. She not only read the prohibited works; she presumed to argue with her husband, and to dispute the decisions of the head of the church. Of all men, Henry was the least disposed to brook the lectures of a female theologian, and he gave orders to have articles prepared against Catharine; but the intelligence was immediately, perhaps designedly, conveyed to the queen; who, repairing to a neighbouring apartment, fell into a succession of fits, and during the intervals made the palace ring with her cries and lamentations. Henry, moved with pity, or incommoded by the noise, first sent his physician, and was afterwards carried in a chair, to console her. In the evening she waited on him, in the company of her sister, and adroitly turning the conversation to the subject of religion, took occasion to express her admiration of his learning, and the implicit deference which she paid to his decisions, which conduct led to their reconciliation.

The king had long indulged without restraint in the pleasures of the table. At last he grew so enormously corpulent, that he could not support the weight of his own body. An inveterate ulcer in the thigh, which had more than once threatened his life, and which now seemed to baffle all the skill of his surgeons, added to the irascibility of his temper.

Of the king's conduct during his sickness, we know little. It is said that at the commencement he betrayed a wish to be reconciled to the see of Rome; that the other bishops, afraid of the penalties, evaded the question; but that Gardiner advised him to consult his parliament, and to commit his ideas to writing. He was constantly attended by his confessor, the bishop of Rochester, heard mass daily in his chamber, and received the communion under one kind.

Of his sentiments on his death-bed, nothing can be asserted with any degree of confidence. One account makes him die in the anguish of despair; according to another, he refused spiritual aid till he could only reply to the exhortation of the archbishop by a squeeze of the hand; while a third represents him as expiring in the most edifying sentiments of devotion and repentance. He died on Friday, the 28th of January, 1547, about two in the morning.

To form a just estimate of the character of Henry, we must distinguish between the young king, guided by the counsels of Wolsey, and the monarch of more mature age, governing by his own judgment, and with the aid of ministers selected and fashioned by himself. In his youth the beauty of his person, the elegance of his manners, and his adroitness in every martial and fashionable exercise, were calculated to attract the admiration of his subjects. His court was gay and splendid; and a succession of amusements seemed to absorb his attention;

yet his pleasures were not permitted to encroach on his more important duties; he assisted at the council, perused the despatches, and corresponded with his generals and ambassadors; nor did the minister, trusted and powerful as he was, dare to act, till he had asked the opinion, and taken the pleasure of his sovereign. His natural abilities had been improved by study; and his esteem for literature may be inferred from the learned education which he gave to his children, and from the number of eminent scholars to whom he granted pensions in foreign states, or on whom he bestowed preferment in his own. As the king advanced in age, his vices gradually developed themselves; and after the death of Wolsey they were indulged without restraint. He became as rapacious as he was prodigal; as obstinate as he was capricious; as fickle in his friendships as he was merciless in his resentments. Though liberal of his confidence, he soon grew suspicious of those whom he had trusted; and, as if he possessed no other right to the crown than that which he derived from the very questionable claim of his father, he viewed with an evil eye every remote descendant of the Plantagenets; and eagerly embraced the slightest pretexts to remove those whom his jealousy represented as future rivals to himself or his posterity. In pride and vanity, he was perhaps without a parallel. Inflated with the praises of interested admirers, he despised the judgment of others; acted as if he deemed himself infallible in matters of policy.

By the obsequiousness of the parliament, the assumption of the ecclesiastical supremacy, and the servility of religious factions, Henry acquired and exercised the most despotic sway over the lives, the fortunes, and the liberties of his subjects. Happily, the forms of a free government were still suffered to exist; into these forms a spirit of resistance to arbitrary power gradually infused itself; the pretensions of the crown were opposed by the claims of the people; and the result of a long and arduous struggle was that constitution which, for more than a century, has excited the envy and the admiration of Europe.

A week before Henry's death, Howard, earl of Surrey, the first whose verse led to the modern style, fell a victim to the tyrant's jealousy. His aged father, Norfolk, escaped by the king having expired a few hours before the time appointed for the duke's execution.

21. EDWARD VI.

Henry had confided the government of the king and kingdom, during the minority of his son Edward, who was only nine years old, to Cranmer and fifteen other guardians. The new king was proclaimed on Monday, January 31, 1547. The council appointed one of their number to transact business with the foreign envoys, and to represent on other occasions the person of the young sovereign. The earl of Hertford, the young king's uncle, was immediately elected to the position of protector of the realm, and guardian of the king's person. The appointment of Hertford was announced by proclamation.

Hertford was created duke of Somerset, and the other members of the council of regency also obtained promotion.

The coronation of Edward took place on the 20th February, 1547. Though the duke possessed the title of protector, he had been compelled to accept it on the condition that he should never act without the assent of the majority of the council; now he procured letters patent under the great seal, conferring on himself alone the whole authority of the crown.

In 1544, Henry, foiled by Cardinal Beaton in an effort to obtain the custody of the young queen, had despatched the Earl of Hertford to invade Scotland at the head of a powerful army; and in that year the cardinal was murdered by some conspirators, who sought thereby to obtain favour with the king of England. The death of Henry made no alteration in the policy of the English cabinet. The protector hastily concluded a treaty with the murderers; by which they bound themselves to procure, with all their power, the marriage of their infant sovereign with Edward VI., and never to surrender the castle during her minority to any Scotsman without a previous licence in writing from the English king and the protector. War soon broke out afresh, in which England succeeded.

Somerset and his associates now undertook to establish the new religious creed.

The kingdom was divided into six circuits, to each of which was assigned a certain number of visitors, partly clergymen and partly laymen. The moment they arrived in any diocese, the exercise of spiritual authority by every other person ceased.

Among the prelates, there was no individual whom the men of the new learning more feared, or those of the old

H

learning more respected, for his erudition and abilities, his spirit and influence, than Gardiner, bishop of Winchester. That prelate commenced a controversy with the protector and the archbishop; the consequence of which was, that, though he could not be charged with any offence against the law, he was committed to the Fleet and detained a close prisoner till the end of the session.

But the ministers were careful to repair many of those breaches in the constitution which had been made by the despotism of the last reign. All felonies created since the first of Henry VIII., and all treasons created since the twenty-fifth of Edward III. were at once erased from the statute-book; the privilege of clergy, with the exception of a few cases, was restored; in convictions of treason, two witnesses were required; the laws against the Lollards, the prohibition of reading the Scriptures, and of printing, selling, or retaining certain English publications; all enactments respecting doctrine and matters of religion, and the statute which gave to the royal proclamations the force of law, were repealed.

The bishops received orders to abolish in their respective dioceses the custom of bearing candles on Candlemas-day, of receiving ashes on Ash Wednesday, and of carrying palms on Palm Sunday. A proclamation also appeared, which required that all images whatsoever should be destroyed. To this succeeded an order for the public administration of the sacrament under both kinds, and in the English language.

It was soon discovered that imprisonment had not broken the spirit of Gardiner. He was again summoned before the council, and the next day, in proof of his submission, was ordered to preach at St. Paul's Cross, in the presence of the king, on the feast of St. Peter. The sermon was preached, and the next day the bishop was committed to the Tower.

The protector had a younger brother, Thomas, whose fate about this time excited much attention. Between them a broad distinction had been drawn by the late king, and while Edward had arisen to the rank of Earl, had obtained the command of armies, and been named one of the governors of his nephew, Thomas had been left without title. The first step towards the improvement of his fortune was his alliance with the queen dowager, who married him, almost before the dead body of Henry was deposited in the grave. With the parson of Catherine, Thomas Seymour became master of her wealth and her dower, and his next object was to win and monopolize the affection of his nephew. With this view, he indulged the young Edward in all his wishes; secretly supplied him with large sums of money, blamed the severity with which he was used by the protector, and hinted that he was kept under undue restraint. The king readily imbibed the opinions of the man whom he loved; and a resolution was taken that he should attempt, with the aid of his partisans, to procure the guardianship for himself. The plot was betrayed to the protector. Thomas condescended to acknowledge his fault; and the two brothers mutually forgave each other. But a new prospect soon opened to his ambition, which, as it sought for power, was not to be satisfied with money. He began to aspire to the hand of the lady Elizabeth, the king's sister, and to condemn that precipitate union with Catherine, which excluded him from the pursuit of so noble a prize.

The protector at length determined to crush so dangerous a competitor. Sherington, master of the mint at Bristol, was examined before the council, on a charge of having amassed an enormous fortune by clipping the coin. To save his life, he said that he had promised to coin money for Seymour, who intended to change the present form of the government. Seymour was committed to the Tower, and in March, 1549, was executed.

In a proclamation, signed by every member of the council, Somerset was charged with divers high crimes and misdemeanours. Edward was not unwilling to be emancipated from the control of his uncle; and the protector was deprived in due form by a writ under the great seal and sign manual. He was committed, and with him five of his confidential advisers. An intimation was given to him, that, if he hoped for pardon, he must submit to an acknowlegment of his guilt. The condition was gratefully accepted. On his knees he confessed his presumption, negligence, and incapacity, and earnestly implored for mercy. Life was promised; but on condition that he should forfeit all his offices, and a large portion of his property. He was discharged and received a pardon.

A treaty was soon concluded with France: and for a sum of money England surrendered all her remaining territory in that country.

The partisans of the new doctrines felt that the reformation still rested on a very insecure foundation. Eleven-twelfths of the nation retained a strong attachment to the creed of their fathers. The council ordered Bonner to preach at St. Paul's. At the appointed day crowds assembled to hear the prelate; many from curiosity, some for the purpose of censure. In his sermon, Bonner broached views different from those held by the council; and Cranmer and Ridley were appointed to try and punish the refractory prelate. Bonner appeared before his judges, with the undaunted air of a man who feels conscious that he suffers in a just cause. The archbishop pronounced the sentence of deprivation; and Bonner was remanded to the Marshalsea, where he remained a prisoner till the king's death; and the bishopric of Westminster was dissolved by royal authority. Gardiner had now been for two years a prisoner in the Tower, without being able to obtain a trial, or even a copy of the charges against him. He was visited by a deputation from the council, and required to approve of every religious innovation which had been established by act of parliament, or by order of the council. Gardiner replied, that he asked for no favour; he sought only a legal trial: he was willing to stand or fall by the law. At length a commission was issued against him for contempt: but he defended himself with ability and perseverance. Cranmer cut short the proceedings, pronouncing him contumacious, and adjudging him to be deprived of his bishopric. By order of the council, he was sent back to a meaner cell in the Tower, with instructions that no man should see him but one of the warders, that all his books and papers should be taken from him and examined; and that he should be refused the use of pen, ink, and paper.

There were two other prelates prisoners in the Tower. Heath, bishop of Worcester, and Day, bishop of Chichester, both distinguished by their learning, their moderation, and their attachment to the ancient creed. Both these bishops were kept in custody till the commencement of the next reign.

There still remained one individual whose conversion, in the estimation of the reformers, would have balanced the opposition of a whole host of bishops—the lady Mary, the sister of Edward, and the presumptive heir to the crown. She had embraced the first opportunity of expressing to the protector her dislike of further innovation. Dr. Mallet, Mary's chaplain, was committed to close custody in the Tower. An active correspondence ensued; Mary demanding the enlargement of her chaplain, the council requiring that she should conform to the law. At length the chief officers of her household were commanded to prevent the use of the ancient service in the house. Having consulted her, they returned to the council, and offered to submit to any punishment, rather than undertake what they could not find in their hearts or consciences to perform. They were committed to the Tower for contempt; and Mary was again urged to conform to the new faith; but she replied: "Rather than use any other service than was used at the death of the late king, my father, I will lay my head on a block and suffer death. If my chaplains do say no mass, I can hear none. They may do therein as they will; but none of your new service shall be used in my house, or I will not tarry in it." Here is the answer not of a proud but of a spiritual woman.

Though the statutes against heresy had been repealed in the first year of the king's reign, still the profession of erroneous doctrine was held to be an offence punishable by the common law of the realm.

The marquess of Northampton proceeded to Paris, in May, 1551, to invest the king of France with the order of the Garter, and to seek a wife for his sovereign. His first demand, of the young queen of Scotland, was instantly refused; his second, of the princess Elizabeth, was as readily granted. The negociators agreed that as soon as Elizabeth had completed her twelfth year she should be married to Edward; but, a difference about her dower suspended the conclusion of the treaty for eight weeks. In November, 1551, Somerset was brought to trial for violent and riotous proceedings, and for conspiring against the nobles who were hostile to his views. It was treason for any persons, to the number of forty or above, to assemble in forcible manner, to the intent to murder, kill, or slay, take or imprison any of the king's privy council; and felony to stir up any persons to the committal of such offences. Somerset was arraigned before his peers, and defended himself with spirit, and acquitted of the treason, but found guilty of the felony, and received the usual sentence of death. After his condemnation, and in the solitude of his cell, he had leisure to compare his situation with that of his brother, not three years before. Every avenue to the throne was closed, his nephew, the king, was convinced of his guilt, and of the expedience of his punishment; and he received for answer, to an appeal for mercy, that he must pay the forfeit of his life, but should have a long respite to prepare himself for death. Six weeks after his trial, January 22nd, 1552, his execution took place, on Tower Hill.

Edward had inherited from his mother a weak and delicate constitution. In the spring of the year, 1552, he was considerably reduced by successive attacks of illness. After a short and delusive interval, Edward relapsed into his former weakness. The symptoms of his disorder grew daily more alarming; and it became evident that his life could not be protracted beyond the term of a few weeks. His danger urged the duke of Northumberland to execute a project, which he had in all probability meditated for some time, of placing the crown, in the event of the king's death, on the head of his own son. By act of parliament, and the will of the last monarch, the next heirs were the ladies Mary and Elizabeth; but, as the statutes pronouncing them illegitimate had never been repealed, it was presumed that such illegitimacy might be successfully opposed in bar of their claim. After their exclusion, the crown would of right descend to one of the representatives of the two sisters of Henry VIII.—Margaret, queen of Scotland, and Mary, queen of France. Margaret was the elder, but her descendants had been overlooked in the will of the late king, and the animosity of the nation against Scotland would readily induce it to acquiesce in the exclusion of the Scottish line. There remained then the representative of Mary, the French queen, who was Frances, married to Grey, formerly marquess of Dorset, and lately created, in favour of his wife, duke of Suffolk. But Frances had no ambition to ascend a disputed throne, and easily consented to transfer her right to her eldest daughter Jane, the wife of Northumberland's fourth son, Guildford Dudley. Northumberland's next object was to secure the person of the princess Mary. To secure his prey, a letter was written by the council to Mary, requiring her, by the king's order, to repair immediately to court. Had she reached London, her next removal would have been to the Tower: but she received a friendly hint of her danger on the road, and hastened back to her usual residence, Kenninghall, in the county of Norfolk.

At this period the care of the king was intrusted to a female, whose medicines aggravated his sufferings. His physicians, when they were recalled, pronounced him to be at the point of death, and on the 6th of July, 1553, the king expired.

The character of Edward is a historical farce. He lived

and died a child. He was used as an instrument to change the popular Christian confidence by aspiring politicians who had not faith of any kind.

22—MARY SIRNAMED TUDOR.

On the evening of July 6, 1553, Edward expired at Greenwich. With the view of concealing his death for some days to gain time to strengthen opposition to Mary, the guards had been previously doubled in the palace, and all communication intercepted between his chamber and the other apartments. Yet that very night, while the lords sat in deliberation, the secret was communicated to Mary, who, without losing a moment, mounted her horse and rode with the servants of her household to Kenninghall, in Norfolk.

The council broke up after midnight; and Clinton, the lord admiral, took possession of the Tower, with the royal treasures, the munitions of war, and the prisoners of state. The three next days were employed in making such previous arrangements as were thought necessary for the success of the plans for the council. On the fourth morning, it was determined to publish the result. The lords, attended by a numerous escort, rode to Sion House, to announce to the lady Jane Grey that she had been appointed to succeed her royal cousin.

Jane Grey has been described to us as a young woman of gentle manners, and superior talents, addicted to the study of the Scriptures and the classics, but fonder of dress than suited the austere notions of the reformed preachers. Of the designs of the duke of Northumberland in her favour, she knew nothing. Her love of privacy had induced her to solicit permission to leave London, and to spend a few days at Chelsea; she was indulging herself in this retirement, when she received an order from the council to return immediately to Sion House, and to await there the commands of the king. She obeyed; and the next morning was visited by the duke of Northumberland, and others. She was told, that the king, her cousin was dead; that before he expired he had named her his lawful heir. She trembled, uttered a shriek, and sank to the ground. On her recovery she observed to those around her, that she seemed to herself a very unfit person to be a queen; but that, if the right were hers, she trusted God would give her strength to wield the sceptre to his honour and the benefit of the nation.

Jane was conducted to the Tower, the usual residence of our kings preparatory to their coronation.

The mass of the people knew little of the lady Jane, but all had heard of the ambition of Northumberland. They said that he had persuaded Somerset to take the life of his brother, and Edward to take that of Somerset. The royal youth was the next victim. He had been removed by poison to make room for the lady Jane, who, in her turn, would be compelled to yield the crown to Northumberland himself. These reports were believed, and the public voice, wherever it might be expressed with impunity, was unanimous in favour of Mary. She was already joined by the earls of Bath and Sussex, and by several other nobles. Northumberland saw the necessity of despatch: but preferring not to leave the capital, he proposed to give the command of the forces to the duke of Suffolk. But he could not deceive the secret partisans of Mary, who saw his perplexity, and to liberate themselves from his control, urged him to take the command upon himself. He gave a tardy and reluctant consent, and, as he rode through the city at the head of the troops, he remarked, in a tone of despondency, "the people crowd to look upon us, but not one exclaims, God speed ye."

Mary left Kenninghall; and, riding forty miles without rest, reached, on the same evening, the castle of Framlingham. There, her hopes were hourly cheered with the most gratifying intelligence. In a few days she was surrounded by more than thirty thousand men, all volunteers in her cause, who refused to receive pay, and served through the sole motive of loyalty.

Northumberland had marched from Cambridge, in the direction of Framlingham, and saw, as he advanced, the enthusiasm of the people in Mary's cause, heard that he had been proclaimed a rebel, and that a price had been fixed on his head. He was arrested on a charge of high treason by the earl of Arundel, and conducted, with several of his associates, to the Tower.

Of Mary's counsellors, the chief were the bishops Gardiner and Tunstall, who, under her father, had been employed in offices of trust, and had discharged them with fidelity and success. The acknowledged abilities of the former soon raised him to the post of prime minister. He first received the custody of the seals, and was soon afterwards appointed chancellor.

The ceremony of Mary's coronation was performed 30th

September, 1553, after the ancient rite, by Gardiner, bishop of Winchester, and was concluded in the usual manner, with a magnificent banquet in Westminster Hall.

Northumberland, Sir John Gates, and Sir Thomas Palmer were selected for execution. Northumberland acknowledged the justice of his punishment, but denied that he was the first projector of the treason. He called on them to witness that he was in charity with all mankind, that he died in the faith of his fathers, though ambition had induced him to conform in practice to a worship which he condemned in his heart.

Under the reign of Edward, Mary had spontaneously preferred a single life; but, from the moment of her accession to the throne, she made no secret of her intention to marry. She asked the advice of the emperor Charles V., and waited with impatience for his answer. It was obviously the interest of Charles that she should prefer his son Philip. He was, however, careful not to commit himself by too hasty an answer. At length he proposed his son, Philip, but told her not to be swayed by his advice; but to consult her own inclination and judgment. Philip was received by the advice of her lords.

The proceedings against the bishops, deprived in the last reign, were reversed; and Gardiner, Bonner, Tunstall, Heath, and Day recovered the possession of their respective sees. A riot was, however, occasioned by the public celebration of mass in a church. The council reprimanded and imprisoned the priest; and the queen, sending for the lord mayor and aldermen, ordered them to put down all tumultuous assemblies. Mary, following the example, of the last two monarchs, prohibited preaching in public without licence, but declared that she could not conceal her religion.

Cranmer now published a declaration, asserting that the mass was the device and invention of the father of lies. Of this intemperate declaration several copies were dispersed and publicly read to the people in the streets. The council sent for the archbishop, and after a long debate committed him to the Tower. A few days afterwards, Latimer was also sent to the same prison.

Such was the situation of affairs when Mary met her first parliament. The two objects which she had principally at heart were, to remove from herself the stain of illegitimacy, and to restore to its former ascendency the religion of her fathers. By the council it was at first determined to attempt both objects by a bill, which should repeal at once all the acts that had been passed in the two last reigns, affecting either the marriage between the queen's father and mother, or the exercise of religion as it stood in the first year of Henry VIII.

That which now chiefly interested and agitated the public mind, was the project of marriage between Mary and Philip of Spain. The projected alliance was unpopular. Protestants and Catholics, postponing their religious animosities, joined in reprobating a measure which, they said, would place a foreign and despotic prince on the English throne. The Commons voted an address to the queen, in which they prayed her to marry, but to select her husband not from any foreign family, but from the nobility of her own realm. But the queen had inherited the resolution, or obstinacy of her father. Opposition might strengthen, it could not shake her purpose. Sending for the imperial ambassador, she bade him follow her into her private oratory, where, on her knees at the foot of the altar, she called God to witness that she had pledged her faith to Philip, prince of Spain. The marriages of her predecessors, she observed, had always been free, nor would she surrender a privilege which they had enjoyed.

Elizabeth remained at court, watched by the imperialists, and caressed by their opponents.

The enemies of the Spanish marriage joined in a rebellion against Mary. The queen ordered her ministers to provide the means of defence, and undertook to fix, by her confidence and address, the wavering loyalty of the Londoners. But the policy of her conduct had been severely arraigned; and, now while her mind was still agitated with the remembrance of her danger, she was induced to sign a warrant for the execution of Guildford Dudley, and lady Jane Grey, whose family had joined in the second rebellion. On the fatal morning, the queen sent them permission to take a last farewell of each other; but Jane refused the indulgence, saying, that in a few hours they should meet in heaven. From the window of her cell she saw her husband led to execution, and beheld his bleeding corpse brought back to the chapel. He had been beheaded on Tower Hill, in sight of an immense multitude; she, on account of her royal descent, was spared the ignominy of a public execution. With a firm step and cheerful countenance she mounted the scaffold, which had been erected on the green within the Tower. Having laid her head upon the block, at one stroke it was severed from the body. Her life had before been spared as a pledge for the loyalty of the house of Suffolk.

That pledge was forfeited by the late rebellion of the duke. The new queen never desired lady Jane's punishment, for she never supposed she was otherwise guilty than as an instrument of Northumberland's party. She assented to the execution accordingly.

Elizabeth was at Ashbridge, labouring, or pretending to labour, under some severe indisposition. Much had come to light which tended to implicate her in the conspiracy: she refused to join the queen in the capital, which was imputed to consciousness of guilt rather than infirmity of body.

Both houses concurred in an act confirming the treaty of marriage, declaring that the queen, after its solemnization, should continue to enjoy and exercise the sovereignty as sole queen, without any right or claim to be given unto Philip. Philip soon arrived at Southampton, escorted by the combined fleets of England, the Netherlands, and Spain. The moment he set his foot on the beach, he was invested with the insignia of the order of the Garter; and instantly a royal salute was fired by the batteries and the ships in the harbour. From Winchester the royal pair proceeded, by slow journeys, to Windsor and the metropolis. The city had been beautified at considerable expense, and the most splendid pageants were devised to welcome the royal party.

Mary now resolved to attempt that which she had long considered an indispensable duty, the restoration of the religious polity of the kingom. She recognised the papal supremacy.

Many had shared the plunder of the church; and they objected to the restoration of that jurisdiction which might call in question their right to their present possessions. It was necessary to free them from apprehension, and for that purpose to procure from the pontiff a bull confirming all past alienation of the property of the church.

This for the peace of the kingdom had been sparingly done. Mary and Philip spoke to the cardinal legate. He absolved all present and the whole nation from all heresy. Next Sunday the legate, at the invitation of the citizens, made his public entry into the metropolis; and Gardiner preached at St. Paul's Cross the celebrated sermon, in which he lamented in bitter terms his conduct under Henry VIII., and exhorted all, who had fallen through his means, or in his company, to rise with him, and seek the unity of the Catholic Church.

The dissolution of the parliament was followed by an unexpected act of grace. The lord chancellor, accompanied by several members of the council, proceeded to the Tower, called before him all state prisoners, and informed them that the king and queen had ordered them to be discharged.

It was the lot of Mary to live in an age of religious intolerance, when to punish the professors of erroneous doctrine was inculcated as a duty. The Protestants had no sooner obtained the ascendency during the short reign of Edward than they displayed the same persecuting spirit which they had formerly condemned.

Though it had been held in the last reign that by the common law of the land heresy was a crime punishable with death, it was deemed advisable to revive the three statutes which had formerly been enacted to suppress the doctrines of the Lollards.

The new year opened to the Protestant preachers with a lowering aspect, and the storm soon burst on their heads. Gardiner presided in a court which was now opened, and was attended by thirteen other bishops, and a crowd of lords and knights. Six prisoners accused of heresy were called before them; of whom four, Hooper, the deprived bishop of Gloucester; Rogers, a prebendary of St. Paul's; Saunders, rector of All-hallows, in London; and Taylor, rector of Hadley in Suffolk, were excommunicated; and their excommunication was followed by the delivery of the recusants to the civil power. Rogers was the first victim. He perished at the stake in Smithfield; Saunders underwent a similar fate at Coventry, Hooper at Gloucester, and Taylor at Hadley. Alphonso di Castro, a Spanish friar, confessor to Philip, preached before the court, and, to the astonishment of his hearers, condemned these proceedings in the most pointed manner. He pronounced them contrary, not only to the spirit, but to the text of the gospel. The bishops, generally declined the hateful task of proceeding against persons accused of heresy.

The last moments of Cranmer, Ridley, and Latimer, deserve special mention. During the preceding reign they had concurred in sending Anabaptists to the stake; in the present, they were compelled to suffer the same punishment which they had so recently inflicted.

To save his life, Cranmer feigned himself a convert to the Catholic creed. He professed to believe on all points, and particularly respecting the sacraments, as the Catholic Church believed. To Ridley and Latimer, life had been offered on condition that they should recant; Cranmer was refused the favour, as the chief author of all the schisms recently broached.

Cranmer, to amuse his admirers at the door of a much extolled martyrdom, conjured the pope to forgive his offences against the Apostolic See, and the king and queen to pardon his transgressions against them. History now proclaims that Mary sought every means to stop those unholy persecutions.

On the deprivation of Cranmer, Pole had been appointed archbishop; and his consecration took place on the day after the death of his predecessor. Pole procured several respites for Cranmer, and thus prolonged his life. The persecution now ceased in the diocese of Canterbury. Pole found sufficient exercise for his zeal in reforming the clergy, repairing the churches, and re-establishing the ancient discipline.

It had at first been hoped, that a few of these barbarous exhibitions would silence the voices of the preachers. Any attempt at defending such persecution can take little from the infamy of the principle. After every allowance, it will be found that, in the space of four years, almost two hundred persons perished in the flames for religious opinion. Heresy was attacked as crime; it is responsible solely to God as sin. In those wretched periods civil *crime* was confounded with private *peccatum*.

If anything could be urged in extenuation of those cruelties, it must have been the provocation given by the reformers.

From the moment of his arrival in England, Philip had sought to ingratiate himself with the natives. But he laboured in vain. The antipathy of the English was not to be subdued. The king grew weary of his stay in England. The queen, believing herself in a state to give him an heir to his dominions, extorted from him a promise not to leave her till after her expected delivery. She was mistaken, however, as to the fact of pregnancy, and Philip departed for Flanders. He left the queen with every demonstration of attachment, and recommended her in strong terms to the care of cardinal Pole.

Secret meetings were now held; defamatory libels on the king and queen, printed on the continent, were found scattered in the streets, in the palace, and in both houses of parliament; and reports were circulated that Mary, hopeless of issue to succeed her, had determined to settle the crown on her husband after her decease. A new conspiracy was formed, which had for its object to depose Mary, and to raise Elizabeth to the throne.

Mary urged Philip to return from the continent without delay. But he, to whom his father had resigned all his dominions in Spain, Italy, and the Netherlands, was overwhelmed with business of more importance to him than the tranquillity of his wife. And to pacify her mind, he made her frequent promises, the fulfilment of which it was always in his power to elude. In March, 1557, he revisited Mary, not so much in deference to her representations, as to draw England into a war with France.

The king of France resolved to besiege Calais. In the month of December, 1558, twenty-five thousand men, with a numerous train of battering artillery, assembled near that fortress. The governor, lord Wentworth, had received repeated warning to provide for the defence of the place, but he persuaded himself that the object of the enemy was not conquest, but plunder. In the depth of winter, and within three weeks, was Calais, with all its dependencies, recovered by France.

The queen felt the event most poignantly.

The reign of Mary was now hastening to its termination. Her health had always been delicate, and from the time of her first supposed pregnancy she was afflicted with frequent maladies. Nor was her mind more at ease than her body. The exiles from Geneva, by the number and virulence of their libels, kept her in a constant state of fear and irritation.

On the morning of Mary's death, mass was celebrated in her chamber. She was perfectly sensible, and expired a few minutes before the conclusion. Her friend and kinsman, Cardinal Pole, who had long been confined with a fever, survived her only twenty-two hours. He had reached his fifty-ninth, she her forty-second year.

The queen was thought by some to have inherited the obstinacy of her father; but there was this difference, that, before she formed her decisions, she sought for advice and information, and made it an invariable rule to prefer right to expediency. Her natural abilities had been improved by education. She understood the Italian, she spoke the French and Spanish languages; and the ease and correctness with which she replied to the foreigners who addressed her in Latin, excited their admiration. Her speeches in public, and from the throne, were delivered with grace and fluency.

The interests of trade were not neglected during her government. She had the honour of concluding the first commercial treaty with Russia. The Russian trade fully compensated the queen and the nation for these efforts and expenses; and the woollen cloths and coarse linens of England were exchanged at an immense profit, for the valuable skins and furs of the northern regions.

23. ELIZABETH.

ELIZABETH ascended the throne without opposition. Immediately after Mary's death a deputation of the council repaired to her residence at Hatfield. She received them courteously and to their congratulations replied in a formal discourse. Cecil was appointed secretary; and through him the queen named the members of her council. Of the advisers of Mary she retained those who were distinguished for their capacity, or formidable by their influence; and to these she added eight others, who had shown attachment to her in her troubles. There was another and secret cabinet, consisting of Cecil and his particular friends, who possessed the ear of the queen, and controlled through her every department in the state.

During the reign of her sister, Elizabeth had professed herself a convert to the ancient faith. The Catholics were willing to believe that her conformity arose from conviction; the Protestants, while they lamented her apostasy, persuaded themselves that she feigned sentiments which she did not feel. It is probable that, in her own mind, she was indifferent to either form of worship: but her ministers, whose prospects depended on the change, urged their mistress to put down a religion which proclaimed her illegitimate, and to support the reformed doctrines, which alone could give stability to her throne.

Elizabeth, by the ambiguity of her conduct, contrived to balance the hopes and fears of the two parties. She continued to assist, and occasionally to communicate at mass; she buried her sister with all the solemnities of the Catholic ritual; and she ordered a solemn dirge, and a mass of requiem, for the soul of the emperor, Charles V. By degrees, however, the secret of the intended change of religion was suffered to transpire. White, bishop of Winchester, was imprisoned for his sermon at the funeral of queen Mary, and Bonner, bishop of London, was called upon to account for the different fines which had been levied in his courts during the last reign. Archbishop Heath either received a hint, or deemed it prudent, to resign the seals, which, with the title of lord keeper, were transferred to Sir Nicholas Bacon. But that which cleared away every doubt was a proclamation, forbidding the clergy to preach, and ordering the Catholic worship to be observed " until consultation might be had in parliament by the queen and the three estates." Alarmed by this clause, the bishops assembled in London, and declared that they could not in conscience officiate at the coronation of a princess, who, it was probable, might object to some part of the service; and who, if she did not refuse to take, certainly meant to violate, that part of the oath which bound the sovereign to maintain the liberties of the church. The question was put, and was unanimously resolved in the negative.

This unexpected determination of the prelates created considerable embarrassment. Many expedients were devised to remove or surmount the difficulty; and at last the bishop of Carlisle separated himself from his colleagues. He was prevailed upon to crown the queen, and she on her part was compelled to take the accustomed oath, to receive the sacrament under one kind, and to conform to all the Catholic rites.

But Cecil soon completed his arrangements. On the 25th of January, 1559, the queen assisted in state at a solemn high mass, which was followed by a sermon from Dr. Cox, a Protestant preacher. The lord keeper then opened the parliament in her presence.

Before the Commons proceeded to any other business, they voted an address to the queen, praying that she would marry. She thanked them, but said that she preferred a single life.

An act was passed, which, without reversing the attainder of Anne Boleyn, restored Elizabeth in blood, and rendered her inheritable to her mother, and to all her ancestors on the part of her said mother. But the subject which principally occupied the attention of parliament was the alteration of religion. It was enacted that the Book of Common Prayer, with certain additions and emendations, should alone be used by all ministers; and that the spiritual authority of every foreign prelate within the realm should be utterly abolished. It next devolved on the queen to provide a new heirarchy for the English Church. She first sent for the bishops then in London, and required them to conform; but they refused and being deprived of their bishoprics, were committed to custody. After the consecration of new bishops, there was little to impede the progress of the reformed worship. The oath of supremacy was tendered by them to the clergy of their respective dioceses, but in general it was refused.

The restoration of Calais was a matter forming, at this time, a ground of negociation. It was agreed that the French king should retain possession during the next eight years, and, that at the expiration of the term, he should restore the town with its dependencies to Elizabeth. The terms were therefore condemned as prejudicial and disgraceful.

Mary Stuart had now completed her fifteenth year. She was married to the dauphin Francis, a prince of nearly the same age, in the cathedral of Paris; he was immediately saluted by his consort with the title of king-dauphin; and to cement the union of France and Scotland, the natives of each country were by legislative acts naturalized in the other.

A war on the subject of religion raged for a long time in Scotland, the details of which possess little interest. John Knox led the party of the new creed, and Elizabeth, though personally disliking Knox, aided his friends.

Francis, a weak and sickly prince, died in 1560. By this event, the near connection between France and Scotland was dissolved, and Mary persuaded herself that she might assume without molestation the government of her native kingdom. Such, however, was not the design of the English ministry. They were aware that she might marry a second time, and that with a new husband her former pretensions might revive, a contingency against which it was their duty to provide. With this view a resolution was taken to prevent, or at least to retard, the return of Mary Stuart to Scotland. Mary had been left a widow at the age of eighteen. She spent the winter among her maternal relatives in Lorrain, and consoled her grief by writing elegies on her departed husband. Having spent a few days with the French royal family at St. Germain en Laye, she proceeded to Calais in great state; whence she sailed in a short time, with two galleys and four transports, accompanied by three of her uncles and many French and Scottish noblemen. On the fourth day, Mary approached the land of her fathers with mingled emotions of hope and apprehension. Her fears were dispelled; with a glad and lightsome heart she mounted her palfry; and entered the capital amidst the shouts and congratulations of her subjects.

There were many, both among foreign princes and subjects, whose vanity or ambition aspired to the honour of marrying the queen of England. Of foreign princes the first was Philip of Spain; but as he received an answer he deemed equivalent to a refusal, he turned his eyes towards Isabella of France, by whom his offer was accepted. The place of Philip was supplied by his cousin Charles of Austria, son to the emperor Ferdinand; but difficulties connected with religion interfered with this alliance: and John, duke of Finland, next solicited the hand of the queen for his brother Eric, king of Sweden. He was received with royal honours, and flattered with delusive hopes, but his suit did not succeed.

The next suitor was Adolphus, duke of Holstein. The prince was young and handsome. On his arrival he was received with honour, and treated with peculiar kindness. He loved and was beloved. The queen made him knight of the Garter; she granted him a pension for life; still she could not be induced to take him for her husband. The earl of Arran next aspired to Elizabeth's hand. During the war of the Reformation he had displayed courage and constancy. To the deputies of the Scottish convention, who urged his suit, Elizabeth, with her usual affectation, replied, that she was content with her maiden state, and that God had given her no inclination for marriage.

The man who made the deepest and most lasting impression on Elizabeth's heart, was the lord Robert Dudley, who had been attainted with his father, the duke of Northumberland, for the attempt to remove Elizabeth as well as Mary from the succession. He had, however, been restored in blood, and frequently employed by the late queen; under the present he met with rapid preferment, was appointed master of the horse, and soon afterwards, to the surprise of the public, installed knight of the Garter. The queen and Dudley became inseparable companions.

A treaty was concluded between Elizabeth, although she was the ally of Charles IX., and the prince of Condé, a subject in arms against that sovereign, and one of the principal leaders of the Protestant party. She engaged to advance money and to land an army on the coast of Normandy, and Condé was to surrender into her hands the town of Havre de Grâce, to be detained by her as a security, not only for the repayment of the money but also for the restoration of Calais.

The English fleet sailed to the coast of Normandy. Havre and Dieppe were delivered to the queen; and the new earl of Warwick, the brother of the lord Robert Dudley, was appointed commander-in-chief of the English army in France. Fired with resentment, the French nobility hastened to the royal army from every province; and to animate their exertions, Charles, the queen regent, and the king of Navarre repaired to the camp before Rouen. The city was taken by assault, and abandoned, during eight days, to the fury of a victorious soldiery.

Elizabeth sent reinforcements to the earl of Warwick, commissioned Count Oldenburgh to levy twelve thousand men in Germany, and ordered public prayers during three days to implore the blessing of heaven upon her cause, and that of the Gospel. She soon afterwards obtained a grant from Parliament to aid in carrying on the war in France. An act highly penal againt the professors of the ancient faith was passed in this year. By the law, as it already stood, no heir holding of the crown could get legal possession of his lands, no individual could obtain preferment in the church, or accept office under the crown, or become member of either university, unless he had previously taken the oath of supremacy, which was deemed equivalent to a renunciation of the Catholic creed. The new act extended to many others the obligation of taking the oath, and made the first refusal an offence punishable by *premunire*, the second by death, as in cases of treason.

When the convocation assembled, matters were submitted to its deliberations of the highest importance to the new church; viz.: an adequate provision for the lower order of the clergy, a new code of ecclesiastical discipline, and the promulgation of a creed to be considered by Protestants as the future standard of English orthodoxy. The Thirty-nine Articles, as they now exist, were drawn up at this period.

The hope of recovering Calais, was one of the chief baits by which the queen had been drawn into the war between the French Huguenots and their sovereign. Her ministers had predicted the restoration of that important place; the prince of Condé had promised to support her demand with his whole power; and the admiral, Coligny, confirmed the engagement made by the prince. It was soon seen how little reliance could be placed upon men who fought only for their own emolument. The duke of Guise was assassinated. Condé aspired to the high station in the government to which he was entitled as first prince of the blood; and the Catholics feared that the English, with the aid of Coligny, might make important conquests in Normandy. The leaders on both sides, anxious for an accommodation, met, were reconciled, and subscribed a treaty of peace, by which the French Protestants promised their services to the king, as true and loyal subjects, and obtained in return an amnesty for the past, and the public exercise of their religion for the future.

Elizabeth received the intelligence with surprise and anger. In her public declarations, she had hitherto professed to hold the town of Havre in trust for the king of France; but now, when he required her to withdraw her forces, she replied that she would continue to hold it as a security for the restoration of Calais. She continued inexorable, till she saw that both parties, the Huguenots, as well as the Catholics, had determined to unite and expel the English troops from the soil of France. But she still had in her power the French hostages, and their bonds for the sum of five hundred thousand crowns.

When the queen of Scots ascended her paternal throne, she was aware that from France, distracted as it was by civil and religious dissension, she could derive no support; and therefore had determined, with the advice of her uncles, to subdue by conciliation, if it were possible, the hostility of her former opponents. The lord James, her illegitimate brother, and Maitland, the apostate secretary, both high in the confidence of the "Congregationists," or Protestant party, and both pensioners of the English queen, were appointed her principal ministers; the friendship of Elizabeth was sought by compliments and professions of attachment; and an epistolary correspondence was established between the two queens.

In a few months, the jealousy or policy of Elizabeth was called into action by a communication from Mary, stating that she had received a proposal of marriage from the archduke Charles of Austria. The announcement put to the test all the ingenuity of Cecil. To prevent the match, he devised two plans, which were instantly carried into effect. By the first, Elizabeth was again brought forward as a rival to Mary. Cecil applied to the duke of Wirtemberg; and that prince, as if of himself, solicited the emperor to make a second offer of his son to the English queen. But Ferdinand replied, that he had once been duped by the selfish and insincere policy of Elizabeth, and that he would not expose himself to similar treatment a second time. The other plan was to induce Mary, by threats and promises, to refuse the archduke. Elizabeth proposed that Mary should marry Robert Dudley, earl of Leicester; but she refused, as Elizabeth evidently expected. In a short time the lord Darnley was set up. Darnley was the eldest son of the countess of Lennox; and it was represented to Mary that a marriage with him could not be degrading, since he was sprung by his father from the kings of Scotland, by his mother from those of England. Mary appeared to listen to this proposal with a willing ear: and the intelligence was immediately conveyed to Elizabeth. The matter hung in suspense till Elizabeth, to the surprise of most men, though she had at first refused, allowed Darnley to proceed to the Scottish court with letters of recommendation. Mary accepted Darnley, but strange to say, this announcement irritated the English queen; and a letter was forwarded to Mary, describing the inconveniences and impolicy of the marriage.

Elizabeth then sent agents to excite rebellion in Scotland. Mary summoned the Scottish nobles to meet her at Perth; Murray and his friends refused to obey. She received secret advice that it was the intention of the discontented lords to make her their prisoner with Lennox and Darnley; but she defeated their object. Mary now, to free herself from the state of uncertainty in which she had so long lived, privately married, July 9, 1565, Darnley.

Both parties began to prepare for the approaching struggle. The lords met at Stirling, and subscribed a bond to stand by each other; a messenger was despatched the next day to Elizabeth, to solicit speedy and effectual aid. Mary immediately acknowledged her choice of Darnley. She ordered the banns to be published, created him duke of Albany, and was married openly to him. Proclamation was made that he should be styled king during the time of their marriage, and that all writs should run in the joint names of Henry and Mary. He was in his twentieth, she had reached her twenty-third year.

The associated lords receiving no aid from England, were unable to withstand the superior force of the royalists, and they retired, some towards Ayr, some towards Argyleshire. The rebel force soon disbanded, and Murray was allowed to proceed to London. At first Elizabeth refused to see him; afterwards he was admitted in presence of the French and Spanish ambassadors, when, falling on his knees, he acknowledged that the queen was innocent of the conspiracy, and had never advised them to disobey their sovereign lady.

Mary, in the ardour of her affection, had overlooked the defects in the character of Darnley. Experience convinced her that he was capricious in his temper, violent in his passions, and implacable in his resentments. He had already contracted habits of inebriety, which led him occasionally into the most scandalous excesses, and made him forget even in public, the respect due to his consort. But his ambition proved to her a source of more bitter disquietude. Darnley insisted that a matrimonial crown should be granted to himself, but Mary refused; and the discontented prince directed his resentment against those whom he supposed to be her advisers, and particularly against David Riccio, one of her secretaries, a native of Piedmont, who had come to Scotland in the suite of the ambassador of Savoy.

Many of the Scotch viewed Riccio with hostility. He was a stranger and a Catholic; two qualities calculated to excite the jealousy both of the courtiers and of the preachers. Maitland, observing the discontent of the king, suggested to him that Mary had transferred her affections to Riccio; and that the refusal of the matrimonial crown had proceeded from the advice of that minion. On Saturday, March 9, 1566, between seven and eight in the evening, eighty armed men, took possession of the gates of Holyrood palace. Mary, who was indisposed and in the seventh month of her pregnancy, was at the time seated at supper in the closet of her bed-chamber with her illegitimate brother and sister. Riccio, Erskine, captain of the guard, and Beaton, master of the household, were in attendance. Suddenly the king entered by a private staircase, and placing himself next the queen, put his arm round her waist. He was followed by Ruthven and others armed. Mary, alarmed at the sight of Ruthven, commanded him to quit the room, under the penalty of treason; but he replied, that his errand was with David; and the unfortunate secretary, exclaiming, "Justitia, justitia!" sprung for protection behind his sovereign. Her prayers and gestures were despised. The table was thrown over in the struggle; and the assassins, dragging their victim through the bed-chamber, despatched him in the adjoining room with no fewer than fifty-six wounds.

Mary had passed the first night and day in fits and lamentations. She was no sooner left alone with her husband than she resumed her former ascendency, and convinced him of the impropriety of his conduct. They both secretly left the palace, and reached in safety the castle of Dunbar. The royal standard was immediately unfurled; before the end of the week eight thousand faithful subjects had hastened to the aid of Mary; and as she approached Edinburgh, the murderers fled to Berwick.

Mary took up her residence in the castle of Edinburgh, where she was delivered of a son. This child lived to ascend the thrones of both kingdoms. Elizabeth was dancing at Greenwich when Cecil whispered the intelligence in her ear. She retired to her chair, reclined her head on her hand, and appeared for some time absorbed in profound thought.

Elizabeth summoned a parliament.

As soon as the motion for a supply was made in the lower house, it was opposed on the ground that the queen had not redeemed the pledge on the faith of which the last grant had been voted; she had neither married nor declared her successor. Elizabeth sent them an order to proceed to other matters. They obeyed with reluctance; but still allowed the bill for the subsidy, which had been read only once, to lie unnoticed on the table. The queen, after the pause of a fortnight, promised to consider the subject. The public business proceeded; and the supply was granted.

In Scotland, the murder of Riccio disappointed the hopes of Darnley. Instead of obtaining the matrimonial crown, and with it the sovereign authority, he found himself an object of scorn and aversion.

Mary about this time got a serious attack of illness, and thinking herself dying, recommended, by letter, her son to the protection of the king of France and of the queen of England. Her symptoms were soon, however, more favourable; she began to recover slowly; and Darnley, who had been sent for at the beginning of her illness, at length paid her a visit; but no advance was made towards a reconciliation. Mary was advised by some of the nobles to seek for a divorce, but she did not consent, and the lords formed a scheme of assassination. The earl Bothwell took upon himself to perpetrate the crime, and the others to save him from the consequences.

It chanced that at this time the small-pock was prevalent in Glasgow, and that Darnley took the infection. When the news reached Edinburgh, Mary sent her own physician to her husband, with a message that she would shortly visit him herself. This promise she fulfilled; their affection seemed to revive; and they mutually promised to forget all former causes of offence. From Glasgow, as soon as he was able to remove, she returned with him to Edinburgh, and, probably, to preserve the young prince from infection, lodged him not in Holyrood house but in a house without the walls, belonging to the provost of St. Mary's, generally called "the Kirk of Field." Here it was that the conspirators prepared to execute their plan. By a door in the city wall their agents obtained access to the cellar of the house, undermined the foundations in several parts, and placed a sufficient quantity of gunpowder under the angles of

and devoting to the flames every house and village which
in his way; while the French, who had been forbidden
to risk an engagement, hovered in small bodies round the
invaders.

The duke of Albany, after his base negociation with Lord
Dacre, had left Scotland; but the principal lords remained constant in their attachment to France, and impatiently expected
his return with supplies of men and money. Henry sought
reconciliation with his sister, Queen Margaret, that he might
set her up in opposition to Albany; and gave the chief command in the north to the earl of Surrey, son to the victor of
Flodden Field, with instructions to purchase the services of the
Scottish lords with money, and to invade and lay waste the
Scottish borders. Margaret gladly accepted the overture,
consented to conduct her son, now in his twelfth year, to Edinburgh, and to announce by proclamation that he had assumed
the government, provided the English general would march a
strong force to her support. Surrey repeatedly entered the
marches, spread around the devastation of war, and at last reduced to ashes the large town of Jedburgh. But on that very
day Albany landed at Dumbarton with two thousand soldiers
and a great quantity of stores and ammunition. The projects
of Margaret were instantly crushed; at the call of the parliament the whole nation rose in arms! and Albany saw at
sixty thousand men arrayed round his standard. Surrey, however, received reinforcements, and Albany, after an ineffectual
attempt to retain the regency, sailed for France, never more to
set foot in Scotland.

Among the different projects which occupied the restless
mind of Julius II., was that of erecting a temple worthy of the
capital of the Christian world, of enormous dimensions and
rivalled magnificence. To raise money for this purpose, he
published an indulgence in Poland and France; which his successor, Leo X., had with the same view extended to the northern provinces of Germany. The papal commission was directed to Albert, elector of Mentz, and archbishop of Magdeburg; and that prelate employed as his delegate Tetzel, a
Dominican friar, whose brethren rapidly spread themselves over
Saxony.

The origin of the revolution which followed may, with probability, be attributed to the counsels of Staupitz, vicar of the
friars of St. Augustine. It has been generally supposed that
he was actuated by a spirit of opposition to the Dominicans

Exactly one month after his
... to the court of session, where, in
... she forgave him; the next day she
..., and was married to him.
... into a confederacy against Both-
... with the murder of Darnley. In
... with his friends, to meet the more
... force of his enemies on Car-
... from Edinburgh. From an
... nine at night, the two armies
... it was agreed that Bothwell
... ion; that the queen should re-
... the associated lords should pay
... ence which was due to the sove-
... mutually ratified, and the army re-
... An hour did not elapse before
... captive in the hands of unfeeling

... nveyed by a body of four hundred
... tal to the castle of Lochlevin, the
..., half brother of Murray.
... med of this extraodinary revolution
... gents, whom she received with the
... pleasure. The insult offered to the
... the doctrines of Knox, which she
... and required severe and immediate
... ards she sent an ambassador to Scot-
... favour.
... called upon to resign the crown in
... when she had yielded to the threat
... was crowned in the High Church
... appointed Regent.
... fered to retire without molestation
... castle of Dunbar. The friends of
... well should proceed through Den-
... it the advice and aid of the French
...; a hostile squadron overtook him;
... interrupted by a sudden storm, which
... Norway, where he was detained a

..., which Mary had inherited from
..., and which she is said to have given
... the possession of the earl Morton. In

the building. The queen visited her husband daily, gave him repeated testimonies of her affection, and frequently slept in the room under his bed-chamber. She had promised to be present at a ball to be given on the 9th of February, 1567, in honour of the marriage of two of her servants; and the certainty of her absence on that night induced the conspirators to select it for the execution of the plot. On that day, Mary went as usual to the Kirk of Field, with a numerous retinue, and remained in Darnley's company from six till almost eleven o'clock. She then returned by the light of torches to Holyrood House; on the termination of the ball she retired to her chamber; and about two the palace and city were shaken by a tremendous explosion. It was soon ascertained that the house of Kirk of Field had been blown up with gunpowder, and that the dead bodies of the king and his page were lying uninjured in the garden.

Judicial inquiries were instituted, and a proclamation was issued, offering rewards in money and land, for the discovery and apprehension of the murderers, with a full pardon to any one of the party who would accuse his accomplices. The same noblemen, however, continued to attend the royal person. Darnley's father, Lennox, expressed his suspicion of Bothwell's guilt, and that nobleman demanded a trial. His request being granted, he proceeded to the Tolbooth, surrounded by two hundred soldiers, and four thousand gentlemen. As no prosecutor appeared, the jury having heard the indictment, and evidence to show that Bothwell could not have been at the Kirk of Field at the time of the explosion, returned a verdict of acquittal.

On the 21th April, Mary rode to Stirling, to visit her infant son, whom, for greater security, she had lately entrusted to the custody of the earl of Marr. On her return, she had reached the Foulbrigge, half a mile from the castle of Edinburgh, when she was met by Bothwell at the head of one thousand horse. To resist would have been fruitless; and the queen with her attendants, the earl of Huntley, Maitland, and Melville, was conducted to the castle of Dunbar. There she remained a captive for the space of ten days: nor was she suffered to depart till she had consented to become the wife of Bothwell. He then left the fortress; but it was to conduct the captive queen from one prison to another, from the castle of Dunbar to that of Edinburgh. The only remaining obstacle, his existing marriage to Janet Gordon, sister to the earl of Huntley, was in a few days removed by a divorce. Exactly one month after his trial, Bothwell led the queen to the court of session, where, in the presence of the judges, she forgave him; the next day she created him duke of Orkney, and was married to him.

Several noblemen entered into a confederacy against Bothwell, and openly charged him with the murder of Darnley. In four days Bothwell ventured, with his friends, to meet the more numerous and well-appointed force of his enemies on Carberry Hill, at no great distance from Edinburgh. From an early hour in the morning till nine at night, the two armies faced each other. At length it was agreed that Bothwell should retire without molestation; that the queen should return to her capital, and that the associated lords should pay to her that honour and obedience which was due to the sovereign. The agreement was mutually ratified, and the army returned towards Edinburgh. An hour did not elapse before Mary learned that she was a captive in the hands of unfeeling adversaries.

The next day she was conveyed by a body of four hundred armed men out of the capital to the castle of Lochlevin, the residence of William Douglas, half brother of Murray.

Elizabeth had been informed of this extraodinary revolution by an envoy from the insurgents, whom she received with the strongest expressions of displeasure. The insult offered to the Scottish queen resulted from the doctrines of Knox, which she had so often condemned; and required severe and immediate punishment. Soon afterwards she sent an ambassador to Scotland to negociate in Mary's favour.

The Queen of Scots was called upon to resign the crown in favour of her son; and, when she had yielded to the threat of force, the royal infant was crowned in the High Church in Stirling, and Murray was appointed Regent.

Bothwell had been suffered to retire without molestation from Carberry Hill to his castle of Dunbar. The friends of Mary resolved that Bothwell should proceed through Denmark to France, and solicit the advice and aid of the French monarch. He put to sea; a hostile squadron overtook him; but the engagement was interrupted by a sudden storm, which cast him on the coast of Norway, where he was detained a prisoner.

In June, a silver casket, which Mary had inherited from her first husband, Francis, and which she is said to have given to Bothwell, came into the possession of the earl Morton. In it, if we may believe him, were found several papers in the handwriting of the queen, which proved her to have been an accomplice in Bothwell's crime.

The Scottish queen was still confined in the Towers of Lochlevin, under the jealous eye of the lady Douglas, mother to the regent. It was in vain that, to recover her liberty, she made repeated offers to her brother and the council. They had resolved that she should never leave her prison alive. But her misfortunes won for her a partisan in George Douglas, the brother of the regent. He introduced a laundress at an early hour into the bedchamber of Mary, who exchanged clothes with the woman, and, carrying out a basket of linen, took her seat in the boat. She had almost reached the opposite bank, when, to secure her muffler from the rudeness of one of the rowers, she raised her arm to her face, and a voice immediately exclaimed, "That is not the hand of a washerwoman." She was recognised, and conveyed back to Lochlevin. In five weeks afterwards she succeeded in escaping, and rode in safety to the castle of Hamilton, where she revoked the resignation of the crown she made in her prison at Lochlevin. At this intelligence, the royalists crowded round their sovereign. On May 13th, 1568, Mary was on her road to the castle of Dumbarton, when Murray, with a small but disciplined force, appeared on an eminence called Langsyde. At the sight, her followers rode in confusion to charge the rebels; but were repulsed. From the field of battle, the disconsolate queen fled precipitately to the court of "her good sister," the queen of England. Mary's unexpected arrival in England opened new prospects to Cecil and his confidential friends in the council. They rejoiced that the prey, which they had hunted for years, had at last voluntarily thrown herself into the toils. After repeated deliberations, it was concluded that to detain her in captivity for life would be the most conducive both to the security of their sovereign and to the interests of their religion. The accomplishment of this object was intrusted to Cecil. Mary was at first assured that Elizabeth would vindicate the common cause of sovereigns, and reinstate her in her former authority; but a hint was given that it was desirable that the Scottish queen should clear herself from the crimes with which she had been charged. Mary, immediately after her arrival, had demanded permission to visit Elizabeth, that she might lay before her the wrongs which she had suffered. But a personal interview might have proved dangerous, not only to Murray and his party but to their friends in the English cabinet; Cecil suggested to his mistress, that she could not in decency admit into her presence a woman charged with murder. Mary, however, refused to submit to a trial, and requested permission to return again or to pass through England to France. The demand was refused. Mary then demanded to be allowed permission to prove her innocence in the the presence of " her good sister," as her friend, but not as her judge. It was resolved that Mary should not be received at court till her innocence had been established; and that she should be transferred from Carlisle to Bolton Castle. Cecil suggested an expedient which served his purpose as well as a trial of Mary—an investigation, not into her conduct, but that of her enemies. Mary assented to this expedient. Murray dared not refuse; and the place of conference was fixed in York. The proceedings were afterwards transferred to London: but it was soon resolved to put an end to the conferences. Murray and his associates were licensed to depart. They had shown no sufficient cause why Elizabeth " should conceive or take any evil opinion against the queen—her good sister." Mary's victory, in argument, appears to have been acknowledged by the chief of the English nobility, who had witnessed the whole of the proceedings.

The Scottish queen was removed to Wynfield.

In November, 1569, an insurrection took place in the northern counties. The object of the insurgents was to march to Tutbury, to liberate the queen of Scots, and to extort from Elizabeth a declaration that Mary was next heir to the throne. They proceeded as far as Branham Moor without opposition. But here dissension insinuated itself into their counsels. Their money was already expended, and all their expectations had been disappointed. Elizabeth, having succeeded in quelling the insurrection, caused a large number of the insurgents to be executed.

In Scotland, at this time, the regent Murray was assassinated; and Lennox, the grandfather of the young king, was, at Elizabeth's recommendation, raised to the regency.

In 1570, a bull was prepared, in which the pope pronounced Elizabeth guilty of heresy, and absolved her subjects from their allegiance. Early one morning a copy was seen affixed to the gates of the bishop of London's residence in the capital. One Felton confessed that he had set up the bull, and was executed.

More than two years had elapsed since the arrival of Mary in England, and she was still a captive. Elizabeth was willing that Mary should perish, but was ashamed to imbrue her own hands in her blood. Hence she offered to transfer the captive to the Scottish regent, provided he would give security that she should be removed out of the way; and hence the earl of Shrewsbury, who had the custody of Mary, was made to engage that she should be put to death on the very first attempt to rescue her.

It had for some time been a favourite object with the leaders of the Huguenots to bring about a marriage between the English queen and the duke of Anjou, the eldest of the two brothers of Charles IX. But Catharine de Medicis, the queen-mother, received the proposal very coldly. Repeated messages induced her at last to view the matter in a more favourable light; but Anjou could not think of disgracing himself by taking for his wife a woman who had no regard for her own honour. More than a fortnight passed before she could extort from her son his assent. Elizabeth received at last a proposal of marriage in due form from Anjou himself.

The Puritans now began to object to the ceremonies which had been retained; and the queen resolved to repress the zeal of these ultra-reformers. By the assumption of the supremacy, it had become the duty of Elizabeth to watch over doctrine, discipline, and public worship. Elizabeth appointed delegates who were authorized to inquire, on the oath of the person accused, and on the oaths of witnesses, of all heretical, erroneous, and dangerous opinions; of absence from the established service, and the frequentation of private conventicles; and to punish the offenders by spiritual censures, by fine, imprisonment, and deprivation. The first victims who felt the vengeance of this tribunal, called the High Commission Court, were the Catholics; from the Catholics its attention was soon directed to the Puritans.

The proposal of marriage between Elizabeth and the duke of Anjou, though entertained on each side, made but little progress. When almost every other article had been settled, the duke required the insertion of a clause securing to him the free exercise of his religion. This the queen was advised to refuse as contrary to law. The marriage was therefore broken off.

In August, 1571, a conspiracy was discovered in which the

duke of Norfolk was implicated. He was conveyed to the Tower. He confessed that he had been made acquainted with several projects of discontented men for the surprisal of the queen, or the deliverance of Mary Stuart; protesting, however, that the idea of injuring the person of the sovereign, had never entered his mind. Norfolk was charged with compassing the death of Elizabeth, by seeking to marry the queen of Scots, who claimed the English throne to the exclusion of Elizabeth. The duke maintained his innocence, but was found guilty. Five months after his condemnation, the duke was led to the scaffold; and in his speech to the spectators, asserted his innocence of treason, and his profession of the Protestant faith.

The death of the queen of Scots was next sought with equal obstinacy. Both houses resolved to proceed against her by bill of attainder; the queen forbade it; they disobeyed; and she repeated the prohibition. Foiled in this attempt, the ministers adopted another course; they introduced a bill, which, by rendering Mary incapable of the succession, secured them from the danger of her resentment if she should survive the present sovereign. They were, however, opposed by a powerful but invisible counsellor, suspected, though not known, to be the earl of Leicester. The queen interdicted all reference to the inheritance of the crown, and seeing that, in defiance of the message, the bill had passed both houses, she prorogued the parliament.

The execution of the duke, and the proceedings in parliament, disheartened the friends of Mary in England, while, at the same time, her interest was rapidly declining in her native country. The earl of Marr had been invested with the regency. His prudence and vigour rendered him formidable; Elizabeth declared openly her intention to support him; and the avowed adherents of Mary dwindled away to a hundred of brave and resolute men, who maintained her cause in the mountains. The duke of Northumberland, one of her firmest friends, was executed without trial at this period.

Elizabeth was next advised to listen to a new proposal of marriage, with the duke of Anjou's younger brother, the duke of Alençon. The former was the leader of the Catholic party; the latter was thought to incline to the tenets of Protestantism. This arrangement was unexpectedly checked by an event which struck with astonishment all the nations of Europe. The young king of Navarre was at this time the nominal, the admiral

Coligny, the real leader of the Huguenots. He ruled among them as an independent sovereign; and, what chiefly alarmed his opponents, seemed to obtain gradually the ascendency over the mind of Charles. He had come to Paris to assist at the marriage of the king of Navarre, and was wounded in two places by an assassin as he passed through the streets. The public voice attributed the attempt to the duke of Guise, in revenge of the murder of his father at the siege of Orleans; it had proceeded, in reality from Catherine, the queen mother. The wounds were not dangerous; but the Huguenot chieftains crowded to his hotel; their threats of vengeance terrified the queen; and in a secret council the king was persuaded to anticipate the designs attributed to the friends of the admiral. The next morning, St. Bartholomew's day, 1572, by the royal order, the hotel was forced; Coligny and his principal counsellors perished; the populace joined in the work of blood; and every Huguenot, or suspected Huguenot, who fell in their way, was murdered.

The news of this sanguinary transaction excited throughout England one general feeling of horror. Burghley again advised Elizabeth to put to death her rival, Mary. The queen did not reject the advice: but that she might escape the infamy of dipping her hands in the blood of her nearest relative and presumptive heir, a messenger was despatched to Edinburgh, ostensibly to compose some differences amongst the nobles; but, in reality, to bring about the death of the queen of Scots, from the hands of her own subjects. He was, however, warned not to commit his sovereign as if the proposal came from her. Marr, the regent, at first, affected to look upon the project as attended with difficulty and peril; but afterwards entered into it most cordially, and sought to drive a profitable bargain with Elisabeth. He died soon after, and was succeeded by Morton, a most determined enemy of Mary, and the tried friend of the English ministers. He obtained troops from Elizabeth, and took the castle of Edinburgh.

One day, however, when the young king was seated at the board with his council, James Stuart, captain of the guard, and son to lord Ochiltree, requested permission to speak to his sovereign. Being admitted, he fell on his knees, and accused James, earl of Morton, of having been guilty act and part of the murder of the king's father, Darnley. He was tried, and found guilty by the unanimous verdict of his peers, and soon afterwards beheaded. He admitted that he knew of the intention to murder Darnley, but declared that he took no part in the act.

In France, the general opinion was, that Mary and James ought to be associated on the Scottish throne; and that the pope and the king of Spain should be solicited to relieve the present pecuniary wants of the young king. But this project was extinguished in its very birth by the promptitude and policy of Elizabeth's cabinet. Under its auspices a new revolution was organized in Scotland. The earl of Gowrie invited James to his castle of Ruthven, secured the person of the unsuspecting prince, and assumed with his associates the exercise of the royal authority. The Scottish lords of the English faction ruled again without control.

It was owing, perhaps, to the peculiar circumstance in which the king of Scotland had been placed from his infancy, or to the education which he had received from his tutors, that he felt none of those generous sentiments which usually glow with so much ardour in the bosom of youth. In 1585, Mary appealed to him. James returned a cold and disrespectful answer, which opened the eyes of the captive to the hopelessness of her situation. Even the son, on whose affection she rested her fondest hopes, had deceived—had abandoned her. In the anguish of her mind she again wrote to Elizabeth, begging, as a last favour, her liberty and life. She was ready to make every sacrifice, except that of her religion. But the English queen, no longer afraid of the interposition of James, committed the custody of her person to Sir Amyot Paulet, a stern fanatic.

A negociation was now opened between Elizabeth and James, and a treaty was concluded, by which the queen of England and the king of Scotland bound themselves to support the Protestant faith against the efforts of the Catholic powers, and to furnish to each other a competent aid in case of invasion by any foreign prince.

The misfortunes of Mary queen of Scots were, at length, drawing to a close. In 1586, a plan for her liberation was arranged. One of the most active in the plot was named Babington, a young man of ancient family and ample fortune. Some years previously he had been page to the earl of Shrewsbury, a situation in which he had learned to admire and to pity his lord's captive, the queen of Scots. His plan embraced the assassination of Elizabeth, and the carrying off of the Scottish queen. It then occurred to him to consult

Mary, and a letter to her was prepared, stating that it was the resolution of himself and friends, to procure a sufficient force to "warrant the landing of foreign aid, her deliverance from prison, and the despatch of the usurping competitor." The letter came into the hands of Walsingham, who communicated it to the queen.

Mary accepted the offer of *liberation* made to her by Babington, and composed instructions for his guidance on that point; but he and several others were soon arrested, tried, and executed for high treason. Mary was removed to the castle of Fotheringhay, in Northamptonshire, the place selected for her trial and death; and a commission was issued to forty-six individuals, peers, privy counsellors, and judges, constituting them a court to inquire into the case. On the 11th of October, 1586, the commissioners arrived at the castle. Mary, on learning their business, said, "I am sorry to be charged by my sister the queen with that of which I am innocent; but let it be remembered that I am also a queen, and not amenable to any foreign jurisdiction. I will not degrade the Scottish crown, nor stand as a criminal at the bar of an English court of justice."

One of the commissioners observed that if she refused to plead, the world would attribute her obstinacy to consciousness of guilt. Mary informed the commissioners that she consented to be tried, though she was refused the aid of counsel.

The charge against the Scottish queen, like that against Babington, had been divided into two parts; that she had conspired with foreigners and traitors to procure the invasion of the realm, and the death of the queen. The papers exhibited to the court as Mary's were only copies. No attempt was made to show what had become of the originals, or when, where, or by whom the copies had been taken. The court was opened at Westminster, in the presence of a numerous assemblage, but Mary was absent, immured in the castle of Fotheringhay. With one exception, the commissioners unanimously gave judgment, that "Mary, daughter of James V., commonly called queen of Scotland, had compassed and imagined divers matters tending to the hurt, death, and destruction of the queen."

On hearing the result, Mary denied solemnly that she had been privy to a conspiracy against the life of their queen. She had, she said, accepted an offer made to rescue her from prison; and where was the person in her situation who would not, after an unjust captivity of twenty years, have done the same? Her real crime was her adhesion to the religion of her fathers, a crime of which she was proud, and for which she would be happy to lay down her life.

James of Scotland felt little for a mother whom he had never known, and whom he had been taught to look upon as an enemy, seeking to deprive him of his authority. He would probably have abandoned her but for the remonstrances of the Scottish nobles, who could not brook the notion that a Scottish queen should perish on a scaffold. James therefore wrote to Elizabeth a letter of expostulation, but it had no effect.

After the sentence, Elizabeth spent two months in a state of apparent irresolution. On the departure of the French and Scottish ambassadors, who had fruitlessly appealed to Elizabeth for mercy, she signed the warrant, telling her secretary, Davison, to take it to the great seal, and to trouble her no more about it; adding with a smile of irony, that on his way he might call on Walsingham, who was sick, and who, she feared, "at the sight of it would die outright." Then suddenly recollecting herself, she said, "Surely Paulet and Drury, (Mary's gaolers,) might ease me of this burthen. Do you and Walsingham sound their dispositions." A letter was accordingly forwarded to Fotheringhay on the same day, in the name of both secretaries. It informed the two keepers, that the queen charged them with lack of care for her service, otherwise they would long ago have shortened the life of their captive. Paulet replied immediately, that his goods, living, and life were at the queen's service; but he would never shed blood without law or warrant. Drury subscribed to Paulet's opinion. Davison put the question to Elizabeth, whether she intended to proceed to the execution of the commission or not. "Yea," with the addition of an oath, was her reply, with more than usual vehemence; but she did not like the form, for it threw all the responsibility on herself.

On the 7th of February, 1587, the earl of Shrewsbury arrived at Fotheringhay; and his office of earl marshal instantly disclosed the fatal object of his visit. The queen rose from her bed, dressed, and seated herself by a small table, having previously arranged her servants, male and female, on each side. The earl entered uncovered; he was followed by the earl of Kent, the sheriff, and several gentlemen of the county; and Beale, after a short preface, read aloud the commission for the execution. Mary listened, without any change of and devoting to the flames every house and village which fell in his way; while the French, who had been forbidden to risk an engagement, hovered in small bodies round the invaders.

The duke of Albany, after his base negociation with Lord Dacre, had left Scotland; but the principal lords remained constant in their attachment to France, and impatiently expected his return with supplies of men and money. Henry sought a reconciliation with his sister, Queen Margaret, that he might set her up in opposition to Albany; and gave the chief command in the north to the earl of Surrey, son to the victor of Flodden Field, with instructions to purchase the services of the Scottish lords with money, and to invade and lay waste the Scottish borders. Margaret gladly accepted the overture, and consented to conduct her son, now in his twelfth year, to Edinburgh, and to announce by proclamation that he had assumed the government, provided the English general would march a strong force to her support. Surrey repeatedly entered the marches, spread around the devastation of war, and at last reduced to ashes the large town of Jedburgh. But on that very day Albany landed at Dumbarton with two thousand soldiers, and a great quantity of stores and ammunition. The projects of Margaret were instantly crushed; at the call of the parliament the whole nation rose in arms! and Albany saw above sixty thousand men arrayed round his standard. Surrey, however, received reinforcements, and Albany, after an ineffectual attempt to retain the regency, sailed for France, never more to set foot in Scotland.

Among the different projects which occupied the restless mind of Julius II., was that of erecting a temple worthy of the capital of the Christian world, of enormous dimensions and unrivalled magnificence. To raise money for this purpose, he had published an indulgence in Poland and France; which his successor, Leo X., had with the same view extended to the northern provinces of Germany. The papal commission was directed to Albert, elector of Mentz, and archbishop of Magdeburg; and that prelate employed as his delegate Tetzel, a Dominican friar, whose brethren rapidly spread themselves over Saxony.

The origin of the revolution which followed may, with probability, be attributed to the counsels of Staupitz, vicar of the friars of St. Augustine. It has been generally supposed that he was actuated by a spirit of opposition to the Dominicans.

...hat have long thirsted
...ooks of water. Com-
... I have done nothing
... of his crown." She
...ight be present at her
... her men and two of
... steward, physician,
...aids. Mary wore the
..., and her countenance
... with that grace and
...d in her happier days,
... her, as she mounted
"I thank you, sir," said
... you, and the most ac-
...d me."
which was prepared for
... assembly. She said
her enemies. She then
...atin language, passages
...er in French, in which
..., declared that she for-
...e was innocent of ever
... of her English sister.
... afflicted church, for
..., all the while holding
... of Kent, "you had
..., and bear him in your
... my hand the repre-
... the same time bear him
... her a handkerchief
..., the executioners, hold-
..., and the queen kneeling
..., "Into thy hands, O
sobs and groans of the
He trembled, missed
... the lower part of the
; and at the third stroke

.... It was afterwards
... room for six months,
... interred with royal
...ch opposite to the tomb

countenance; then, crossing herself, she bade them welcome; the day, she said, which she had long desired, had at last arrived; she had languished in prison near twenty years, useless to others, and a burden to herself; nor could she conceive a termination to such a life more happy or more honourable, than to shed her blood for her religion. Placing her hand on a Testament which lay on the table, "As for the death of the queen your sovereign," said she, "I call God to witness, that I never imagined it, never sought it, nor ever consented to it." The earl of Kent exhorted her to accept the spiritual services of the dean of Peterborough, a learned divine appointed by the queen. Mary requested that she might have the aid of Le Préau, her almoner, who was still in the house; but this, which was the last and only indulgence that she had to demand, was cruelly refused. Mary asked when she was to suffer. The earl of Shrewsbury answered, but with considerable agitation, "To-morrow morning, at eight o'clock."

Mary heard the announcement of her death with perfect serenity of countenance, and dignity of manner, which awed and affected the beholders; but her attendants burst into tears and lamentations.

The last night of Mary's life was spent in the arrangement of her domestic affairs, the writing of her will and of three letters, and in exercises of devotion. About four she retired to rest; but it was observed she did not sleep. Her lips were in constant motion, and her mind seemed absorbed in prayer. At the first break of day her household assembled around her. Weeping, they followed her into her oratory, where she took her place in front of the altar; they knelt down and prayed behind her.

In the midst of the great hall of the castle had been raised a scaffold, covered with black serge, and surrounded with a low railing. Before eight a message was sent to the queen, who replied that she would be ready in half an hour. At that time the sheriff entered the oratory, and Mary arose, taking the crucifix from the altar in her right, and carrying her prayer-book in her left hand. Her servants were forbidden to follow.

Mary was now joined by the earls and her keepers, and descending the staircase, found at the foot Melville, the steward of her household, who for several weeks had been excluded from her presence. "Good Melville," said Mary, "I pray thee report that I die a true woman to my religion, to Scotland

and to France. May God forgive them that have long thirsted for my blood, as the hart doth for the brooks of water. Commend me to my son, and tell him that I have done nothing prejudicial to the dignity or independence of his crown." She made a last request, that her servants might be present at her death. It was resolved to admit four of her men and two of her women servants. She selected her steward, physician, apothecary, and surgeon, with her two maids. Mary wore the richest of her dresses. Her step was firm, and her countenance cheerful. She advanced into the hall with that grace and majesty which she had so often displayed in her happier days, and in the palace of her fathers. To aid her, as she mounted the scaffold, Paulet offered his arm. "I thank you, sir," said Mary; "it is the last trouble I shall give you, and the most acceptable service you have ever rendered me."

The queen seated herself on a stool which was prepared for her; and in an audible voice addressed the assembly. She said that she pardoned from her heart all her enemies. She then repeated with a loud voice, and in the Latin language, passages from the book of Psalms; and a prayer in French, in which she begged of God to pardon her sins, declared that she forgave her enemies, and protested that she was innocent of ever consenting in wish or deed to the death of her English sister. She then prayed in English for Christ's afflicted church, for her son James, and for Queen Elizabeth, all the while holding up the crucifix. "Madam," said the earl of Kent, "you had better leave such popish trumperies, and bear him in your heart." She replied, "I cannot hold in my hand the representation of his sufferings, but I must at the same time bear him in my heart." One of her maids taking from her a handkerchief edged with gold, pinned it over her eyes; the executioners, holding her by the arms, led her to the block; and the queen kneeling down, said repeatedly, with a firm voice, "Into thy hands, O Lord, I commend my spirit." But the sobs and groans of the spectators disconcerted the headsman. He trembled, missed his aim, and inflicted a deep wound in the lower part of the skull. The queen remained motionless; and at the third stroke her head was severed from her body.

The body was embalmed the same day. It was afterwards enclosed in lead, and kept in the same room for six months, till August, when Elizabeth ordered it to be interred with royal pomp in the abbey church of Peterborough, opposite to the tomb of Catharine, queen of Henry VIII. It was transferred to Westminster by order of James I., in 1612.

When one of Elizabeth's ladies mentioned before her, as it were casually, the death of Mary Stuart, she affected the most violent indignation, and indulged in threats of the most fearful vengeance against the men who had abused her confidence and usurped her authority, by putting the queen of Scots to death without her knowledge or consent.

A full month elapsed before the king of Scotland received any certain intelligence of the execution of his mother. At the news he burst into tears, and talked of nothing but vengeance. His indignation gradually evaporated; and his mouth was sealed with a present of £4,000.

That spirit of commercial enterprise which had been awakened under Mary, seemed to pervade and animate every description of men during the reign of Elizabeth.

In 1562, Sir John Hawkins commenced the trade in slaves. He made three voyages to the coast of Africa; crossed the Atlantic to Hispaniola and the Spanish settlements in America; and in exchange for his captives returned with large quantities of hides, sugar, ginger, and pearls. This trade was, however, illicit; and during his third voyage he was surprised by the Spanish fleet. Hawkins lost his fleet, his treasure, and the majority of his followers.

The queen had almost annually offered injuries to the king of Spain. She had intercepted his treasure, and given aid to his rebels in the Netherlands.

Policy taught him to dissemble for a long time. At length he resolved to invade England with 135 sail of men-of-war, carrying 8,000 seamen and 19,000 soldiers, who obeyed the command of the Marquis of Santa Cruz, an officer whose brow was shaded with the laurels of numerous victories.

Lord Howard of Effingham, admiral of England, took the command of the fleet. Drake was appointed lieutenant.

Under the duke of Medina Sidonia, 1587, the Armada sailed from the Tagus. Off Cape Finisterre, the southerly breeze was exchanged for a storm from the west, and the Armada was dispersed along the shores of Gallicia. To collect and repair his shattered fleet detained the duke three weeks in the harbour of Corunna. The English had scarcely moored their ships in the harbour of Plymouth, when the duke of Medina was discovered off the Lizard Point. The Armada formed in the shape of a crescent, the horns of which lay some miles asunder, and with a gentle breeze from the south-west proudly advanced up the Channel. The lord admiral had already formed his plan. To oppose might be dangerous; but he followed and annoyed the Spaniards from a distance. The Spanish admiral completely baffled, resolved to return home, by sailing round Scotland and Ireland, and in his voyage lost many of his largest vessels by storm. Such were the contemptible results of that prodigious armament.

In 1588, the earl of Leicester died. He was one who as a statesman or a commander, displayed little ability: but his rapacity and ambition knew no bounds. This great favourite of the pious queen, was one of the basest of men.

After the defeat of the Armada till the death of the queen, during the lapse of fourteen years, the Catholics groaned under the pressure of incessant persecution. Sixty-one clergymen, forty-seven laymen, and two gentlewomen suffered capital punishment for some or other of the spiritual felonies and treasons which had been lately created. Generally the court dispensed with the examination of witnesses: by artful and ensnaring questions an avowal was drawn from the prisoner, that he had been reconciled, or had harboured a priest, or had been ordained beyond the sea, or that he admitted the ecclesiastical supremacy of the pope or rejected that of the queen. Any one of these crimes was sufficient to consign him to the scaffold.

Robert Devereux, earl of Essex, the rival of the Cecils, had once been a prime favourite of the queen. He had greatly distinguished himself in command of the land forces, at the capture of Cadiz. To put down the revolt of Hugh O'Neill, earl of Tyrone, he was sent to Ireland to act as lord-deputy, and conduct the war against the stubborn chieftain of Ulster. His campaign there was a disgraceful failure. Abandoning his office and shattered army, he returned to court without leave; and was strongly suspected of having come to a treasonable understanding with Tyrone. He was deprived of all his employments. Having failed in an attempt to raise an insurrection in his favour, and seize the queen, his enemies persuaded Elizabeth to consent to his death. It is said that his melancholy fate influenced her health and hastened her death, which took place March 24, 1603; unattended by a single circumstance creditable to her memory.

CHAP. VII.—HOUSE OF STUART.

24. JAMES I.

James was thirty-seven years old at his accession. He was crowned at Westminster, July 25th, 1603. By both parents he was descended, in the third degree, from Henry VII.

Scarcely had he ascended the throne than a conspiracy to seize his person had been formed, in which lords Cobham and Grey, and Sir Walter Raleigh, had a hand. After unfair trials they were condemned to death. Having confessed their guilt on the scaffold, pardon was granted to all but Raleigh, who was sent to the Tower, where he languished for fifteen years, at the end of which term he was brought to the block, at the instigation of Gondemar, the Spanish ambassador.

From James the Catholics had formed great expectations, in consequence of his mother's religion. They were much disappointed. James had been educated a Presbyterian, and consequently, his principles were as hostile to the old creed as were those of Lutherans or Puritans.

The fines levied on Catholics had become excessive. A gentleman, named Catesby had suffered so severely that he resolved to be avenged, and accordingly, projected the design of blowing up both king and parliament. His principle associate was Guy Fawkes, a soldier of fortune. They hired the vaults under the houses of parliament; and, pretending to use them as stores for coals, conveyed thither a large quantity of gunpowder. But it was resolved that the Catholic peers, and such others as were friendly to Catholics, should be forewarned. One of the conspirators sent a letter earlier than need be to his brother-in-law, lord Mounteagle, who laid it before the king. It was an advice not to attend the coming parliament. Vague as the information was, precautions were taken sufficient to secure Fawkes just as he had arrived to explode the mine, November 5th, 1605. The conspirators suffered the last penalty. The Jesuits were accused of being privy to this atrocious attempt, but nothing worthy the name of proof was ever adduced for the accusation; except a confessional secret entrusted to father Garnet, who also forfeited his life.

As may be expected, the persecuting spirit of the times was inflamed to the highest degree; and the penal code against Catholics rendered still more exasperating and excruciating.

James had early desired a complete incorporation of his two kingdoms, but the proposal was disagreeable to the people of both. All that he could affect was that there should be a common naturalization, and a free commercial intercourse. He then assumed the style of King of Great Britain.

Through jealousy of her proximity to the throne James committed to the Tower his cousin lady Arabella Stuart, under pretence of having married without his permission. She died in the fourth year of her confinement. Her husband had made his escape.

Immediately after the mourning for his eldest son, whose death he is suspected of compassing, had ceased, he married his only daughter, Elizabeth, to Frederic, count palatine of the Rhine.

James is somewhat notorious for having had two favourites who possessed extraordinary influence over him. One was Robert Carr, whom he created earl of Somerset; but afterwards merely disgraced, instead of hanging, for having instigated the poisoning of Sir Thomas Overbury, a prisoner in the Tower, whither Somerset persuaded the king to send him.

The next favourite was George Villiers, at first the king's cup-bearer, but soon duke of Buckingham, and father of him who was stabbed in the next reign by Felton.

As the Irish knew that James was descended from Fergus I., the founder of the Scottish monarchy, a prince of Antrim, whose great ancestor was Conn of the Hundred Battles, they were confident of great favours at his hands; instead of which he multiplied the penal statutes, and confiscated the province of Ulster, by a series of the most nefarious acts that ever disgraced the annals of crime.

Three very remarkable men lived in this reign; Raleigh, already noticed, a philosophical historian and a poet, whose purity of diction has not been surpassed since, was suffered to leave the Tower, and fetch gold from Guiana, where he pretended to have seen a mountain of it. When he could not find the treasure, he attacked the Spanish towns, which proved empty. Count Gondemar, complained to James, who had Raleigh beheaded on his former sentence. Coke and Bacon were great lawyers, with very little integrity. Bacon was a man of fine literary taste. His essays are almost the best in the language; but as a philosopher he is greatly overrated. He was fined £40,000 for taking bribes as lord chancellor.

James died, March 27, 1625. He was married to Anne,

daughter of Frederick II. of Denmark. By her he had seven children, of whom only Charles and Elizabeth survived.

25. Charles I.

Charles, the heir of Egbert and of William the Conqueror, was in his twenty-sixth year when he mounted the throne. He was crowned at Westminster, February 6, 1626. He was married to Henrietta, daughter of Henry IV. of France, by Mary de Medici.

The misfortunes of this king are easily explained. For centuries the royal prerogative was in an unsettled state; and a spirit of enquiry touching the theory and practice of government had set in, just as its reins had fallen into his hands, extremely hostile to monarchy. What was operating in men's minds respecting politics, was also operating with respect to religion. There prevailed a general resistance to authority. Every one was a patriot and a theologian. The rights of man and the liberty of the gospel kindled flames and spread fever in every direction. In the controversies arising from the various questions connected with church or state, there was one prominent peculiarity. While all contended for liberty, and proclaimed its principles, not one sect or party could tolerate another. There was, however, a happy unanimity on one point: all agreed to hate cordially the Catholics. The hostility to the king, if not quite so general, was much more fatal; for the king's friends did him almost as much mischief as did his foes.

As Charles found himself burthened with the debts of his father, he was completely at the mercy of his very first parliament: but when he asked for money, they recommended him to put into immediate execution all the laws against Papists and Missionaries; an answer which reveals much of the future of this reign.

The English kings, since the time of Henry VI., had been granted tonnage and poundage for life; Charles could get them voted only for a year. He told them if they were not more liberal "it would be worse for them." They were not dismayed, and as they would not yield he levied taxes by royal authority, threats and force. But the danger and difficulty of such modes becoming daily more apparent and palpable, he had once more recourse to parliament, who withheld the subsidy until he had assented to the "Petition of Rights," declaring illegal, "forced loans, and benevolences, taxes without the consent of parliament, billeting of soldiers and martial law."

The early embarrassments of the king were much increased by a war with France, undertaken in consequence of a breach of religious toleration, complained of on both sides. Richelieu was besieging Rochelle, the stronghold of the French Protestants, and Buckingham, who was sent out to relieve it, returned in disgrace. The year following Buckingham was assassinated at Portsmouth by Felton.

Buckingham had been superintending a new expedition, the ships for which had been raised and equipped by shipmoney. Hampden disputed his share (20s.) of this tax; but seven out of the twelve judges decided against him; a result which the public regarded as a victory.

Having found parliament so refractory, Charles resolved to do without them. He appointed archbishop Laud to manage the church, and Wentworth, earl of Stafford, the state; the same Wentworth, whose tyranny, fraud, and spoliation had rendered him infamous in Ireland, when he governed it. Parliament brought both to the block. The attempt to force episcopacy on the Scotch, hastened their end. Laud designed the project, and Stafford was sent with an army to execute it. Leslie, the Presbyterian general, drove him out of Scotland. The Scotch immediately affiliated with the English revolutionists.

Charles was now driven to the most violent measures. He attempted to seize five members in the very house, and had afterwards to apologize. But by way of reprisal, the commons demanded that he should surrender the command of the army and navy to officers appointed by parliament. In reply the king raised his standard at Nottingham, August 22, 1642, when the herald-at-arms read his proclamation.

From Nottingham Charles despatched deputies to London, the bearers of a proposal, that commissioners should be appointed on both sides, with full powers to treat of an accommodation. The two houses, assuming a tone of conscious superiority, replied that they could receive no message from a prince who had raised his standard against his parliament.

There was one class of men on whose services the king might rely with confidence—the Catholics—who, alarmed by the fierce intolerance and the severe menaces of the parliament, saw that their own safety depended on the ascendency of the sovereign. But Charles hesitated to avail himself of this resource. His adversaries had allured the zealots to their party, by representing the king as the dupe of a popish faction, which laboured to subvert the Protestant, and to establish on its ruins the popish worship. While higher classes repaired with their dependents to the support of the king, the call of the parliament was cheerfully obeyed by the yeomanry in the country, and by the merchants and tradesmen in the towns. Both parties soon distinguished their adversaries by particular appellations. The royalists were denominated Cavaliers; and they on their part gave to their enemies the name of Roundheads, because they cropped their hair short. The command of the royal army was intrusted to the earl of Lindsey, that of the parliamentary forces to the earl of Essex.

Waller reduced Portsmouth, while Essex concentrated his forces, amounting to fifteen thousand men, in the vicinity of Northampton. From Northampton he hastened to Worcester, to oppose the advance of the royal army.

At Nottingham the king could muster no more than six thousand men; but he left Shrewsbury at the head of thrice that number. By a succession of skilful manœuvres he contrived to elude the vigilance of the enemy; and had advanced two days' march on the road to the metropolis before Essex became aware of his object. That general saw his error, and followed the king with expedition. His vanguard entered the village of Keynton on the same evening on which the royalists halted on Edgehill, only a few miles in advance. At midnight Charles held a council of war, in which it was resoved to turn upon the pursuers, and to offer them battle. In the contest which ensued, both parties claimed the advantage.

The king's situation daily became more critical. His opponents had summoned forces from every quarter to London, and Essex found himself at the head of twenty-four thousand men. The two armies faced each other a whole day on Turnham Green; but neither ventured to charge, and the king, understanding that the corps which defended the bridge at Kingston had been withdrawn, retreated first to Reading, and then to Oxford.

After several messages from the parliament, he removed from Reading and fixed his head-quarters at Tame. One night Prince Rupert, making a long circuit, surprised Chinner in the rear of the army, and killed or captured the greater part of two regiments that lay in the town. In his retreat to Oxford, he was compelled to turn on his pursuers at Chalgrove; they charged with more courage than prudence, and were repulsed with considerable loss. It was in this action that the celebrated Hampden received the wound of which he died.

In 1643, Charles invested Gloucester, but was compelled to raise the siege. A battle took place soon afterwards, at Newbury. It raged till late in the evening, and both armies passed the night in the field, but in the morning the king allowed Essex to march through Newbury to London; and having ordered Prince Rupert to annoy the rear, retired with his infantry to Oxford. Lucius Cary, lord Falkland, fell at Newbury.

It was at this period the Catholics of Ireland framed the confederation of Kilkenny: it exercised all the authority without the name of Parliament. An oath and covenant was ordered to be taken, binding the subscribers to protect, at the risk of their lives and fortunes, the freedom of the Catholic worship, the person, heirs, and rights of the sovereign, and the lawful immunities and liberties of the kingdom of Ireland, against all usurpers and invaders whomsoever.

To counterpoise the rebel assembly at Westminster, Charles summoned by proclamation both houses to meet him at Oxford on the twenty-second of January, in the succeeding year. Forty-three peers and one hundred and eighteen commoners obeyed. The king's principal resource was in the courage and activity of Prince Rupert, his nephew. He ordered that commander to collect all the force in his power, to hasten into Yorkshire and fight the enemy. He did so, and on 2nd July, 1644, was fought the battle of Marston Moor. Rupert, at the head of the royal cavalry on the right, charged with his usual impetuosity, and with the usual result. He bore down all before him, but continued the chase for some miles, and thus, by his absence from the field, suffered the victory to slip out of his hands.

The line of the confederates was pierced in several points; and their generals, Manchester, Leven, and Fairfax, convinced that the day was lost, fled in different directions. By their flight the chief command devolved upon Cromwell, who improved the opportunity to win for himself the laurels of victory. Ordering a few squadrons to observe and harass the fugitives, he wheeled round on the flank of the royal infantry, and overwhelmed it. When the royal cavalry returned, the aspect of the field struck dismay into the heart of Rupert. His thoughtless impetuosity was now exchanged for an excess of caution; and after a few skirmishes he withdrew, leaving Cromwell in possession of the field.

In January, 1645, archbishop Laud, who had been a considerable time in prison was attainted and executed. An attempt at negociations soon afterwards took place between the king and parliament, but without success. War was resumed and Montrose, acting for the king, gained some advantages in Scotland.

Charles took the field again, in May, 1645. Fairfax had appeared with his army before Oxford, where he expected to be admitted by a party within the walls; but the intrigue failed and he received orders to proceed in search of the king. On the evening of the seventh day his van overtook the rere of the royalists between Daventry and Harborough. Early in the morning, the royal army formed in line about a mile south of Harborough. Till eight, they awaited with patience the expected charge of the enemy; but Fairfax refused to move from his strong position near Naseby, and the king, yielding to the importunity of his officers, gave the word to advance. Prince Rupert commanded on the right. The enemy fled before him; but the lessons of experience had been thrown away upon Rupert. He urged the pursuit with his characteristic impetuosity, and, as at Marston Moor, by wandering from the field suffered the victory to be won by the masterly conduct of Oliver Cromwell.

After the battle of Naseby, the campaign presented little more than the last and feeble struggles of an expiring party. Charles himself after various wanderings, not marchings, reached Downham; and not being able to escape by sea, surrendered at Kelham to the Scottish army, on a promise of safety. The Scots gave up Charles to the Parliamentarians for £400,000.

The parliamentary commissioners conducted the captive king to prison at Holmby. To disband the army was now the main object of the Presbyterian leaders. Their rivals for power, the Independents, to whom Cromwell belonged, instigated the army to another course. Cromwell sent Colonel Joyce to take possession of the king, as a treasure he may for some time use to serve his purposes; and next day he rendezvoused at Newmarket. The soldiers now appointed Oliver commander-in-chief, and under the pretence of an intention of seeing all grievances redressed, entered on a systematic series of proceedings which plainly foreshadowed a military tyranny. Among the soldiery there was a set of men called *agitators*, who were altogether moved by Cromwell. They were composed of a few inferior officers, for the most part sergeants. They introduced a representative system, by which the com-panics selected men of their choice, independently of their regimental rank, to give expression to their passions and inclinations. By this device the authority of a commission was superseded; the control of the civil power annihilated; and the army subjected to the most absolute sway of its commander-in-chief. The military parliament thus elected put forward two orders of grievances: first, those connected with the public; and, secondly, those relating to themselves; and they vowed not to disband till they saw both kinds redressed—a very unpromising declaration for the speculative patriots assembling at Westminster. But these men were stiff enough in their own way. They passed a few ordinances with the hope of satisfying the army; and then resolved on withstanding any more mutinous demands. Between these two authorities the breach grew wider every day, and the contest warmer. This is what Cromwell wanted, and what he shrewdly foresaw.

Charles was transferred, August, 1647, to Hampton Court, where he was allowed free intercourse with his family and friends. From this he made his escape to the Isle of Wight, where Hammond, the governor of Carisbrook Castle detained him. Having renewed his attempts at escape, parliament resolved to have no further intercourse with him, and that it should be treasonable to bring any message from him.

The most violent of the regimental representatives were called *Levellers*. They called loudly for judicial vengeance on the king, and the establishment of a commonwealth. The public showed symptoms of alarm and dissatisfaction at these proceedings. Partial risings took place in the king's favour. The duke of Hamilton led a Scottish army over the borders; which was, however, defeated by Cromwell at Preston. At the same time a small fleet, under the prince of Wales, sailed from Holland, with the view of liberating the king, and was grossly mismanaged. The officers, and, no doubt, many others beside, felt that their safety was incompatible with any compact with the king. Kings, they knew, never find themselves obliged to keep their word with rebels; for they pretend not to be bound by bargains made under restraint; a principle which has been always pleaded, but which is, in such cases, base, immoral, and illogical. The clamour of men fearing for their lives prevailed; and the Commons appointed a court of one hundred and thirty-three persons, over whom Serjeant Bradshaw presided, to try Charles Stuart for levying war against parliament, an offence which had been declared treason for the purposes of the prosecution. The king was condemned, and beheaded on a scaffold which could be reached from the windows of the banquetting room of Whitehall, January 30, 1648, in the forty-ninth year of his age.

THE COMMONWEALTH.

IMMEDIATELY after the king's death, royalty and the house of lords were abolished by vote of the commons. Government was entrusted to a council of state consisting of forty-one members, whose authority was to last for twelve months. But in Scotland this scheme did not meet the views of the Presbyterian ministers. It shut them out from the ascendency they so much coveted. They, therefore, as a mere artifice, had recourse to the counter policy, and proclaimed Prince Charles: but with this proviso, that he should accept the solemn league and covenant. Commissioners were sent to Charles in Holland, but they did not yet arrive at an understanding with him.

As the royalists were very strong in Ireland, Cromwell was sent over as lord lieutenant, with an army of twelve thousand men to secure it. He opened his campaign with the siege of Drogheda, which was held by sir Arthur Aston. At the end of eight days, it was taken by assault, and the garrison, after the surrender of their arms, put to the sword. In Wexford a similar cold-blood slaughter was perpetrated; but to add to the horrors of the tragedy, three hundred women were butchered, who had gathered round the great cross in the centre of the town.

Several garrisons shortly declared for the parliament, and Cromwell with an army swelled to twenty thousand, swept over the whole face of the country. Blood, devastation, and rapine, marked his furious progress. Never was conquest more complete. With him there was no "Treaty of Limerick;" he overwhelmed and annihilated all opposition; confiscated two-thirds of the whole country; bestowed his conquests on whom he pleased, and left his friends in secure possession of his triumphant plunder. And all this was owing to the bigotry, the meanness, and selfishness of the *great* duke of Ormond, who, had he trusted in the *Confederation of Kilkenny*, would assuredly have saved the king.

The raising of the royal standard in Scotland, by Montrose, called Oliver thither, who left the remnant of his work to be finished by Ireton, his son-in-law. Montrose was easily quelled;

He was able to muster but a handful, so that his own romantic daring and noble devotion went for nothing. He perished on the scaffold in his thirty-eighth year. To augment his friends in Scotland, Chrales signed a treaty binding himself to the solemn league and covenant, to disavow and annul the Irish peace; to forbid the free exercise of the Catholic religion in Ireland, and all other parts of his dominions; and to be governed by the Kirk in religious matters. Baser conditions there could not be; but baser still, Charles had no intention of keeping them. In the first battle, which was fought after the prince's arrival in Scotland, Cromwell was victorious. He gave Leslie a ruinous overthrow at Dunbar, 1650. Nevertheless Argyle and the preachers had the young man crowned at Scone. He was then put in command of the army, with Leslie and Middleton for his lieutenants.

Seeing that his Scotch affairs were in a hopeless condition, he formed the bold resolution of marching into England. Cromwell pursued with great celerity: overtook Charles at Worcester: and extinguished his hopes for many a weary, gloomy day. The battle was fought on the auspicious anniversary of Dunbar, Sept. 3rd, 1651. After long wandering, much suffering by cold, and hunger, and journeying; after many perils, anxieties, and escapes, borne with manly endurance for one-and-forty days, he landed safely at Feschamp in Normandy.

At this juncture war was declared against the Dutch, who had declined a proposal of alliance made them by St. John, agent of the commonwealth. To make way for a rupture the *Act of Navigation* was passed, which prohibited the importation of goods from Asia, Africa, and America, in foreign vessels. This had soon the desired effect. In the naval engagements which ensued, the English admirals, Blake and Monk, greatly distinguished themselves. Off Portland, in February, 1653, they captured almost the entire Dutch fleet, commanded by Tromp, Ruyter, and De Witt.

Cromwell now felt his power so bulky, that a parliament incommoded it. He doggedly determined to put it out of his way. On April 20, 1653, he went to the house accompanied by some of his *ironside* soldiers. Leaving them on the lobby he entered; and asperging the members in every direction with their vices and backslidings, he declared the Lord had done with them; showed them the door, and bidding the bauble of a mace to be taken away, put the keys in his pocket.

Such was an expeditious and easy dissolution of the famous long parliament, which, under various aspects and auspices, had sat for twelve years.

The dictator next formed a provisional government, composed of four civilians and eight officers of high rank, under himself as lord president; and, dispensing with election, issued writs of summons to 139 representatives for England, 6 for Wales, 6 for Ireland, and 5 for Scotland, to serve as members for particular places, and to attend on the 4th of July, at Whitehall. When they met he delivered to them, under his hand and seal, an instrument authorizing them to sit for fifteen months, and then to chose their successors. In this assembly were several opulent and able men; but, as may be expected, many of those fanatics that rejoiced in such pious cognomens as *Praise-God Bare-bones*, a style of appellation frequently assumed by the *saints* of the period. One of the members, a leather-seller, from Fleet-st., who was distinguished by the euphonious form mentioned, had the honour of imparting his nickname to this appointed parliament. Bare-bone's legislature began with many salutary reforms; but the cant of their harangues, the quaintness of their language, and the wild absurdity running generally through their sentiments, rendered them obnoxious to the perpetual shafts of ridicule and joke. Cromwell, who was at bottom a wag, saw all this, perhaps foresaw it, no doubt chuckled over it. Having led the valour of his ironsides to ruin the royalists, it was but fair to use the humour of the public to laugh down the fanatics. At all events, matters turned out as he wished; so that no one murmured, and thousands held their sides, when the consul dismissed, amidst roars of jocularity, Praise-God Bare-bone's conscript fathers. He quickly hatched another constitution clutch, and from one of the eggs issued the lord-protector of the commonwealth of England.

Three ordinances appeared incorporating Scotland with England, absolving the Scotch from their allegiance to Charles Stuart, abolishing the kingly office and Scottish parliament, and granting a free pardon to the whole nation, with the exception of numerous delinquents, who deserved or were likely to deserve, his special resentment.

The parliamentary faggot which Cromwell bundled together in September, 1654, concealed many thorns; of these the most troublesome and refractory were Bradshaw, Hazlerig, and Scot, who boldly questioned the competency of government, and contrasted the assembly in which they sat with a legitimate parliament. Oliver threw this bundle into the oven.

Nothing remained but a strong tyranny, masked by an elective senate. He tried the experiment, but the new parliament was more prickly than the former one. Whichever side he turned, he was stung. Manifestly driven to madness, he thought the crown would be a helmet. What his ambition had long coveted his judgment now approved. The theory was sound, but the trial insanity. The country could be content with nothing but the royal authority. But was not the protector mad when he fancied it could be vested in him? It was not in the least probable that a people familiar with the names of Alfred, Edward, Henry, would ever approve of Oliver for one of the royal family; nor was it at all likely that so much of republican blood would fructify into king Cromwell.

In the year 1656, being in want of money, he called a parliament, for which he had contrived an ingenious experiment. His friends had managed the passing of an address under the name of the *Humble Petition and Advice*, in which he had been recommended to take a higher title. This leven was allowed to ferment for a considerable period in public. The title of king was pressed on the protector from several quarters; but he observed minacious frowns where he had most to fear. Still he wavered. And it was commonly reported that he was about to fill the "empty bauble," when Lambert, Fleetwood, and Desborough told him that they and several others had determined to withdraw from his counsel and service the moment he assumed the detested dignity. Henceforth he gave up all hopes of practising kingcraft according to prescription.

Public affairs were now administered in his name, mostly by military chiefs. His government was to all intents a military organization. The whole country was divided into twelve districts, superintended each by a major-general. There was authority, but no content; obedience, but not assent. Time revealed the man: he had worn through his mask. All his admirers turned aside with disgust; all his friends with bitterness and disdain. Amongst every party there was something to be apprehended. On this side he shrunk from the scowl of scorn: on that from the dagger of vengeance. From a miserable life of perpetual anxiety this great, unprincipled, man was relieved by a tertian ague, in 1658, on the 3rd Sept., his well-known *lucky* day.

Cromwell left two sons, Richard and Henry. After the establishment of the commonwealth, Richard married, and, retiring to the house of his father-in-law, in Hampshire, devoted himself to the usual pursuits of a country gentleman. Henry accompanied his father in the reduction of Ireland, which country he afterwards governed, first with the rank of major-general, afterwards with that of lord-deputy.

The moment Oliver Cromwell expired, the council assembled, and the result of their deliberation was an order to proclaim Richard Cromwell protector, on the ground that he had been declared by his late highness his successor in that dignity. Not a murmur of opposition was heard.

The royalists, who had persuaded themselves that the whole fabric of the protectoral power would fall in pieces on the death of Cromwell, beheld with amazement the general acquiescence in the succession of Richard; and the foreign princes, who had deemed it prudent to solicit the friendship of the father, now hastened to offer their congratulations to his son. Fair and tranquil as the prospect appeared, the elements of an approaching storm may have been easily discerned. Between Richard and the "long" parliament, which had re-assembled, disputes arose, and the country was soon in a state of anarchy. The intentions of the armies in Scotland and Ireland remained uncertain; and the royalists, both Presbyterians and Cavaliers, were exerting themselves to improve the general confusion to the advantage of the exiled king. Richard exercised no real authority, though he continued to occupy the state apartments at Whitehall. By repeated messages, he was ordered to retire; and, on his promise to obey, the parliament granted him the privilege of freedom from arrest during six months; transferred his private debts to the account of the nation, gave him two thousand pounds as a relief to his present necessities, and voted that a yearly income of ten thousand pounds should be settled on him and his heirs.

Ever since the death of Oliver Cromwell, the exiled king had watched with intense interest the course of events in England; and each day added a new stimulus to his hopes of a favourable issue. In Cheshire the royal standard was unfurled by sir George Booth, a person of considerable influence in the country, and a recent convert to the cause of the Stuarts. At Chester, the parliamentary garrison retired into the castle, and the royalists took possession of the city. Each day brought to them a new accession of strength. But when they learned that they stood alone, that the other risings had been either prevented or suppressed, their confidence was exchanged for despair. After the fall of the protector, Richard Monk, who commanded in Scotland, became an object of distrust. Lord Fairfax was also become a convert to the cause of monarchy; to him the numerous royalists in Yorkshire looked up as leader; and he, on the solemn assurance of Monk that he would join him within twelve days or perish in the attempt, undertook to call together his friends, and to surprise the city of York. On the first day of the new year, each performed his promise. The gates of York were thrown open to Fairfax by the Cavaliers confined within its walls; and Monk, with his army, crossed the Tweed. In parliament the Presbyterian party now ruled without opposition. They appointed Monk commander-in-chief of the forces in the three kingdoms, and joint commander of the fleet with admiral Montague.

Monk had now spent more than two months in England, and still his intentions were covered with a veil of mystery which no ingenuity, either of the royalists or of the republicans, could penetrate. He soon sent a message to Charles, who was at Brussels, advising him to promise a general, or nearly general pardon, liberty of conscience, the confirmation of the national sales, and the payment of the arrears due to the army, and that he would aid in his restoration. By Charles the messenger was received as an angel from heaven. But when he communicated the glad tidings to Ormond, Hyde, and Nicholas, these councillors discovered that the advice, suggested by Monk, was derogatory to the interests of the throne and the personal character of the monarch, and composed a royal declaration which, while it professed to make to the nation the promises recommended by Monk, in reality neutralized their effect, by subjecting them to such limitations as might afterwards be imposed by the wisdom of parliament. Notwithstanding the alterations made at Brussels, Monk professed himself satisfied with the declaration. Though he still declared himself a friend to republican government, he now ventured to assume a bolder tone. The militia of the city, amounting to fourteen thousand men, was already embodied under his command; he had in his pocket a commission from Charles, appointing him lord-general over all the military in the three kingdoms; and he resolved, should circumstances compel him suddenly to throw off the mask, to proclaim the king, and to summon every faithful subject to repair to the royal standard. A new parliament met on the 25th of April. Charles's letter was delivered to the two houses and was well received. Encouraged by the bursts of loyalty with which the king's letter had been received, his friends made it their great object to procure his return to England before limitations could be put on the prerogative. The two houses voted, that by the ancient and fundamental laws of the realm the government was and ought to be by king, lords, and commons; and they invited Charles to come and receive the crown to which he was born. Charles was as eager to accept, as the houses had been to vote, the address of invitation. As soon as the weather permitted, he set sail for Dover, where Monk, at the head of the nobility and gentry from the neighbouring counties waited to receive the new sovereign. From Dover to the capital the king's progress bore the appearance of a triumphal procession. He entered London on the 30th May, his birth day, 1660. Thus was the ancient constitution restored without the spilling of one drop of blood.

26. Charles II.

Charles was born in 1630, and crowned at Westminster, April 23, 1661.

In England, the demands of justice were satisfied with the blood of several regicides; to expiate the guilt of Scotland, a more illustrious victim was selected, the marquis of Argyle. Charles seemed inclined to save him, but his enemies were inexorable. He was tried and executed in May, 1661.

In Ireland a new race of proprietors had arisen, soldiers and adventurers of English birth, who, during the late revolutionary period, had shared among themselves the lands of the natives, whether royalists or Catholics. On the fall of Richard Cromwell, a council of officers was established in Dublin; these summoned a convention of deputies from the Protestant proprietors; and the convention tendered to Charles the obedience of his ancient kingdom of Ireland. The present was graciously accepted; and the penal laws against the Irish Catholics were ordered to be strictly enforced.

In 1660, James, duke of York, was married to Anne, the daughter of the chancellor Hyde. In 1662, Charles married Catherine, sister of the king of Spain. The princess brought a dower of five hundred thousand pounds, the possession of

Tangier on the coast of Africa, and of Bombay in the East Indies, and a free trade to Portugal and the Portuguese colonies. Charles's conduct towards her at first was attentive, but he soon forgot his duty to God and his wife, by plunging into a life of licentiousness.

Charles, who wanted money, sold Dunkirk, in 1663, to the king of France, by the advice of Clarendon. This sale of Dunkirk had no small influence on the subsequent fortune of each. The possession of it had flattered the national pride; for it was looked on as a compensation for the loss of Calais.

In 1665, Charles entered on a war with the Dutch, on account of commercial disputes respecting the African trade. The most formidable fleet that England had as yet witnessed sailed under James. An easterly wind drove the English to their own shores, and the Dutch fleet immediately put to sea under admiral Opdam. Early in the morning of the 3rd June, 1665, the hostile fleets descried each other near Lowestoffe. Opdam was killed, and the Dutch, alarmed at the loss of their commander, fled.

In the depth of the previous winter, two or three isolated cases of plague had occurred in the outskirts of the metropolis; and, about the end of May, under the influence of a warmer sun, and with the aid of a close and stagnant atmosphere, the evil burst forth in all its terrors.

In January, 1666, the French monarch Louis, though with many expressions of regret, declared war against England, by virtue of a treaty which had linked France and Holland, in 1662.

The great fire which consumed a large portion of London, broke out at two in the morning of Sunday, the 2nd of September, 1666. By this deplorable accident two-thirds of the metropolis, the whole space from the Tower to the Temple, had been reduced to ashes. The number of houses consumed amounted to 13,200; of churches, including old St. Paul's, to 89. A pillar called the "Monument," was raised to commemorate this great calamity. Its origin, although unknown, was falsely attributed to the detested Papists, in a disgraceful inscription, which was removed in 1829.

In May, 1667, the Dutch fleet appeared off the coast of England. For six weeks De Ruyter, the Dutch admiral, continued to sweep the English coast. But his attempts to burn the ships at Portsmouth, Plymouth, and Torbay were successively defeated. A treaty was soon afterwards concluded between England and Holland.

In 1668, lord chancellor Clarendon having, by haughty and overbearing conduct, created many enemies, was deprived of his office, and driven into exile, having been accused of malpractices.

In 1668, Charles received an important communication from his brother James. Hitherto that prince had been an obedient and zealous son of the church of England. He communicated to the king in private that he was determined to embrace the Catholic faith; and Charles, without hesitation, replied that he was of the same mind, and would consult with the duke on the subject in the presence of some peers. James, with all the fervour of a proselyte, urged his brother to publish his conversion without delay, while Louis XIV., on the contrary, represented to the English king, that a premature declaration might endanger his crown and his person. Thus, time passed away without Charles avowing any change to his subjects.

In 1672, Louis and Charles, as allies, made war on Holland; which was brought to a conclusion by the duke of York's victory over the Dutch admiral De Ruyter, in Southwald bay, May 28, 1672.

In 1673 a bill was passed into a statute, known as the "Test Act," requiring, not only that the oaths of allegiance and supremacy should be taken, and the sacrament received, but also that a declaration against transubstantiation should be subscribed by all persons holding office, under the penalty of a fine of five hundred pounds, and of being disabled to sue in any court of law or equity, to be guardian to any child, or executor to any person, or to take any legacy or deed of gift, or to bear any public office. James refused to take the test, and soon afterwards voluntarily resigned all the offices which he held under the crown.

The earl of Carlisle moved, in 1674, that, to a prince of the blood, the penalty for marrying a Catholic should be the forfeiture of his right to the succession. Though this motion was lost, the duke of York, who had just married Mary of Modena, a Catholic princess, had but a cheerless prospect before him. The opponents of James fixed their eyes on the young duke of Monmouth, a natural son of Charles. A second rival was William, prince of Orange, the next in succession to the crown after the duke of York and his children.

William was a Protestant; and his exertions in defence of his country had exalted him in the eyes of all who dreaded the ambitious designs of the French monarch.

About this time, 1675, it was agreed that the king of France should pay a yearly pension to the king of England.

During the long prorogation, and with the aid of his foreign pension, Charles enjoyed a seasonable relief from the cares and agitation in which he had lived for several years. He retired to Windsor, where he spent his time in the superintendence of improvements, the amusement of fishing, and the company and conversation of his friends.

Of the celebrated *Popish Plot* this was the simple origin. Several Jesuits in the month of April, 1678, held a private meeting in London. On this foundation, however, frail and slender as it was, Oates, a degraded chaplain of a man-of-war, contrived to build a huge superstructure of malice and fiction. The meeting was in reality the usual triennial congregation of the order. Oates said that it was a consultation on the most eligible means of assassinating the king, and of subverting by force the Protestant religion. A bill was passed for the exclusion of all Catholics, and consequently of the duke of York, both from parliament and from the presence of the sovereign. An address to exclude him from the presence and the councils of the sovereign was moved by Lord Shaftesbury in the house of Lords, by lord Russell in the house of Commons. James announced from his seat in the Lords that he was no longer a member of the council.

So violent was the excitement, so general the delusion created by the perjuries of the informer, that the voice of reason and the claims of justice were equally disregarded. Several innocent persons were executed on the perjured evidence of Oates, and an accomplice named Bedloe. A bill to exclude James from the throne was now introduced. While the debates on the bill were progressing, Charles prorogued parliament. It was at this time that the Habeas Corpus Act was passed.

In England the executions on account of the pretended "popish plot" continued. The commons selected the lord Stafford for trial, who, on account of his age and infirmities, appeared the least able to make a powerful defence. On the 13th of November, 1680, this venerable nobleman was placed at the bar; he was found guilty of treason on perjured evidence, and suffered with fortitude on the 20th December, 1680.

In 1681, the succession bill was revived, but Charles suddenly dissolved the parliament. In the same year was executed Oliver Plunket, the Catholic archbishop of Armagh, the last victim of the " popish plot."

At a farm-house, called the Rye House, a plot was hatched for the assassination of Charles and James, 1683. By means of lord Howard an indirect communication had all along been maintained between these men and the more discontented among the Whig leaders, the duke of Monmouth, the earl of Essex, the lord Grey, lord William Russell, Algernon Sydney, and Mr. Hampden, who, though they refused to hear any mention of assassination, were willing to employ the services of those among whom the notion originated. Russell, Sydney, and others were arrested and committed to the Tower. The trial of lord William Russell excited general interest, as it promised a solution of the important question, whether the Whig leaders were implicated or not in the plans of the minor conspirators. Lord Russell made but a feeble defence. The jury returned a verdict of guilty. Posterity has long ago absolved Russell from seeking to dip his hands in the blood of the king. But there were other charges against him. He was a party to the design of compelling the king by force to banish and disenherit James, the presumptive heir to the crown, and concurred in the design of raising an insurrection in Scotland to co-operate with another in England for the same purpose. The succeeding trial, that of Algernon Sydney, soon took place before sir George Jeffreys, of infamous memory. Sydney was found guilty.

Monmouth was pardoned. Sydney was soon led to the scaffold, 1683.

On Monday, the 2nd of February, 1685, after a feverish and restless night, Charles rose at an early hour. To his attendants he appeared drowsy and absent; his gait was unsteady, his speech embarrassed. It soon became evident that his dissolution was rapidly approaching. The duke of York, though aware of his brother's secret preference of the Catholic worship, had hitherto been silent on the subject of religion. Having motioned to the company to withdraw to the other end of the apartment, James knelt down by the pillow of the sick monarch, and asked if he might send for a Catholic priest. " For God's sake do !" was the king's reply ; " but," he immediately added, "will it not expose you to danger?" James replied, that he cared not for the danger. In a short time, Hudleston, a priest, was led through the queen's apartments to a private door on the right hand of the bed. Hudleston, having received his confession, anointed him, administered the eucharist, and withdrew. During that night the king suffered at times the most distressing pain; but in the intervals between the paroxysms his mind was calm and collected, and he spoke of his approaching death with composure and resignation. About two o'clock, looking on the duke, who was kneeling at the bed-side, and kissing his hand, he called him the best of friends and brothers, desired him to forgive the harsh treatment which he had sometimes received, and prayed that God might grant him a long and prosperous reign. About six on the following morning he complained of pain in the side accompanied with a difficulty of breathing: to remove which eight ounces of blood were taken from his arm. Three hours later he lost the faculty of speech, and about noon, 6th February, 1685, calmly expired.

27. JAMES II.

James, the second son of Charles I., was born in 1633, and crowned at Westminster, in 1688, along with his queen, by Sancroft, the primate.

Titus Oates was brought to trial, and condemned to pay a fine of 2,000 marks, to be stript of his canonical habit, to be twice publicly whipped, and to stand every year of his life five times in the pillory.

The duke of Monmouth landed on the coast of Dorsetshire, on the 15th June, 1685, in order to assert his right to the throne, as son of Charles II., by a queen whom he asserted to have been lawfully married. He was immediately attainted, and a price set upon his head. The earl of Argyle, who was appointed to a high command in the invading force, had sailed from Holland to Scotland, landed in Lorn, and afterwards in Cantire, and published in both places a declaration against James which he brought back with him from Holland. But each day was marked by new disappointments, and new causes of dissension between the earl and his associates. Argyle was soon defeated and taken prisoner. He was executed in Edinburgh, on the 30th June, 1685.

Monmouth had engaged to follow Argyle in the course of six days; yet three weeks elapsed before he left Amsterdam.

He soon took on himself by solemn proclamation the title

of king James II., and set a price on the head of the "usurper of the crown, James duke of York."

Monmouth reaped little benefit from the assumption of royalty. He wandered from place to place without any apparent object. No person of quality offered his services, and his friends in the capital and the country remained quiet. When he became acquainted with the fate of Argyle, his last hope was gone. He was soon defeated in the battle of Sedgemoor, and having fled, was in a short time taken and conducted to London. He wrote to James a supplicatory letter, expressive of the deepest remorse for his ingratitude and rebellion, attributing the blame to the counsels of "false and horrid" companions; and soliciting the favour of a personal interview. The king received him in the presence of Sunderland and Middleton, the two secretaries of state. He threw himself on his knees, and implored forgiveness in the most passionate terms; but James replied, that by usurping the title of king he had rendered himself incapable of pardon. He was beheaded in two days after the interview with the king.

Several Protestant clergymen at this time adopted the Catholic creed, of whom were Obadiah Walker, master of University College, Oxford, and Boyce, Dean, and Bernard, fellows of different colleges. To these James granted dispensations, by which they were empowered to enjoy the benefits of their respective situations without taking the oaths, or attending the established worship. This dispensing power was regarded as a violent attack on the laws. He had prepared an effectual check to the ebullition of popular resentment by the presence of an army of about sixteen thousand men, consisting of twelve battalions of infantry and thirty-five squadrons of cavalry, encamped on Hounslow Heath. It was remarked that several of the officers were Catholics; the piety of all good Protestants was scandalized by the public celebration of mass in the tent of lord Dunbarton, the second in command.

James soon addressed the privy council. During the four last reigns, he said, law upon law had been passed to enforce uniformity of doctrine. But experience had shown the uselessness of such enactments. Conscience could not be forced; persecution was incompatible with the doctrines of Christianity; and it was, therefore, his resolve to grant religious liberty to all his subjects. But nothing was less popular than religious liberty; which certainly was not the Protestantism of the period.

A year had elapsed since his proclamation of liberty of conscience. James now ordered it to be republished, and appended to it an additional declaration, stating his unalterable resolution of securing to the subjects of the English crown "freedom of conscience for ever," and of rendering thenceforth merit, and not oaths, the qualification for office. Several prelates prayed to be excused from reading the declaration, not because they were wanting in duty to the sovereign, but because it was founded on the dispensing power which had often been declared illegal in parliament; whereupon James ordered them into custody. While the public attention was absorbed by the proceedings against the bishops, the king was blessed with what he so ardently wished for, the birth of a son, the apparent heir to his crown. The disappointment and vexation of his opponents were marked. But they quickly rallied; they had prepared the people to expect a supposititious birth, and they maintained that their predictions had been verified.

On the appointed day the seven prelates were brought from the Tower, to their trial. The jury had been fairly chosen. Differing in opinion among themselves, they left the court, and spent the night in loud and violent debate. In the morning they returned, and pronounced a verdict of not guilty. It was received with deafening shouts which spread till they at length penetrated to the camp of Hounslow Heath, where it is said that the king himself, who chanced to be dining with the general, lord Feversham, was surprised and alarmed at the loud acclamations of the soldiers.

The prince of Orange had never lost sight of the English crown, the great object of his ambition. On the afternoon of the 19th of October, 1688, he sailed from Helvoetsluys, but was driven back by a storm.

William sailed again from Holland, on 1st November, and in two days reached Torbay, in Devonshire. To oppose the prince by land James resolved to collect his army in the neighbourhood of Salisbury. The prince, though he had been permitted to land without opposition, did not meet with the reception which he had been taught to expect. At his approach to Exeter, the bishop and dean fled from the city; the clergy and corporation remained passive spectators of his entry; and though the populace applauded, no addresses of congratulation, nor public demonstrations of joy, were made by the respectable citizens. William was disappointed; he complained that he had been deceived and betrayed; he threatened to re-embark, and to leave his recreant associates to the vengeance of their sovereign. Still, however, his hopes were kept alive by the successive arrival of a few stragglers from a distance: in a short time they were raised almost to assurance of success by the perfidy of lord Cornbury, son of the earl of Clarendon, who went over to him with part of the army.

The princess Anne privately left London. On the receipt of the intelligence James burst into tears, and exclaimed, "God help me! my very children have forsaken me!" The queen had hitherto refused to separate her lot from that of her husband; but when he had made up his mind to leave the kingdom, and that he solemnly promised to follow her within twenty-four hours, she consented to accompany her child. The time for their escape was fixed for two after midnight. A yacht, with lord and lady Powis, and three Irish officers on board, was ready to receive them; and thence they pursued their course in safety to Calais. The king soon fled from London, and the news of his flight created surprise and consternation.

James returned to London for a time, but soon was obliged to leave it again, and join his queen in Ambleteuse, on the coast of France. Thence he hastened bringing his wife and child to the castle of St. Germains, where he was received by Louis with expressions of sympathy and proofs of munificence, which did honour to that monarch.

The lords and commons continued to sit at Westminster, and by them an address was voted to the prince of Orange, begging of him to assume and exercise the government of the realm till the meeting of a national convention on the 22nd of January, 1689.

The English convention met on the appointed day. Care had been taken to direct writs to none but Protestant peers. It was contended in the commons, that the voluntary withdrawal of James, without any provision for the government of the realm during his absence, was equivalent in law to a demise of the crown; by others that it was in fact an abdication of the sovereignty, and it was resolved that the throne was vacant. In the lords a protracted and angry debate took place, and the friends of James showed that they still possessed considerable influence. When the prince saw the crown sliding from his grasp, he complained of the time which had been wasted in useless debate. If any persons, he observed intended to appoint him regent, they might spare themselves the trouble, for the regency was an office which he would never accept; adding, in allusion to a plan to make his wife the sole sovereign, that while he was her husband, he would never be her subject. It was then agreed on, in compliance with the alleged wish of the princess, that, though William and Mary were to be equal in rank as king and queen, yet the exercise of the royal authority should be vested in William exclusively during his life.

An instrument known as the "Declaration of Right" obtained the approbation of both houses. It stated that, whereas the late king James II. had assumed and exercised a power of dispensing with and suspending laws without consent of parliament; and had committed other arbitrary acts which were set forth, it was necessary to declare such conduct subversive of right. It was next resolved that William and Mary, prince and princess of Orange, should be declared king and queen of England, France, and Ireland; and that the sole and full exercise of the royal power should be only in, and executed by, the prince of Orange in both their names during their joint lives, and that after their decease the said crown should descend to the heirs of the said princess, and for default of such issue, to the princess Anne of Denmark and her heirs, and in default of such issue, to the heirs of the prince of Orange.

28. WILLIAM and MARY.

William and Mary were crowned at Westminster, April 11, 1689. He was grandson of Charles I., by his eldest daughter, Mary; and born at the Hague, November 14, 1650. His father was styled the Prince of Orange, or Nassau.

In Scotland, an act had been passed distinctly affirming that James had forfeited the crown. That unfortunate monarch had, however, a strong party still amongst the Scotch, especially in the Highlands. Viscount Dundee, formerly Graham of Claverhouse, raised an insurrection in his favour. At Killiecrankie, a memorable battle took place in May, 1690, in which the adherents of James gained the advantage. As, however, Dundee was killed in the moment of victory, the Highlanders were not in a position to follow up what they had begun, and in a short time the clans were induced to yield, at all events, a nominal obedience to William and Mary.

It was destined that Ireland should be the battle-ground in which William and James were to contend for the crown. The king of France furnished James with a fleet, with which he sailed to Ireland, where he arrived on the 22nd March, 1689, and landed at Kinsale. The lord deputy, Tyrconnell, was a devoted adherent of James, and received him with an army of nearly 40,000 men. All Ireland declared for James with the exception of Derry and Enniskillen. Derry was besieged, but the inhabitants held out till the city was relieved. In August, William sent an army of 16,000 men to Ireland, under Schomberg, who kept James in check for some time. In the summer of 1690, William himself landed in Ireland with 36,000 men, and hastened to take steps for giving battle to James. The hostile armies met on the 1st July, 1690, on the banks of the Boyne, near Drogheda. A sanguinary engagement took place in which Schomberg was killed. The soldiers on both sides fought with the most determined courage; but the Irish army was not equal, in point of numbers, to that which William commanded. 1,500 of James's troops were killed before victory declared for William. James, considering his cause hopeless, fled to the south and embarked for France, where he passed the remainder of his life.

But the Irish army, though defeated at the Boyne, retreated in good order to the centre of the island. Dublin and the entire eastern coast yielded to William, but he soon sailed for England, as news had reached him that his fleet had been defeated by that of James. His generals, however, continued to prosecute the war. In June, 1691, Athlone was taken by De Ginkle, and shortly afterwards the defeat at Aughrim, where James's general, St. Ruth, and a very large number of troops were killed, gave to his cause a still gloomier aspect. Limerick, however, remained firm to the cause of the Stuarts. When William returned from England he besieged that city, but the bravery of Sarsfield having led to the destruction of a large part of his artillery, and to the repeated repulse of the besieging forces, he again left Ireland, having abandoned the siege on the pretended plea that the excessive rains had caused disease amongst his troops.

But when almost all Ireland had yielded to William's generals, and the flower of the Irish army had fallen at Aughrim, Limerick was again besieged, and after some time, capitulated, on the condition of honourable terms. According to the "Treaty of Limerick," memorable for its being soon violated by Act of Parliament, the king undertook to obtain for the Irish Catholics the free exercise of their religion and the peaceable enjoyment of their estates. Permission was given to those who wished to retire to France to do so, and it is said that 14,000 persons availed themselves of this privilege, and with Sarsfield embarked for the Continent, where such as were soldiers formed themselves into a corps, which became famous under the title of the "Irish Brigade."

James still indulged the hope of recovering his crown, and having obtained a fleet from Louis, prepared to make a descent upon England. He was, however, anticipated, and his fleet was defeated with great loss in May, 1692, by admiral Russell, off Cape La Hogue. This was the last attempt made by James to reinstate himself in the throne of his ancestors. It was not, however, till 1697, that Louis acknowledged, by the treaty of Ryswick, William as king of England.

William had frequent disputes with his parliament, on the subject of money; and at last threatened to return to Holland unless his applications for taxes were more generously met. There was also much jealousy entertained by the English respecting the foreign troops maintained by William; a feeling to which he was, after some time, obliged to yield.

In 1701 James II. died, having passed several years in religious retirement. He had spent a portion of each year with the monks of La Trappe, and had adopted a demeanour which showed that he felt at last reconciled to his fall from worldly greatness. His last advice to his son was an injunction to forgive his enemies. On his death, Louis XIV. proclaimed his son king of England; for though he had acknowledged William, events had occurred which caused a renewal of hostilities between France and England. Charles of Spain having died, leaving no children, bequeathed his crown to Philip the grandson of Louis. William formed an alliance with the states of Holland and the emperor of Germany, to prevent this union of the monarchies of France and Spain, and to obtain Spain for the emperor. But the king of England did not live to carry on the war, for he soon afterwards broke his collar-bone by a fall from his horse, and died, 8th March, 1702, in the 58th year of his age.

William was very unpopular with the people of Scotland. Their feelings were greatly irritated by the horrid commission he signed for the extermination of the Macdonalds of Glencoe, and his heartless conduct towards the Scotch colony of Darien. This was a project for colonizing the Isthmus of Darien, into which the people of Scotland had warmly entered about the close of the eighteenth century, and which at first received the approbation of the king and the sanction of parliament. Commercial jealousies intervened, and William was induced not only to withdraw his favour from the plan, but to assist the Spaniards in their opposition to the colonists who ventured their lives and properties in making the attempt to carry it into execution. Some of the colonists, after suffering great privations, succeeded in reaching their country, where their account of all they endured roused a feeling of resentment against England to which many writers trace the growth of the strong feeling in favour of the Stuarts which so long prevailed in Scotland.

It was in the reign of William, that the standing army of England was first established by act of parliament, and under the same monarch, the national debt commenced.

29. ANNE.

The second daughter of James II., by his first wife, Anne Hyde, was crowned at Westminster. She was married to prince George of Denmark, who was not allowed any official share in the royal authority.

She declared that her foreign policy would be guided by the same principles which had actuated her predecessor, and that she would maintain her place in the " Grand Alliance," as the combination of England, Germany, and Holland, against Louis XIV. was termed. Subsequently it was joined by Portugal and the duke of Savoy. Marlborough was sent with a large force to the continent, and entered on that career which has rendered his name so distinguished in the military annals of England. Marlborough commenced operations in the Netherlands, and soon succeeded in taking Liege, where he found a large amount of treasure. In 1704, he gained the memorable victory of Blenheim. Marlborough, in 1706, defeated the French under marshal Villeroy, at Ramillies.

In Spain, lord Peterborough, aided by Portugal, gained some important advantages, and even drove Philip from the capital. The important fortress of Gibraltar was, in 1704, taken by Rooke and Shovel, who commanded the English fleet on the Spanish coast.

Louis, finding that he could not resist the allies, made overtures, in 1706, for peace. Such, however, was the desire, on the part of England, to humble France, that the war was universally popular, and negociation distasteful to the national mind. Hostilities were protracted, and as a consequence, the national debt was largely increased.

In 1707, the union between England and Scotland took place. This measure principally owed its origin to the course which the Scottish parliament had begun to adopt on the subject of the succession. That body had by the "Act of Security," decreed that the successor of Anne should not, as regarded Scotland, be the same person whom England might accept, unless Scotland obtained certain commercial privileges which were then withheld. An act for arming Scotland was passed at the same time. These proceedings alarmed the English ministers, and commissioners were appointed to draw up articles of union. The articles were presented to the Scottish parliament, and led to very angry debates. By these articles the two nations were declared to be united under the one government and legislature, but each was to retain its own legal forms. The Presbyterian church was to be guaranteed to Scotland, which country was to send forty-five representatives to the British house of commons, and sixteen to the house of lords. The union was very unpopular in Scotland, for the people regretted the loss of their legislature, but, by threats and bribery, the project was carried, and, from the 1st May, 1707, the two countries have been united under the title of Great Britain.

The discontent of Scotland was observed in France, and roused the hopes of the son of James II., who, under the name of James III. resided at the French court. He was known also by the title of the Chevalier de St. George, and was by the English termed the Pretender. Louis assisted him with an armament, and, 1707, he sailed for Scotland, to which country many of the Scottish nobility invited him. "I hope I shall never see you again," were the parting words of the king of France, who expected that by giving England some military affairs to attend to in Scotland, he would divert her armies from himself. The Stuart squadron was, however, destroyed by some English ships of war under admiral Byng.

About the close of the year 1709, intense popular excitement prevailed in England, in consequence of the impeachment of a clergyman named Sacheverell, who had preached a sermon containing language so violent against the whig party, then in office, that ministers resolved on punishment. He was impeached for asserting that the revolution of 1688 was not an act of resistance to the supreme power. He was suspended for three years; he declaimed violently against dissenters and Catholics.

Shortly after the trial of Dr. Sacheverell, two tories were, through court influence, introduced into the ministry. These were Harley, afterwards earl of Oxford, and St. John, afterwards lord Bolingbroke. Disputes having arisen between these two statesmen and the prime minister, Godolphin, he dismissed them, which course gave such displeasure to the queen, that she soon afterwards recalled them to power, and directed them to form a ministry. At the general election which shortly took place, the whigs were left in a considerable minority. Marlborough, about this time, was recalled through the influence of court enemies.

Negociations for peace were soon commenced by the tory adminstration, who were by no means so hostile to France as their whig predecessors in office. After some resistance in the house of Lords, these negociations were supported by parliament; and, in 1713, Great Britain and Holland, without the concurrence of Germany, concluded the peace of Utrecht. The principal article in this treaty was, that Philip should be king of Spain, but neither he nor any of his descendants, king of France, and that no king of France should ever inherit the crown of Spain. England was to retain Minorca and Gibraltar. Thus, after a lavish waste of life and treasure, a war was brought to an end, by which, although England added to her military name, she largely increased her national debt, and obtained very inadequate advantages.

Shortly after the peace of Utrecht, Queen Anne died suddenly, 1st August, 1714, and with her terminated the direct Stuart line. The Hanoverian descendants of James I., another branch of the Stuart line, succeeded to the throne. There is every reason to believe that Anne was anxious to cause the Act of Settlement to be repealed, and to promote the restoration of her own family to the crown.

CHAP. IX.—HOUSE OF BRUNSWICK, OR HANOVER.

30. GEORGE I.

George, eldest son of Ernest Augustus, elector of Hanover, by Sophia, granddaughter of James I., born in 1660, was crowned at Westminster, October 20, 1714.

He called the whigs to office under the earl of Halifax, ap-

THE RISING OF 1715. 163

pointing Marlborough commander-in-chief of the army. The house of commons prepared articles of impeachment against Oxford, Bolingbroke, and others of their party. Bolingbroke fled to France, but Oxford remained to stand his trial. As there were serious differences between the lords and commons on the subject of his guilt, he was acquitted.

The popular feeling against the whigs encouraged the tories to choose this period for making an attempt to place the Chevalier on the throne. Accordingly, in September, 1715, the earl of Mar raised the banner of the Stuarts in Scotland, and was joined by 10,000 Highlanders. At the same time, the earl of Derwentwater and some other noblemen took up arms in Northumberland, and having received reinforcements from Scotland, proceeded towards the south and endeavoured to rouse the people of England against George I. The adherents of the Stuart cause, who were called Jacobites, were obliged to submit to the government troops at Preston, in Lancashire. At the same time, the earl of Mar came to an engagement at Sheriffmuir, in Scotland, with the duke of Argyle, on which occasion neither army obtained a victory.

The Chevalier sailed for Scotland, in December, 1715, but in a short time it became apparent that his cause was desperate, and he returned to France, accompanied by the earl of Mar. The earl of Derwentwater and many others of various ranks in society, were executed for appearing in arms; many families lost their estates; and several persons of a high position in society were sent from Great Britain in exile to America.

Although the attempt against the throne was defeated, still there soon arose considerable popular discontent, and ministers felt this to such an extent that, in 1716, they carried the "Septennial Act," which increased the duration of parliament from three to seven years. The king soon afterwards paid a visit to his German dominions, which were threatened by Charles of Sweden. On his return he arrested the Swedish ambassador, who was proved to be implicated in a fresh attempt on behalf of the Stuart dynasty.

In 1719, the king of Spain made an attempt to regain the portion of Italy which formerly had belonged to that country, and England interfered to prevent his success by despatching admiral Byng to the Mediterranean, who gained a decided victory over the Spanish fleet. France soon afterwards joined in the war against Spain.

It was about this period that the remarkable delusion

known as the "South Sea Bubble," began to influence the public mind. It was projected by a Scotchman named Law, and ended in the ruin of thousands.

Sir Robert Walpole was now prime minister, and maintained himself in power for twenty years. During the latter part of the reign of George I., public attention was principally occupied with preparations for naval and military armaments, which the king endeavoured to collect for the purpose of opposing Austria and Spain. In June, 1727, George left England again to visit Germany, and on this occasion returned no more; for during the journey he was seized with paralysis, and died at Osnabruck, on the 11th July, in the 68th year of his age, and 13th of his reign, leaving two children, a son and a daughter, to survive him. He was married to his cousin, Sophia Dorothea, daughter of George, duke of Brunswick. He kept her in prison for forty years, at Ahlden, in Hanover.

31. GEORGE II.

The only son of the late king, born at Hanover, in 1683, was crowned at Westminster, October 11, 1727.

A contest with Spain, which lasted for a considerable period, was one of the principal circumstances attending the reign of George II. This war took its rise from some efforts made by Spain to check the trade between England and the Spanish colonies of America. Two fleets were despatched, one to the coast of Spain, and another to America. The latter, under the command of admiral Vernon, succeeded in taking Portobello, a town of considerable importance in the West Indies. Carthagena was bombarded, but without success, and a large number of British soldiers perished in the attempt. A third fleet, commanded by admiral Anson, sailed to Spanish America to assist Vernon; but Anson lost several ships, and, being unable to render effective aid to his brother admiral, he cruized along the eastern coast of South America, and took several prizes. He even crossed the Pacific to China and refitted his ships at Canton. Anson was the first navigator who sailed round the world.

When the emperor, Charles VI., died, his daughter, Maria Theresa, queen of Hungary, was entitled to his throne, by right of inheritance. She was opposed by several princes, one of whom, the elector of Bavaria, was crowned emperor as Charles VII., and received the support of France. George II., considering that the increase of French influence in Germany would endanger his Hanoverian dominions, took part with Maria Theresa, and found the people of England willing to support him in his views. Sir Robert Walpole, held a different opinion, and refusing to be a party to the war, ceased to be minister in 1742. He was, on his retirement, created earl of Orford.

In 1743, George II. joined the army which fought for Maria Theresa, and appeared in person at the battle of Dettingen, which was the last occasion on which a king of England entered the field. The British and Hanoverian troops compelled the French to retreat, but the advantage was not followed up. Soon afterwards Charles VII. died; but, in order to prevent the grand duke of Tuscany, the husband of Maria Theresa, from being elected emperor, the French continued to prosecute the war. Count Saxe, a general of great ability, commanded the French army, and the duke of Cumberland, son of George II., led the British and Hanoverian forces. Tournay was besieged by Saxe, and in order to save that city, the British army advanced to Fontenoy, where, May, 1745, a fierce battle took place, and the French gained the victory, principally in consequence of the courage of the "Irish Brigade." Soon afterwards, however, the grand duke of Tuscany was elected emperor of Germany.

In 1745, another attempt was made by the Stuarts to regain the British throne. The son of James II. had married, in 1719, the princess Clementina Sobieski, granddaughter of the great John Sobieski, king of Poland. They had two sons, the elder of whom, Charles Edward, resolved, in his twenty-fifth year, to make an effort for his family. In 1744, he was declared by a proclamation, which his father, then at Rome, issued, regent of the British islands, and he immediately took steps to carry into effect the designs he had formed. In June, 1745, Charles Edward sailed for Scotland, with a few friends, and landed on the coast of Inverness, where he was soon joined by several Highland chieftains at the head of their respective clans. In August he took the field with a considerable force, and, having proclaimed his father king of Great Britain, he marched to Edinburgh, of which he obtained possession without opposition.

The prince beat Sir John Cope at Prestonpans, but did not follow up his advantage with rapidity. The Stuart prince entered England in November, crossing the border with 5,000 men. He easily took Carlisle, and marched unchecked through the north of England as far as Derby. Here he learned that George II. was at the head of a large army which was encamped near London, and which was each day increasing in number. But it was deemed advisable to return to Scotland, as the duke of Cumberland came over with 6,000 Dutch soldiers.

The duke having soon arrived in Scotland, prepared to take the field without delay, as he was at the head of a large army. He remained at Edinburgh for a short time, and in February marched to Aberdeen, where he received reinforcements, and soon moved against Charles, who drew up his troops at Culloden, near Inverness, and offered battle to the duke. They engaged on the 16th April, 1746. Charles had 8,000 men; but the duke had the advantage in numbers, and obtained a complete victory over the Stuart forces. The conquerors stained their arms by the indiscriminate and remorseless slaughter of the vanquished, and, contrary to the practice of civilized war, spared not even the wounded who lay disabled on the field. Charles, after wandering for several months in the Highlands, escaped to France though a large reward, £30,000, was offered for his capture.

When the civil war had thus been brought to a close, several noblemen were tried for high treason and executed, amongst whom were lords Kilmarnock, Balmerino, and Lovat.

During the events which we have been considering, the war continued with unabated vigour on the continent, till 1741, when peace was concluded at Aix-la-Chapelle.

In 1756, war broke out between England and France, in consequence of disputes which took place on the subject of the western boundary of the North American colonies.

The troops under general Wolfe took Quebec, in 1759, but he was killed during the assault.

At this period, although the East India company had been a long time formed, the French possessions in the Indies were very extensive. When war broke out between England and France, India became one of the scenes of the contest. Colonel Clive, afterwards lord Clive, commanded the British troops. His victory at Plassey, in June, 1756, mainly contributed to the downfall of French influence in India, and after a severe struggle France lost almost all her eastern possessions.

It was during this war that the awful tragedy took place in Calcutta, of the suffocation of 123 Europeans in a narrow dungeon called the "Black Hole."

While the British colonies in each hemisphere were thus the

CONQUESTS FROM THE SPANIARDS.

scenes of most important contests, England was also engaged in war upon the European continent. She formed an alliance with Frederick the Great, king of Prussia, against the combined forces of France, Russia, Austria, and Poland, with a view to protect Hanover. At sea, Great Britain at this period maintained her high character in consequence of the numerous victories gained by Hawke, Rodney, and other distinguished admirals.

Amongst other naval engagements which took place about this time, was one between captain Elliott and the French commodore Thurot, who had attacked and taken Carrickfergus, in the north of Ireland. Thurot, hearing that a large force was advancing, returned on board ship and set sail. He was met by Elliott, and after a severe engagement near the Irish coast, in which Thurot was killed, the French were defeated, and their ships taken.

George II. died suddenly, on the 25th October, 1760, in consequence of the bursting of the left ventricle of the heart.

32. GEORGE III.

George, eldest son of Frederick, prince of Wales, and grandson of George II., was born June 4th, 1738, and crowned at Westminster, September 22nd, 1761. He married, exactly a fortnight before, Charlotte Sophia, of Mecklenburgh Strelitz.

Lord Bute, a Scotchman, who exercised vast influence over the young king, and Pitt, were appointed joint secretaries of state. Lord Bute was in favour of peace, but Pitt considered that a warlike policy was demanded by the interests of Britain. On learning that France was about to receive aid from Spain, Pitt advocated a declaration of war against the latter country, but being overruled in his opinion he resigned. The king conferred on him a pension of £3,000 a year, and created his wife a peeress under the title of Baroness of Chatham. It was not till some years afterwards, that Pitt, as earl of Chatham, became a peer. Negociations soon commenced, but they were unsuccessful, and not only did war continue between France and England, but Spain commenced hostilities, as Pitt had foretold. England took from Spain, Havannah, Manilla, and the Philippine Islands. In Portugal also, which had been invaded by Spain, England triumphed over the Spanish troops. In Germany, the Marquis of G. anby commanded the British troops, and succeeded in gaining many advantages. Notwithstanding the success which had attended British arms, both at sea and on land, ministers found it so difficult to provide the supplies necessary for the support of so many armaments that negociations were again entered upon, and a peace, known as the "Treaty of Paris" was concluded in 1763. By this treaty England surrendered many of the conquests which she had made during the war, amongst which were Martinique, Guadaloupe, Havannah, and other places of importance. She retained Canada, Vincent's, Tobago, numerous large tracts of the Coromandel coast in the East Indies, Minorca, and East and West Florida. This war called by historians the "seven years war" had caused an addition of sixty millions sterling to the national debt which was now almost one hundred and forty millions.

At this period John Wilkes, member for Ailesbury and editor of a paper called the *North Briton*, in the 45th number, went so far as to impeach the veracity of the king. A general warrant was issued against the editor, printers, and publishers of the *North Briton*, and, by force of this, a king's messenger entered the house of Wilkes and apprehended him. He brought an action against the secretary of state for seizing his person, and obtained damages; the judge, chief-justice Pratt, laying it down as law that general warrants were illegal.

In the year 1765, Mr. Grenville, prime minister, brought in a bill to impose a tax on the North American colonies in the form of a stamp duty. The stamp act was founded on the principle that as the expenses of the war had been increased by the defence of the American colonies, the colonists ought to pay a portion of the national debt. As they were not represented in parliament, their indignation rose to such a height, that they resolved to resist the operation of the act, especially as they observed that their cause was advocated by Pitt, and other distinguished members of the British legislature. Mr. Townsend, one of the ministers, subsequently proposed the imposition of taxes on tea, glass, and some other articles imported into America from Great Britain, which measure kindled afresh the flame throughout the North American colonies.

In 1768, Wilkes, who had been outlawed, returned to England, and, having surrendered, was fined and imprisoned. He was expelled from the house, on the ground that having been solemnly censured by the preceding parliament he was disqualified for life. Wilkes was repeatedly elected. In 1776, he was allowed to take his seat, and soon afterwards a motion was carried to erase from the journals of parliament the record of the various decisions against his being permitted to act as a member.

In 1770, Lord North became prime minister, which position he occupied for twelve years. It was during his administration that the contest took place which made the North American colonies an independent power.

England might have conciliated the colonies by repealing the three-penny tea duty act. Her most distinguished senators advised such a policy, and foremost amongst them was Edmund Burke. But ministers could not submit to the humiliation of yielding. As the colonists were equally resolved not to concede, there was of course no alternative but war, and accordingly, in spring, 1775, hostilities commenced.

The first military encounter between the royalists and the Americans took place at Lexington, near Boston, in April, 1775, on which occasion the latter gained the advantage. A much more important engagement took place on the 7th June, in the same year, at Bunker's Hill, also near Boston. The Americans inflicted severe injury on the British army; but the latter maintained their position.

George Washington was appointed, in June, 1775, to command the American forces, and the war began to assume an aspect which caused the British ministers to offer pardon to those who would lay down their arms; but the "Declaration of Independence" announced to the world, on the 4th July, 1776, that the North American colonies were free and independent states.

In December, 1777, the Americans compelled a considerable force, under general Burgoyne, to surrender at Saratoga.

The cause of the Americans continued to succeed, and, in 1778, ministers sent out commissioners to treat of peace, but failed to obtain it. In 1778, Franklin, the American philosopher, was sent to France, which country soon acknowledged the independence of America, and sent out troops under La Fayette to assist the republicans. Soon afterwards Spain and Holland adopted the same course. In 1781, lord Cornwallis was defeated at Yorktown, in Virginia, by Washington, which event terminated active hostilities. In the February of 1783, lord Shelbourne being prime minister, a treaty was concluded at Paris, between England and the United States of America, which henceforth ranked as one of the independent powers of the world.

In 1778, some mitigation took place in the severity of the laws against Catholics in England. A society, called the Protestant Association, was formed in England, for the purpose of endeavouring to cause the repeal of the recent act in favour of the Catholics. At the head of this confederacy was lord George Gordon, who inflamed the mob to that degree that for several days the rioters had possession of the greater portion of London, but at length they were put down by the military, whom the king had ordered out, and several were killed. Lord George Gordon was tried for high treason, but was acquitted on the ground of insanity. He was afterwards, however, imprisoned for libel, and died in gaol.

In 1779, by the exertions of Flood, Grattan, and other popular leaders, the commercial restrictions which had interfered with the trade of Ireland were removed. A powerful military association, the Irish Volunteers, had been formed, under the command of the duke of Leinster, for the defence of the kingdom from the threatened invasion of the French. The Volunteers soon turned their attention to the questions which had long been the sources of difference between their country and Great Britain. Supported by the *Volunteers*, in 1782, the popular leaders gained the recognition by England of the parliamentary independence of Ireland.

At the early age of twenty-two, Wm. Pitt, son of the great Chatham, was appointed chancellor of the exchequer. Lord Shelbourne was censured by parliament for having made peace with France and Spain on bad terms and resigned. In the April of 1783, the coalition ministry was formed, of which the duke of Portland was the head. Fox and North became colleagues in office, each taking the place of one of the secretaries of state. Pitt was succeeded as chancellor of the exchequer by lord George Cavendish.

The coalition ministry was destined to be but of short duration. In the November of 1783, Fox introduced a bill placing the government of India under the control of seven directors chosen by the house of Commons. This measure was much disliked by the king. The bill passed the house of Commons, but was lost in the house of Lords, and the king sent orders to the ministers to deliver up the seals of office. He immediately appointed Pitt prime minister, in which position he continued without intermission for eighteen years.

In 1786, Warren Hastings was impeached by the house of Commons for " high crimes and misdemeanors," alleged to have been committed by him as governor-general of India. The leader in the prosecution was Edmund Burke, with whom were associated Fox, Sheridan, and other distinguished members of the house. Pitt was at first inclined to defend Hastings, but was forced by public opinion to join in the impeachment. The proceedings lasted for seven years and terminated in the acquittal of Hastings.

The French revolution commenced in 1789, but England was not involved in its agitation till 1792.

The war against France began in Holland, the Duke of York taking the command. At first the French sustained some reverses; but they subsequently succeeded in driving the English army out of the Netherlands. Lord Howe defeated the French fleet near Brest; several of the colonial possessions of France were taken, and the French commercial shipping sustained severe losses.

The English obtained numerous victories at sea in 1797. It was in this year that admiral Jervis and commodore Nelson defeated the Spanish fleet off Cape St. Vincent, and that admiral Duncan attacked with success the Dutch fleet near Camperdown, on the coast of Holland, and took many of the enemy's ships.

In 1798, the French Directory sent Napoleon at the head of an expedition to Egypt, for the purpose of commencing an attack on the British power in the East Indies. Napoleon proceeded through the Mediterranean, and passed over to Egypt. Nelson, however, attacked the fleet on the 1st August, at one of the mouths of the Nile, and gained one of the most complete naval victories on record. In Ireland the enrolling of members of the society of United Irishmen went on with activity until March, 1798, when several of the leaders were arrested in Dublin and executed.

In 1799, ministers proposed a Legislative Union with Ireland, which was passed into law in 1800, by the extensive use of the open and undisguised bribery of the members of the Irish parliament.

On the 21st October, 1805, Nelson fought the celebrated battle of Trafalgar, off the Spanish coast, and defeated the combined fleets of France and Spain. In this battle Nelson fell.

Pitt's administration was succeeded by a ministry of which lord Grenville was the head, and Fox and Sheridan mem bers. It also contained several other eminent men, and was called the ministry of "All the Talents."

An army was sent to the Peninsula, in 1808, under sir Arthur Wellesley, afterwards duke of Wellington.

The first battle which Wellesley fought was with marshal Junot, whom he repulsed, on the 21st August, 1808, at Vimiera, in Portugal.

Sir John Moore was sent out to take command of the army. He fell at Corunna, having repulsed the French under Soult.

Towards the end of 1810, the king lost his reason. The Prince of Wales was appointed regent, and exercised full regal powers from 1812 to 1820.

The French army, under Soult, was driven out of Portugal by Wellesley, who rapidly advanced towards Madrid. He defeated Marshal Victor at Talavera, in July, 1809, and was rewarded with a peerage by the title of Wellington.

In 1810, Marshal Massena led the French troops against Wellington, who retired to a strongly fortified position at Torres Vedras. From 1812 to the capture of Thoulouse, April, 1814, the Peninsular war was a series of British victories, which contributed to the abdication of Napoleon.

On Sunday, the 18th June, 1815, was fought the memorable battle of Waterloo, which finally decided the fate of Napoleon. The British and allies were commanded by Wellington, the French by the Emperor, who was condemned to imprisonment for life in the isle of St. Helena.

George III. died on the 29th January, 1820. His queen had died in 1819, and his son the Duke of Kent, father of Queen Victoria, on the 23rd January, 1820.

33. GEORGE IV.

The regent was proclaimed king, January 31, 1820. His coronation, which was deferred chiefly by the differences existing between him and his wife, did not take place till July 19, 1821.

Shortly after the proclamation a plot for the assassination of the ministers of state was brought to light. It was concocted by one Thistlewood, who had been some time before tried on a charge of treason. With him were associated a set of mean wretches, as destitute and desperate as himself. They met in an obscure den in Cato-street, which has given its name to the conspiracy. When the ministers were assembled at a cabinet dinner at lord Harrowby's, it was the design of the plotters to obtain admission on some pretence, and murder them all. As spies had been put on them in due time, in consequence of the betrayal of their plans, they were surprised by the police and a detachment of the guards just as they were making ready to perpetrate their project. The greater part were captured on the spot. Thistlewood, with a few others, effected a temporary escape. The principal was seized, a little after, in Moorefields. Five of the leaders were executed; some were transported; and here the pursuit of justice halted.

George, who was born August 12, 1762, was twice married. His first wife was a colonel's widow, the beautiful Mrs. Fitzherbert, whom he cruelly abandoned. Next, in 1795, he wedded Caroline of Brunswick, whom he did not more kindly use. Their friendly intercourse was of short duration. Whatever may have been the origin of his dislike, his separation from her was accompanied with such marks of aversion and contempt, as could have been openly exhibited by no good or honest man. Whatever may have been the grounds of blame, the accusations were brought forward in a manner so base, and the persecution of the helpless woman conducted so unrelentingly, that public experience found it impossible to believe them elicited by real guilt.

The king had prepared for his coronation, which he had hoped to get through without being troubled by the presence of his wife, whom he was resolved to exclude from the ceremony. Caroline was on the continent, where she had been travelling or residing for the six years preceding her consort's accession. News of the approaching event having reached her, she set out for England, and landed at Dover, June 5. Her reception was thoroughly popular, and her appearance in London, an ovation. But the bustle about the crowning suddenly ceased, and a message was sent to both houses requesting an enquiry into her conduct. As she had many zealous friends in the Commons, who obstructed the ministers not a little, a bill of "pains and penalties" was introduced into the Lords, to deprive Caroline of her rights and dignities as queen of England, and to divorce her from her husband. Her trial lasted forty-five days. The second reading of the bill was carried by a majority of twenty-eight, which dwindled to nine on the third reading. It was not thought safe to act on so small a majority. Besides the public excitement was general, intense, and threatening. The queen resided at Hammersmith.

The approaches to her house were covered with incessant cavalcades. Banners streaming to banners floated round her. Vociferations of attachment rent the air; and acclamations of joy hailed her presence. Affectionate and encouraging addresses poured in from all quarters. The morning and evening papers shook the breasts of every house in Britain. Never was there such honest enthusiasm, or burning indignation. The man had a bad character, the woman a slandered one. The libelled was not convicted, but ruined; the libeller, not baffled, but blasted. As long as the queen lived the agitation lasted, and the dangers to the public peace were always imminent. No one could foresee the trifle that would cause an outbreak. For the victim there was in all this generous manifestation that victory which burns but does not warm; not warm the broken and bleeding heart. It gave her courage but not strength; confidence but not hope. In the queen's case, it detracts something from the picture, that she drew from the sympathy which flowed round her, a certain degree of audacity not favourable to a good opinion. This it was that prompted the attempt to force her way into Westminster when the coronation of her cruel husband was going on. It ought to have been the last place to which delicacy would have accepted an invitation, or where anguish would have sought a moment's relief. Caroline had no business there, unless she had been mad; nor is this improbable. Many are wronged for misconduct whose errors are the offspring of misfortune. And it seems as if Caroline more or less illustrated the reflection. When, after this ill-judged display, her better judgment secluded her more, and concealed her griefs from the broad gaze, Caroline pined in the gloom of solitude, and perished in the dignity of retirement. She survived the repulse at Westminster Abbey but three weeks; her remains were carried home to Brunswick. Assuredly guilt does not die so easily.

The king's visit to Dublin was projected immediately after the coronation. Its intention was easily divined. It was to create a diversion in his favour; and for this purpose it was extremely successful; for the display of Irish loyalty knew no bounds. The journey to Hanover, which followed directly, was undertaken with the same view, and attended with like results; and the same may be said of that made to Scotland the following summer, August 10, 1822.

While the king was in Scotland the foreign secretary, the marquis of Londonderry, formerly lord Castlereagh, committed suicide, and Mr. George Canning, a man of letters, and some oratorical abilities, succeeded to his office. The latter distinguished himself not a little by his zeal and forwardness in recognising the Spanish republics of south America, and acknowledging the independence of all those states that broke loose from the Spanish monarchy.

The despotic princes of the continent entered into a silly scheme of checking the march of liberal ideas, with a view not merely of better securing thrones, but of exercising their wills without any legal restraints or constitutional trammels. The league formed amongst them for those purposes received the name of the Holy Alliance. One of the first exploits undertaken in furtherance of their objects was the suppression of the efforts of the Spanish patriots to secure liberal institutions and a representative system. The congress of Verona entrusted the execution of it to France. The duke of Angoulême, at the head of a powerful army, entered Spain, and fell upon the constitutionalists in every direction. The struggle was fierce and bloody. The Spaniards were beaten; but the obstinacy of the contest redeemed their character all over Europe.

The Greeks, after groaning for ages under the merciless and scornful tyranny of the Turks, broke out into open insurrection in 1822. They were secretly encouraged and assisted by the Russians, not from any elevated sympathy, but from very sincere selfishness. For a considerable time the efforts of the Greeks were desultory and isolated, so that the Turks gratified their vengeance by a series of bloody massacres. The accounts from Greece shocked all Christendom, and roused the ardour of all educated society. Of the volunteers who went to aid the Greek cause was Lord Byron, the poet, but before he could be of any service beyond his purse, which was freely given, he caught fever, and died at Missolonghi, in 1824. The heroism of the Greeks was doomed to stand the test of three tedious years of bloody conflict and miserable suffering, in defiance of a numerous foe, pouring on them an incessant torrent of slaughter. At length the humanity, the shame, the classical reminiscences of England, France, and Russia, were roused, and by the treaty of London, July 6, 1827, the triple Alliance was effected for the pacification of Greece. The allied admirals forthwith sailed to the Morea, and demanded a cessation of hostilities from Ibrahim Pasha, the Turkish commander. On the 20th October, the united fleet, under sir Edward Codrington, afterwards Lord Collingwood, sailed into the harbour of Navarino, to intimidate Ibrahim. As he still obstinately refused, a blockade was formed which was of short duration, for one of the Turkish vessels having fired a gun, a general action commenced, and ended in a glorious victory for the allies and the total annihilation of the enemy's fleet. Greek independence was thus virtually secured, but it was not acknowledged by the Porte. On the contrary, this government declared war against Russia. In the beginning numbers, situation, and the possession of fortresses and outposts, gave a preponderance to the Sultan, but the scales were soon turned. The Danube passed, the Balkan forced, Adrianople captured, Russia stood with raised hand, at the gates of Constantinople. It was only knock, and it shall be opened, when the submission of the Turk averted the ruinous clang, and obtained peace and safety at Adrianople. There he signed a treaty, acknowledging the independence of the land of Pindar and Demosthenes, of Miltiades and Timoleon, and ceding to his conqueror those broad provinces that enrich the banks of the noblest of European rivers.

The year 1825 was signalized by the expedition to Birmah, under the command of sir Archibald Campbell. The Birmese had for some time been the cause of much uneasiness to our north-eastern provinces of Hindustan. They had evinced a dangerous spirit of aggression and conquest, and it became necessary to check their enterprises. On the failure of remonstrance, a small force of about 6,000 men was sent to Rangoon, which advanced up along the banks of the Irrawaddy, which is, as it were, the high road of the Birmese empire. The progress was neither fast nor smooth for the handful that found every inch of ground pre-occupied by thousands led by their famous general Bandoolah, the faith in whom diffused a dangerous confidence and energy into troops otherwise timid, yet neither feeble nor undisciplined. Some of the best constructed and strongest stockades ever faced by British soldiers had to be taken at the point of the bayonet. The invading army, however, by dint of fighting and daily successes, advanced as far as Prome, the third city, and in the heart of the empire. Then the barbarian sued for peace, and ceded Rangoon, Arracan, Amherst, and Tenasserim.

In the latter year an expedition was sent out to Portugal to support Donna Maria, and the new constitution, framed on liberal principles, and lately granted by Don Pedro, heir to John VI. At the death of John, Pedro was governor of Brazil. In concert with him, a scheme of separation was derised, by which Brazil was to be constituted into an empire, independent of the crown of Portugal, which was conferred on his daughter, Donna Maria. To obviate family jealousies and the misfortunes of a disputed succession, he betrothed little Maria to his brother Don Miguel, who was naturally appointed regent. But Miguel was not satisfied with the free constitution that was to limit his authority, and there was a large party of the same temper longing to restore the old *regime*, and ready to make Miguel as absolute as he pleased. This knave deposed his betrothed niece and lawful queen the moment the English troops had turned their backs: Portugal, however, was not without patriots, who rallied round their young queen and young constitution; and the English government allowed enlistment and equipment here in their favour. The British legion greatly contributed to the triumph of the liberals, and the safety of Donna Maria's throne.

It rarely happens that a minister's talents are sufficient of themselves, and independently of some concurrent though, perhaps, casual event, to entitle his name to a place in history. Premiers X, Y, and Z, who may be great in cabinet, may be small indeed in a historical paragraph. Passing by, therefore, the changes of administration till 1829, it must not be forgotten that Wellington and Peel were then the king's advisers. This year is rendered memorable by the introduction of "The Roman Catholic Relief Bill," or "Emancipation Act," by which the civil disabilities of the Catholics of the empire were removed, and religious toleration established. Wellington and Peel commenced their political career as bitter Tories; nor was there any chance of their being in the least sweetened by their subsequent mixture. Wellington was open to conviction when he saw a fact. Peel was much more accessible to a reason than his colleague. The former observed the deep clouds of a civil war rising above the horizon, and rapidly darkening the hemisphere. The latter felt the arguments of the greatest statesmen at home, and the voice of all intelligent Europe ringing in his ears. There was no time to be lost; no opportunity to quibble; the era of shedding blood in support of a civil tyranny had gone, and a successful atrocity was now very doubtful. The ministers brought in their bill, and it passed. If that bill has not made Ireland rich, it has done better. It has humanized every class of society within her limits. The very Orangeman has been improved by it, in spite of fate and of himself.

N

But the name of the man to whose mind and labours that famous bill can be traced, will ever be the most memorable amongst the great advocates of the same measure—the Floods, the Grattans, the Burkes, the Plunkets, the Currans. To O'Connell must be referred the unity of opinion, the sincerity of purpose, and the iteration of effort, which resulted in the Catholic Association, the simultaneous meetings, the great Protestant Petition, and the surrender of Peel and Wellington. To him, to his eloquence, his understanding, his wisdom, be all the honour of Catholic Emancipation. If after that achievement there were many who thought their time of service had expired, and left his colours, still there is not this day one thinking candid man in Ireland who would not lay a laurel on his tomb; praise him for his glory, and forget about what they differed.

George IV. bore a long illness with patience, but it does not appear that his conduct in his sufferings was, in other respects, exemplary. He lived a gross sensualist. A perception of moral good or a touch of gentle feeling, never, perhaps, reached his mind or his heart in the whole course of his life. Being thoroughly selfish, he could not be said ever to have had social enjoyments; and for mental he had little inclination, and less capacity. Literature he could not endure, beyond conversation; and the liking for this did not survive his middle age. Then he indulged in every looseness and luxury that could gratify depravity or kill time. He was a studious epicure, and would spend hours debating the relative merits of pleasures before he decided which to enjoy. In early life he was given to excess, but afterwards he restrained himself to protect his health and relish. To affections of every kind he was as insensible as a lump of chalk. I have been told by one who knew him well, that he loved neither man, woman, nor child—dog nor cat, beyond the minute. He bought vice dearly and cheerfully; but rather than be a benefactor he would have you pick his pocket. He hated nothing so much as friends; because those folks are always troubling you for something. Yet he could not have been much troubled, for he has scarcely been ever known to do a service. He was shrewd and logical, and had an excellent memory. Notwithstanding his vices, had he occupied a less conspicuous place, he would have slided through life without much reproach; quite as blamelessly as some of the best by whom his youth was surrounded. Nay, he may have gained more credit amongst his neighbours, than many of your steady fox-hunters; for even in that sour and nasty book, *The Four Georges*, he is not charged with any personal malice or vindictiveness. No vice admits defence, no turpitude extenuation. He never made amends for his heartless abandonment of Mrs. Fitzherbert; it remains an ineffaceable blot on his memory. As for his treatment of Sheridan and other literary companions, it may be left to Moore's *Monody*, without further notice. Such conduct is still common enough to be put down as anything more than a mere peccadillo. The worst part of George's life is its close. He seems to have reflected little on his accountability. He has left us no legacy of an instructive regret. He breathed no aspiration above the reek of the mire in which he lived. He had a long warning, and showed himself insensible of it until it was expiring. He died, June 26, 1830.

34. WILLIAM IV.

The princess Charlotte, married to Leopold of Saxe-Cobourg, late king of the Belgians, died in childbirth, November 6, 1817. Frederick, duke of York, second son of George III., died in 1827. The third son, William, duke of Clarence, therefore, succeeded his brother George. He was born, August 21, 1765, and crowned at Westminster, September 8, 1831. He espoused Adelaide, the amiable daughter of the duke of Saxe Meiningen, in 1818, and had by her two daughters, of whom the first died on the day of her birth, and the other when four months old.

In this short and peaceable reign, there occured scarcely two events of a purely historical character to be recorded. On the continent there was a stir of unusual interest, from which Great Britain wisely withheld herself. Matters of this kind are not fitly introduced here; but to relieve the barrenness of the situation, a word or two may be bestowed on them.

On the fall of Napoleon, the restoration of the ancient dynasty of the Bourbons, was accompanied with a charter of French rights, voluntarily granted by the late king Louis XVIII. His brother, Charles X, who succeeded in 1824, was no way friendly to this instrument. The administration at the head of which was prince Polignac, had been a long time unpopular, and it was strongly suspected that he contemplated, in concert with the king, the abrogation of the charter, and the restoration of arbitrary power. With a view of suppressing the hostility they everywhere provoked, they published, July 28, three ordinances in direct violation of the charter; the first dissolved the chambers before their meeting; the second deprived a great body of the electors of the franchise; and the third ordered a rigid censorship of the press. The printers resisted, the Parisians joined them; and after three days' fighting, Charles X. was once more an exile. The chambers met as they had been originally convened, on August 3rd, and elected Louis Philip, duke of Orleans, the representative of the junior branch of the Bourbons, to the vacant throne, under the style of Louis Philip I. king of the French. Charles X. found an asylum at Holyrood house, Edinburgh, and subsequently retired to Germany, where he died in 1837.

Three weeks after, a revolution broke out in Belgium, which had been united to Holland by the treaty of Vienna. It began by a riot in Brussels, on the night of the 25th of August, provoked by the oppressive conduct of the Dutch authorities. The final result was the independence of the Belgians, but not without much hard fighting. The Dutch garrison at Antwerp made an obstinate resistance; nor did it surrender till it had been reduced almost to powder by a besieging army of 70,000 French, who came to the aid of the Belgians. Leopold, who had been husband of the princess Charlotte, was chosen for their king.

Those revolutions gave an immense impulse to the public mind all over Europe. Princes were dethroned, constitutions changed, and the standard of revolt raised in every direction. But the most remarkable movement was that which took place in Poland. The Poles, who had long been the victims of oppression, rose against their Russian tyrants, and began a struggle never surpassed in fury, bravery, and endurance. The contest terminated in the terrible siege of Warsaw, and the slaughter of almost all the fighting men of the nation. The general ardour reached Ireland, and greatly animated the agitation for the repeal of the legislative union between Great Britain and Ireland. In defiance of a highly penal and arbitrary enactment passed to put down meetings for that object, an enactment O'Connell happily designated the Algerine Act, he continued to hold breakfast or tea meetings which caused almost as much agitation as the celebrated assemblages of 1846. It was on occasion of those meetings he was put on his trial for the first time. He was convicted, but the sentence was not carried out.

THE REFORM BILL OF 1832.

The king, who was a whig and a reformer, and was therefore not a little gratified when the Wellington ministry, in consequence of their declaration against any change in the constitution of parliament, was compelled to tender him their resignation. He very justly called earl Grey to his counsels, who gave the great seal to Henry Brougham. On the 1st March, 1831, lord John Russell introduced a bill of greater amplitude than the most sanguine had expected. A majority of one told that the bill had been read a second time. The king stood firm to his ministers; dissolved the parliament in person; and took the opinion of the country. The appeal was successful. Two-thirds of the new house were reformers. The reform bill was sent from the lower to the upper house on September 22, where a majority of forty-one negatived the second reading. Flames of discontent and vengeance burst forth in sundry districts, especially Derby, Nottingham, and Bristol. Bristol was set on fire, the prisons forced, and the private dwellings wrecked. Manchester was preparing to march to London, where she would have received the welcome of two hundred thousand wrathful men. The spirit of resistance was rising above all control when it was allayed by a timely resolution of the commons, on the motion of lord Ebrington, to support ministers and their measure. At the commencement of the following year the bill was again introduced, and passed the lower house by decisive majorities. In the lords earl Grey, observing that it was again menaced, asked the king to strengthen him by a creation of peers. On being refused, he resigned, and Wellington was sent for to fill his place. The duke was unable to organize an administration. The earl returned to power. Several of the hostile peers, seeing the danger of resistance, abstained from attending the house. Thus the reform bill at last obtained a third reading from their lordships, and became law, June 7, 1832.

Of the remaining events to which allusion may be appropriately made, the briefer the summary the better. Ten bishoprics of the Established Church were suppressed in Ireland, and tithes were commuted into a rent-charge. The freedom of the negroes was purchased from their owners at a cost of twenty millions sterling. The charter of the Bank of England was renewed with some beneficial modifications. A bill for reforming municipal corporations was carried by the Melbourne Ministry. A sytsem of National Education for the humble classes in Ireland was adopted in 1831. The charter of the East India Company was remodelled in 1834, and its monopoly abated. The first English railway, between Liverpool and Manchester, was opened September 15, 1830.

The king died in the seventy-second year of his age, June 20, 1837, of a general break up of his constitution. He was a good man; reared to the naval profession, he evinced to the last, the frankness and cordiality of the sailor; long accustomed to the association and influence of a virtuous woman, his fine disposition grew to a fixed integrity and evenness of life. His talents were confined; his understanding, clear; his ambition, inert; his pretension, modest. If he did not give splendour to the diadem, he gave it, what it had long wanted, decency.

85. VICTORIA.

The queen, who was born at Kensington Palace, May 24, 1819, eight months before the death of her father, the duke of Kent, ascended the throne June 20, 1837, when she was five weeks beyond the legal age for taking the reins of government into her own hands.

She succeeded under circumstances highly calculated to diffuse satisfaction throughout her kingdoms. She was the daughter of a prince of great popularity in his time, and who was reputed to be the most amiable man of his family, and whose character was still fresh and sweet eighteen years after his decease. Her mother, to whom the nation had entrusted the superintendence of the moral culture and mental discipline of her minority, was a woman of prudence, earnestness, and pure principles. Her rule and mode of life were known to all. As a mother she was respected in every domestic circle. She bore the character of the woman high above the splendour of her position. There was not a lady of rank in Britain thought less about it than she did of hers. Even in the ordinary and innocent gaieties of life she participated sparingly; and no fashionable frivolity of her time or her sex ever reached her. Her movements occupied a small space in the court news. She was always at home, where her maternal duties were her pleasures, and her virtues sprinkled their dews on her girl's dawn. From such rearing as she gave by precept and example, the people augured well for the morality of the coming reign, and happily they have not been disappointed. All classes rejoice in having for thirty years witnessed a virtuous court, illustrating all the domestic relations and obligations as fully and simply as any private household in the empire.

Victoria's coronation took place at Westminster Abbey, June 28th, 1838. She was married to her cousin-german, Albert of Saxe Coburg-Gotha, February 10, 1840; with whom she enjoyed twenty-one years of uninterrupted conjugal felicity.

As the *Salic* law prevailed in Hanover, the queen's uncle, the duke of Cumberland became entitled to the crown of that little kingdom. Accordingly the link between England and the German *dominions* was severed. This was an event very agreeable to the country at that time. Other events have recently occurred which must make observing men truly thankful for this providential severance. From the accession of the house of Brunswick, in 1714, for a period of eighty years, almost every war was undertaken for the preservation of those miserable *dominions*; which were always preferred to the honour and interests of England; even by George III. himself, who, "born and educated in the country, gloried in the name of Briton." It is no exaggeration to say that Hanover cost this realm three hundred millions of money, and one million and a half of men by land and sea. Nothing more probable than that we have had lately a narrow escape from a repetition of such losses. In the war between Austria and Prussia, just concluded, had the crowns of England and Hanover been on one head, it would have been scarcely possible to have avoided entanglement in the dispute. The very fact of our having to defend the rights of a woman would have inflamed the courage and animosity of the whole nation. Thanks to the *Salic* law.

The administration existing at the close of the late reign was retained in the new. In the commons it was strong; in the lords not violently opposed; parties were rather nearly balanced; and all sides were in unusually good temper. By the courtesy of faction a quiet honeymoon was permitted to the royal couple, and a pleasant festive spirit diffused itself over all society. Up to this period, England since the conquest never once felt conscious of such repose.

But in so large an empire, with a people involved in such a variety of interests, and in contact with such restless and ambitious neighbours, it cannot be hoped that rest and ease will be of long continuance. Canada, indeed, did not partake of the general quiet. It had long been in a disturbed state.

Lower Canada was occupied by a population almost exclusively French. They were a gentle race, of rural habits, rural tastes and morals. They were easily contented but the dominant party wronged them. A rebellion burst forth, which, had England been engaged in any other war, would have been truly formidable. As it was, the revolt was not suppressed without a great display of force on the part of Upper Canada and the mother country. To allay the discontents the earl of Durham, a statesman of a good judgment and a mild temper, was sent out as governor-general of all the British possessions in North America. In pursuance of the policy he recommended, the two provinces, which had heretofore been administered separately, were united into one government. This arrangement removed many of the causes of animosity and jealousy. But what most contributed to heal those sores which rebellion necessarily leaves behind, and calm those agitations of spirit which impede and perplex the interests of society, the past was forgotten, and the future honestly viewed. From that period to the present, it would be impossible to name any other people on the globe, whose affairs, abroad and at home, have been conducted with so much integrity and success. Whatever advantages may be derived practically or speculatively, from a monarchy or a republic, are to be seen combined both in the government and in the social condition of the Canadian provinces. A still greater improvement is now, (1867,) on the eve of being consummated. All the local governments of the dependencies of the crown in North America are to be fused into one, with a common representative legislature of similar authority, functions, and dignity, to the imperial parliament.

An expedition was sent to Afghanistan, under lord Keane, with a view of checking the designs of the Russians, who appeared to have inveigled Persia into projects injurious to our Indian interests. It was organized on a large scale, and furnished with munitions of war and an abundant commissariat, calculated to inspire the greatest confidence. Sir John Keane rapidly advanced against inconsiderable resistance till he occupied Candahar. Having taken the stronghold of Ghazni by storm, he entered Cabul, and deposed the reigning prince Dost Mohammed. To fill the place of this powerful chief he selected Shah Soojah, who was willing to take all that was offered, but had not much to give in return; for he possessed narrow local influence, and slender military skill. What rendered his friendship still less profitable was that he had not the address of making friends and attaching them to his person or purposes. On the return of Keane to India he committed the object of his mission to the care of Messrs. Macnaghten and Burnes, who were left in Cabul, with a competent staff of civil and military officers. But Akhbar Khan, the son of Dost, was not idle. He roused and organized the whole country against the invaders, and postponed his operations till he could turn the severity of the winter of a mountainous region to the best account. When he had counted his strength, and examined his arrangements, he calculated upon nothing short of the massacre of the whole of the Anglo-Indian force, or their piecemeal ruin by hardship and harassing attacks. As he desired it happened; nor do the annals of England record a larger or more melancholy disaster than the attempted retreat from Cabul. The work of destruction commenced with the slaughter of the agents, their officers, and servants. This was the crisis when a bold decision would have been the best shield. But instead of standing, defending themselves, and selling life at its highest price, the army began a retreat, a flight with twelve thousand camp followers, women, and children. The consequence of this movement through one of the most difficult countries imaginable, a thousand miles removed from any certain asylums in the unrelenting season of the year; through snow and ice, torn by crags, breasted by mountains, and swallowed by valleys, may be easily conjectured. The sword, the climate, and the way spread havoc till nothing was left to be destroyed. Twenty-five thousand perished; less than three hundred escaped. During the Afghan war, the Ameers of Scinde finding us in trouble, played false. Sir Charles Napier was sent to call them to order for their breach of faith in sundry particulars connected with that event. The defeat of those chiefs, at Hydrabad, was followed by the annexation of their territories. In the same year, and for similar offences, signal punishment was inflicted on the Mahrattas at Maharajpoor, Punniar, and Gwalior. Those victories, however, did not deter the Sikhs, a brave race of Mahommedan fanatics, from crossing the Sutlej, in 1845, with a fixed determination of driving us out of the northern parts of the Peninsula. It exacted the utmost efforts of European skill and valour to reap the laurels of Ferozeshah, Aliwal, and Sobraon, conducted by sir Henry Hardinge and sir Harry Smith. The seizure of Lahore and the utter discomfiture of the Sikh army promised British rule a long rest, when a war of equal magnitude almost immediately called forth all the energy and resources of the Indian government. This was closed by the unexpected and decisive battle of Chillianwallah won by lord Gough.

On the removal of lord Auckland, lord Ellenborough was appointed governor-general of India. The invasion of Afghanistan was renewed under general Pollock. The country was overrun, and ample, though worthless vengeance inflicted. As the Afghans were soon left to themselves all that can be found consolatory in this second enterprise is, that the British arms were vindicated, and that several British officers and ladies who had been made prisoners, were fortunately rescued as they were about being deported into Jurkistan, and put almost out of the reach of relief. Our army returned in 1842.

The war with China, which was undertaken in consequence of the seizure, in 1843, by the Chinese authorities, of two millions' worth of opium belonging to our merchants, does not appear justifiable on any ordinary moral principles, or reconcilable with the admitted rights of nations. The Chinese have been for some time accustomed to take opium as an intoxicating drug, instead of the spirituous liquors used by Europeans. Their government, which is not very thrifty of their lives, having observed the ravages of this poison, entered on laudable efforts to circumscribe its consumption as much as possible. To prevent the supply became a leading object. The great bulk of the narcotic was derived from India through our merchants. The culture of the poppy in China had been prohibited, to import its dried juice from abroad had been declared illegal. The Indian traders, however, had contrived to introduce it clandestinely on an incredible scale, as the amount mentioned plainly shows. The loss they sustained was from a seizure of contraband goods; and if those had been chocolate, instead of opium, they had no right whatever to indemnification. Our government was not influenced by such a consideration. The opium traffic was a set off against the tea traffic; and so they resolved to keep the trade with China *open*—open to a ravaging poison. Accordingly an expedition was fitted up and despatched, which soon imposed our conditions on the celestial emperor. Canton was captured; Hong Kong retained; and the Chinese made pay for the opium, and the trouble of reducing them to obedience. Our subsequent intercourse with China was carried on in an angry mood. Hostilities broke out again in 1856, when admiral Stopford received orders to punish an insult offered to the British flag, which he did effec-

THE CRIMEAN WAR. 187

tually. But the chastisement did not extinguish the wrath. The imperial government had determined on discouraging Europeans altogether. In 1860, the French united with the English in a grand campaign designed to *open* China for ever. The allies took Pekin, drove out the emperor, and sacked his palace. They returned with vast plunder, and peace to the present.

In 1853, the designs of Russia on Turkey became intelligible to the cabinets of France and England, by means of her own obscure intrigues. The Porte declared war against the Czar, September 27, and on the 28th March, the year following, Victoria and Napoleon did the same. During the interval, the Russians had gained several advantages, and had almost the entire command of the Danube. They received a vexatious check at Silistria, from which they had to retire in consequence of their rear being threatened by the allies. The united fleet, however, had accomplished little, and was, if we may believe Marshal St. Arnaud, the French commander-in-chief, on the point of returning home, when it ran into his head to propose an attack on Sebastopol. The consequences of this whim were that a landing was effected in two or three favourable harbours, lodgments made, and Sebastopol tried from the sea. The entrance into this port was so defended by numerous and powerful batteries, that the combined fleets found it absolutely impenetrable. The approach by land was scarcely less difficult, when we consider the inequalities of the ground, the strength of the enemy, his numerous forts, and extensive lines of multiplied and almost impregnable earthworks. The Russians made an obstinate stand at every point, nor lost a battle without covering themselves with glory. From the first great engagement, however, they must have learned that they had not much to expect from the field. The heights of Alma, whose batteries poured a shower of shot, "very like hail, but much thicker," were carried, September 23; the battle of Balaklava was won, October 26, and that of Inkermann, November 5. The last was fought when the allies had been much enfeebled by their losses in the trenches from the severity of the weather, the necessary labours of the lines, the furious sorties of the besieged, and the deficient supplies and inhospitable accommodations of the besiegers. After this the approaches were pushed forward with wonderful perseverance, and under incredible sufferings and privations. The Russians repelled with immense slaughter the repeated assaults of their defences. Never were the courage and firmness of man better tried, than on both sides during this protracted siege. But the storm and the ruin were coming to a climax. On the night of September 6, 1855, the allies opened that *feu d'enfer*, which devoured the city, the ramparts and the defenders. Earth and air were on fire. The ground quivered beneath the incessant shocks of guns and mortars. The boom of shells soaring in flocks, kept up an awful concert in the skies. To this picture add that almost as terrible, as hideous, and as sublime on the other side, where the indefatigable, inexhaustible Todelben, replied with a thousand thunders. The firmament quaked. Nature stood aghast. "It was a night," said one of the combatants, "that left behind an impression, but not a description!" The dawn of September 8, disclosed Sebastopol torn asunder, laid in heaps, and deserted even by her heroic soldiers, whose last bands were seen departing from the desolation by a bridge of boats, drawn across the harbour. Such is the magnificence of war, such the devastations of ambition. But where shall we find colours to paint the groans of death, the agonies of wounds, the wails of widows, the tears of mothers, the cries of children; the woes and sorrows of the thousands who lost all by a bloody and worthless conquest?

While the war was raging in the Crimea, a fleet in the Baltic, under Sir Charles Napier, performed services quite inconsistent with its strength and its admiral's name. It has been said that he was more attentive to Bacchus than to Mars. At any rate, after some vaunting promises, all the noise he made was the destruction of the fortress of Bomarsund, which could have had no effect on the campaign, and the bombardment of Sveaborg, an equally idle exploit. An attack on Revel or Riga would have instantly occurred to any serious tactician. St. Petersburgh should have been threatened at the outset; but the war was replete with blunders. After a congress held at Paris, peace, which cost the British taxpayers thirty-three millions, was proclaimed March 30, 1856.

But the clang of arms had scarcely ceased in Europe, when the sound of the trumpet was heard from India. There a mutiny of the sepoys broke out, May 11, 1857, at Meerut, which began with the murder of some of their officers. The spirit of revolt soon infected almost the whole of the native troops. They were guilty of many atrocities of peculiar wantonness and infamy. Their conduct to British ladies, women, and children, at Cawnpore, spread with horror over all

Europe. A bloody repayment, still not commensurate with the deed, was exacted by Havelock and other English officers. The most memorable events of the war were the sieges of Lucknow and Delhi. In the former city a mere handful of European soldiers and civilians defended themselves with unparalleled fortitude against an immense beleaguering host till delivered by sir Colin Campbell, afterwards lord Clyde.

During the last quarter of a century the commerce and manufactures of the empire have advanced by gigantic strides. The wonderful rapidity of the development may be referred to four prominent causes: (1) the improvements in machinery of all kinds; (2) the abolition of the corn-laws; (3) our neutrality with respect to the differences arising between foreign states; (4) the treaty of commerce lately effected with France, through the exertions of Cobden.

Those great exhibitions of human industry and ingenuity, which have become such serious objects of interest all over Europe, besides their general utility in exciting emulation, and diffusing practical instruction and artistic skill, have indirectly the effect of highly stimulating invention and enterprise, ingenious trades, and useful commerce.

The first London Exhibition, organized by Prince Albert, was opened May 1, 1851; the Dublin one, projected by Mr. Dargan, May 12, 1853.

The most distinguishing feature of the age, is the general effort to ameliorate the condition of the humbler of the working and reproductive classes. Laws have been passed for the protection of children employed in factories; for the promotion of health in towns, and for the general education of the children of the people. Societies have been formed for the collection and diffusion of information on social subjects, and for the correction of various social abuses. Reformatories have been legally established for the reclamation of juvenile delinquents. The discipline of prisons has been greatly improved. The use of masks and silence is, however, very questionable. Respecting silence there are very serious ethical objections, unless it be employed religiously.

The measure that will make the year 1867 memorable in constitutional history, is the large and unhoped for extension of the elective franchise by the Reform Bill, passed by the ministry of the earl of Derby.

There are but few domestic occurrences suitable to these pages; in general they partake too much of the nature of politics; and this is specially the case with regard to Ireland. It is, therefore, necessary to be reserved in her regard. Of the past thirty years, one half has been spent in an excited activity, attended by no beneficial results, and the other half has been passed in quiet; but the tranquillity has been that of exhaustion or despair. The rest has not been that which follows useful labour; nor the peace, that of prosperity and content. It is impossible to separate the remembrance of the political outbreak in 1848 or 1867 from the long continued neglect and mis-government of that country. It is a simple fact that during the thirty years her Majesty has been on the throne little has been wisely done for the direct benefit of Ireland. As she found it at her accession, so it is, or rather much worse. It could not be otherwise. During this long period there has been an annual absentee drain of four millions, to make up for which nothing in return has been *commercially* received. This drain for thirty years amounts to £120,000,000, abstracted directly from the capital and industry of the country; or to £213,000,000, if simple interest be calculated at 5 per cent.

Yet the public expenditure in Ireland is of the most parsimonious and begrudging character. It seems to have become the settled policy to do nothing for that portion of the empire but supply her with plausible viceroys, always ready with a vapid harangue on the fine arts or the fine weather, on poetry or poultry, on the cultivation of flax or of the belles-lettres. If the lieutenancy of Ireland be not intended for a mockery, or a snare, it is serious politicians should fill it, not puerile rhetoricians; deep legislators, not shallow lecturers. It is easy to please, to astonish the comfortable classes, whose humour and judgment are better prepared for the reception of a peer than for the appreciation of talent or learning; but such artifices will, in the long run, prove unprofitable if not ruinous.

QUESTIONS ON LEADING POINTS IN ENGLISH HISTORY.

CHAP. I.

1—When and where did Cæsar land in Britain?
2—For what commodity was Britain famous?
3—Describe the primitive inhabitants.
4—Who was Cassivalaunus? Caractacus? Boadicea?
5—What Roman emperor appeared in Britain?
6—What do you know of Ostorius Scapula and Paulinus?
7—Who constructed the wall or ditch of Antorienus?
8—What do you know of Carausius? of Allectus?
9—Where did Severus die? Describe the Picts' Wall.
10—Who founded the Scottish monarchy? Who called in Hengist and Horsa? Why?

CHAP. II.

1—Who founded the kingdom of Sussex? Name the other kingdoms of the Heptarchy.
2—What was the principal king called?
3—Who was Gildas? Venerable Bede?
4—Who laid the foundation of the kingdom of England?
5—Name the sons of Ethelwolf; and the kingdom of St. Edmund.
6—Give a general account of Alfred, his life and policy.

CHAP. III.

1—What was the *Witenagemot*?
2—What do you know of Athelstan and Anlof?
4—How did Edward the *martyr* lose his life? Who was the instigator?
5—Give an account of Danegelt? Who was Sweyn? Canute?
6—Who had a better right than Harold Harefoot?
7—What do you know of Godwin? Harold? Editha?
8—Describe the transactions between Harold and William duke of Normandy? What do you know of Malcolm? Of Siward? Of
9—Name the brothers of Harold. Describe the battle of Hastings.
10—How long did the Anglo-Saxon period last?

CHAP. IV.

CHAP. IV. 1—From whom did the Saxons derive their institutions?
2—What were *eorl, ceorl, oyning? thane? shire-reeve, lada, ordeal?*
3—Give some account of the early importance of London and York.

1. WILLIAM I.

1—Name the *Conqueror's* mother and wife.
2—Who was Atheling? To whom was his sister married?
3—What do you know of the Conqueror's children? Of the new forest? Of *couvre-feu*? Of Gerberoi? Of Lanfranc? Of Stigand?
4—What was the manner of William's death?

2. WILLIAM II.

1—Mention some particulars of Odo: Malcolm III.; Peter the Hermit, and Anselm.
2—What was the manner of William's death? For what purpose was Westminster Hall built?
3—What was William's conduct towards the Church?

3. HENRY I.

1—What means did Henry use to win the affections of his subjects?
2—What was the agreement made near Winchester between Robert and Henry?

3—When was Robert made prisoner? Where confined? How long?
4—Describe the right of *investiture*; and detail Henry's dispute with Anselm
5—Who was Robert's heir? Who gained the battle of Brenville?
6—Describe the circumstances attending Henry's return to England.
7—What do you know of Fulk of Anjou? Of Burchard de l'Isle?
8—Who was Matilda's second husband? How did Robert's son come by his death? Who was Bloet?

4. STEPHEN.

1—Describe the pretensions of Stephen; the interference of David I.; and why he became neutral.
2—Give an account of the battle of Northallerton; of the duke of Gloucester; and of Eustace.

5. HENRY II.

1—What were the possessions of Henry II.? his relations with Malcolm IV.? Who was his wife?
2—State the dispute with Becket; defend his conduct. Who was Pope? How did Becket come by his death?
3—What led to the invasion of Ireland? Who were the principal actors?
4—What do you know of Henry's children?
5—Who was made prisoner at Alnwick? Give the king's character.

6. RICHARD I.

1—What happened in Sicily? at Acre? at Jaffa? at Zara?
2—Who was Adelais? Berengaria? Leopold? Saladin?
3—Mention something of the marquis Montferrat; of William de Longchamp; of Hugh de la March; and of Prince Arthur.
4—What were the proceedings of John in Richard's absence? Of Philip Augustus, respecting Richard's return home?
5—Instance Richard's ingratitude. What do you know about Bertrand of Haute-fort? Of the title, *Dauphin*? Of William Longbeard? Of Richard's death?

7. JOHN I.

1—What affairs took place between Philip and John? Name Arthur's mother. What happened at Mirabeau?
2—Describe John's losses in France; his quarrel with the pope?
3—What was the *Interdict*? Who was Pandulph? Langton?
4—On whom did the pope bestow England? How did Louis offend the English? How did the contest end?
5—Relate all the particulars connected with *Magna Charta*.

8. HENRY III.

1—Who was appointed Henry's guardian? What happened at Lincoln? Off the coast of Kent?
2—What were the causes of discontent? To whom was Jane married?
3—State what you know of Simon de Montfort; of Thomas de Clare.

9. EDWARD I.

1—Where was Llewellyn slain? Why was Edward called the English Justinian?
2—Who was the Maid of Norway? To what dispute did her death lead?
3—What do you know of Wallace, Bruce, and John Baliol?
4—Where was Warrenne defeated? and by whom?
5—Where did Edward beat Wallace? What was Wallace's fate? Who took the regency in Baliol's name? Who was Oliphant?
6—What do you know of Bohun and Bigod? What happened at the confirmation of the Charter? To what years is the formation of Parliament referred? State the particulars.

7—What do you know of the younger Bruce, and of John Comyn? Of the battle at Methuen? Of queen Eleanor's funeral? Of the statute *de tallagio non concedendo?*

10. EDWARD II.

1—Who was Gaveston? Thomas, earl of Lancaster? Who won Bannockburn? In what year was it fought? Who was Phelim O'Connor? Where was he beaten?
2—Detail the adventure of the Bruces in Ireland.
3—To whom was Edward II. married? What was her conduct? Who was Hugh de Spencer? Roger Mortimer?

11. EDWARD III.

1—What arrangement was made respecting Scotland? What was done to the earl of Kent? to Mortimer? Who was Montacute? What happened at Halidon Hill?
2 What was the *Salic* law? the pretensions of Edward III. to the crown of France? How can you show that Edward acknowledged the *Salic* law?
3—Who were Edward's allies on the Continent? Give an account of Creci. Who was John of Luxemburgh?
4—Who was Eustace St. Pierre? What exchange did Edward propose to Philip? What bargain did he enter into with Baliol? State the circumstances connected with Poitiers. Where was king John lodged? What is the date of the great peace of Bretigni?
5—State the particulars of the Black Prince's, and of the king's death.

12. RICHARD II.

1—Of what did the *Villeins* complain? Who was Wycliffe? What were his doctrines?
2—Give an account of Wat Tyler, and John Ball. Who was Sudbury? Walworth? Jack Straw? What good resulted from the disturbances?
3—Who was Jane of Kent? To whom was Richard I. first married? Who was declared heir presumptive? What about the council of Nottingham? about Lancaster and Gloucester? Tresilian, and Brembre? about the statute of Kilkenny?
4—What favours were conferred on Oxford? Describe the transactions in Ireland. Who were the Lollards?

13. HENRY IV.

1—How did Henry act towards Scotland? What do you know of Owen Glendower? Of Henry Percy? Of Gascoigne? Of Mary de Bohun? Of Sir Edward Mortimer?

14. HENRY V.

1—What reply was given to the French ambassadors? What is the date of the battle of Azincourt? Who was Henry's wife? Whom did she marry when a widow?
2—What was the surname of Charles VI. of France? What of sir John Oldcastle? The character of Henry?

15. HENRY VI.

1—Describe the particulars of the accession of Henry VI. Who were Gloucester and Bedford? Who Bandricourt? Joan of Arc? Her fate?
2—Who was Dunois? What party was espoused by Gloucester and cardinal Beaufort? What was the origin of "The Wars of the Roses?" Which was the rose of Lancaster?
3—Who was the representative of the Mortimers? Why did Richard, duke of York, leave Ireland?

4—To whom was Henry VI. married? What became of Suffolk? Who was Jack Cade? Who won the battle of Ludlow? Who was made prisoner at Northampton? Who fell at Wakefield? Who who Mortimer's cross? What year?

16. EDWARD IV.

1—What was the decisive battle between the Roses? Describe Henry's fate? Whom did Edward marry? After what battle was Edward made prisoner?

2—Where were Warwick and Montague slain? What became of queen Margaret and her son?

17. EDWARD V.

Detail the actions of their uncle Richard towards the royal children. Who proposed Richard for king?

18. RICHARD III.

What part did the bishop of Ely take? What Northumberland and Stanley? How did Richard conciliate the Yorkists? What was Richard's fate?

19. HENRY VII.

Who were Simnel and Warbeck? and what became of them? Of Warwick? What about Estaples? about the *Badge*? How was the House of Stuart introduced? To whom were princes Arthur and Henry married? Who first explored Newfoundland? The king's character and death?

20. HENRY VIII.

1—In what battle did James IV., of Scotland, fall? Who commanded the English who took Tournay? Who succeeded Louis XII.? Tell the particulars of Wolsey's rise and fall. What do you know of Thomas Cromwell? Sir Thomas More? Fisher? Campeggeo and Luther?

2—Whom did James the fourth's widow marry? Who was the duke of Albany? What about the " Field of the cloth of gold?" about the intrigues of Charles V. of Germany?

3—What was the issue of the dispute between Albany and Margaret? Who were Tetzel and Staupitz? What do you know of Julius II., and Leo X.?

4—What was the origin of the title "Defender of the Faith?" Why did Henry seek a divorce from Catherine of Arragon? Give an account of the court appointed to try the validity of Henry's first marriage? Where did it meet? How did Wolsey act? How the queen? How Campeggio? How the court of Rome?

5—What was the first charge brought against Wolsey? In what year was he charged with high treason? What events followed? How and where did Wolsey die?

6—Who succeeded the cardinal in the chancery? Who suggested to Henry to declare himself head of the Church? What did Reginald Pole think of the divorce? How was the sentence of divorce pronounced, and by whom? Who excommunicated Henry and Anna Boleyn?

7—What enactments were hostile to the court of Rome? What do you know of Frith and Hewet? Who proposed the plunder of the monasteries? Give some particulars of the two visitations.

8—What led to Anna Boleyn's death? What can you tell of Jane Seymour? Who succeeded her? Name the children of Catherine of Arragon, Anna Boleyn, and Jane Seymour.

9—What was the "Pilgrimage of grace?" What embassy did Henry send to Germany? What was the nature of Pole's mission to the emperor, and the king of France? Who was Anne of Cleves? What led to the fall of Cromwell? When was Catherine Howard married? What was her fate?

10—Give an account of the state and affairs of Ireland. Who was David Beaton? What policy did Henry's nephew, James, adopt? What took place at Salway Moss? Relate what you know of Catherine Parr, of Norfolk, of Surrey, and of the king's latter days.

21. EDWARD VI.

1—Who were the competitors for power? What was the fate of Thomas Seymour? Of Somerset? Of Northumberland? How was the kingdom divided for spiritual government?

2—What ameliorations were made in the laws? Why was Gardiner sent to the Tower? To whom was Thomas Seymour married? What ambitious views did he entertain? Before whom was Bonner tried? Who was Heath? Day? Mallet?

3—Describe the princess Mary's resolution. What were the negociations about Edward's marriage? Describe Northumberland's intrigues; and Edward's illness and death.

22. MARY.

1—Describe the progress of Mary's cause. Who was Tunstall? Who arrested Northumberland? Who were executed with him? What confession did he make? How did Cranmer endeavour to save himself? To whom was Mary married? What immediately led to the execution of Dudley and Jane Grey?

2—How was Philip received? What steps did Mary take for restoring the ancient worship? What do you know of Hooper, Rogers, Ridley, and Latimer? What of Alphonso di Castro?

3—Who succeeded Cranmer in his archdiocese? What became of Calais? How was the Spanish marriage liked?

23. ELIZABETH.

1—Who were the queen's chief advisers and favourites? Describe the caution with which she proceeded. Who crowned her? How did the body of the bishops act respecting her coronation?

2 Mention particulars of Nicholas Bacon; of Cecil; of the bishop of Carlisle. Who were the husbands of Mary Stuart? Give an account of her residence in France, and of the state of Scotland at her return.

3—What do you know of Ruthven? Of Knox? Of Lennox? Of Bothwell? Of Murray? Of Douglas? Of Adolphus of Holstein? Of the earl of Arran? Of Robert Dudley?

4—What can you tell of Charles of Austria? Of Eric of Sweden? Of the duke of Anjou? Of Condé? Of Rouen?

5—What penal statutes were passed against the Catholics? Give an account of Babington's conspiracy. What were the charges against Norfolk? Who was Davison? What means of getting rid of Mary did Elizabeth suggest?

6—Who was Shrewsbury? Kent? Paulet? Devereaux? Give the details of Mary's execution; and of Elizabeth's dissimulation. What do you know about the "Kirk of Field?" Langsyde? Carberry Hill? Lochlevin? Of Riccio? Mar? Janet Gordon?

7—Who was Elizabeth's principal secretary of state? Who commanded the English fleet against the Spanish Armada? Who were next in command? What do you know of sir John Hawkins, and of the duke de Medina Sidonia?

8—Who was appointed commander-in-chief of the English army in France? What towns were delivered up to Elizabeth? What town in France was taken by storm? What French leaders promised Elizabeth support? What combination in France exasperated Elizabeth?
9—Who was Maitland? How did Cecil act with regard to the match proposed by the archduke Charles? Who was Darnley's mother? What honour did Mary refuse Darnley? Give Darnley's character; and an account of the inquiry made as to his murder?
10—What title was conferred on Bothwell? What about the silver casket? Mention the particulars of the unsuccessful attempt at escaping from Lochlevin Castle. Under what pretence was Mary refused an interview with Elizabeth? What occurred at Branham Moor? Why was the match with the duke of Anjou broken off? To what party did the duke of Alençon incline?
11—Who accused Morton of Darnley's murder? Where, and to whom? What was the conduct of James towards his mother? How did he act after her death? Why did Mary consent to plead before the commissioners? How many were on the court of inquiry? Describe Elizabeth's conduct for some time after the sentence on Mary. How did Paulet and Drury act? What is the date of Mary's execution? Who was Le Préau? Specify the victims of the persecution under Elizabeth.

24. JAMES I.

1—Who was Gondomar? What do you know of Grey, Cobham, and Raleigh?
2—Why had Catholics expectations from James? How was James educated? What oppression did Catesby resent?
3—With whom did Catesby conspire? What led to the arrest of Fawkes? Is there any proof of the complicity of the Jesuits in the "Gunpowder Plot?" What do you know of Garnet? Of Arabella Stuart?
4—Who planned the poisoning of sir Thomas Overbury? From whom was James descended? How did James act towards Ireland? Who instigated James to send Overbury to the Tower?
5—Who was Coke? Bacon? Why was Bacon fined? How many children had James? Which survived him?

25. CHARLES I.

1—What were Charles's rights of descent? Who was Henrietta Maria? What explanation can you give of the king's position?
2—There was a common point of agreement between all parties: what was it? To what does this observation refer: "an answer which reveals much of the future of this reign?" Under what circumstances did Charles use the words, "it would be worse for them?" What was the tenor of the "*Petition of Rights?*" Name the stronghold of the French Protestants? Who slew Buckingham? Who brought ship-money to a legal trial?
3—What persons did Charles select to manage public affairs when he dispensed with parliament? Who was sent to enforce episcopacy in Scotland? What do you know of Leslie? about the five members? and Nottingham?
4—On what grounds did the rebel parliament reject the king's first message? What was the position of Catholics in those disputes? Who were the *Cavaliers?* the *Roundheads?* the *Levellers?*
5—Who reduced Portsmouth? What was the result of the battle of Edgehill? Who was Essex? Prince Rupert? What was Rupert's character?

ENGLISH HISTORY. 197

6—Mention particulars respecting Chalgrove, Field, and Newbury. What eminent men fell in those engagements? What do you know of the Confederation of Kilkenny? What was the error of the duke of Ormond?
7—In what year was Laud executed? What was the cause of the royalists' defeat at Marston More and Naseby? Who had command of the rebels at Naseby? What do you know of Manchester, Leven, and Fairfax?
8—In what battles did Oliver Cromwell distinguish himself? How did the Parliamentarians get possession of the king? Who was sent to seize Charles at Holmby? Who were the agitators? Whose purposes did they serve?
9—How did relations stand between the army and the parliament? Mention particulars of Hampton Court, and Carisbrook Castle. Where was the duke of Hamilton beaten, and by whom?
10—How many were on the court for the king's trial? Who presided? What was the charge against him? Where was the scaffold erected? How old was he at his death?

THE COMMONWEALTH.

1—How was the new Government constituted? What proposals were sent to prince Charles? What do you know of sir Arthur Aston?
2—What occurred at Drogheda? at Wexford? What do you know of Ireton? of Montrose? What agreement did the prince enter into with the preachers? Who defeated Leslie at Dunbar? What do you know of Middleton?
3—Who fought at Worcester? What was the date? What became of Charles? Why was the *Navigation Act* passed? What Dutch admirals were beaten off Portland? What happened April 20, 1653?
4—How was Cromwell's first parliament constituted? Why was it called *Barebone's* parliament? What policy was pursued towards Scotland?
5—Who were Scot, Hazlerig, and Bradshaw? Give an account of the *Humble Petition and Advice*. Whose remonstrances alarmed Cromwell? What anxieties beset Cromwell? What was the manner of his death? Relate the events subsequent to it.
6—Describe the efforts of the royalists. Who had the command in Scotland? How did Fairfax and Monk act? What arrangements were made with Charles? What is the date of his entry into London?

26. CHARLES II.

1—How did the king act towards his adherents in Ireland? To whom was Charles married? What dowry did he get? Why, and by whose advice, did the king sell Dunkirk?
2—What gave rise to the war with the Dutch? What are the dates of the *Great Plague* and the *Great Fire*? What was done to commemorate the *Great Fire*? Who was the ally of Charles in the next Dutch war? Who commanded the English fleet at Southwold Bay? Who the Dutch?
3—Who were Anne Hyde and Mary of Modena? What was the *Test Act*? What effect had it on James? Give an account of Monmouth, Russel, and Algernon Sydney. What was the *Popish Plot*? Who got it up? Name some of its victims? Who was the last victim?
4—Who moved the *Exclusion Bill* in the Lords? who in the Commons? Who was Huddlestone? Describe the king's last days. What do you know of Argyle?

27. JAMES II.

1—To what punishment was Oates condemned? What was Argyle's fate? Monmouth's? Where was he defeated? Why did the bishops refuse reading the declaration for liberty of conscience? How was their acquittal received?
2—Give the particulars of William's invasion, and James's subsequent proceedings. What do you know of Cornbury? Of the princess Anne? How did Louis XIV. act?
3—Give an account of the Convention; and of the "Declaration of Rights."

28. WILLIAM AND MARY.

1—Who fell at Killiecrankie? at Aughrim? Who was Tyrconnell? De Ginkle? Schomberg?
2—What do you know of Derry? the Boyne? Of the *Treaty of Limerick*? Of the *Irish Brigade*? Of James's last years? Of William's death?

29. ANNE.

1—To whom was Anne married? What about the "Grand Alliance?" Liege? Blenheim? Ramillies?
2—Who was Peterborough? Villeroy? Who took Gibraltar? In what year? What do you know of the "Act of Security?" What measure did it hasten?
3—Mention the terms of the Union between England and Scotland. What do you know of Sacheverel? Of Byng? Of Harley? Bolingbroke? Godolphin? Of the *Treaty of Utrecht*?

30. GEORGE I.

1—From which of the Stuart kings was George descended? What party did he call into office? What do you know of Mar and Derwentwater?
2—Who were the Jacobites? Who came to lead them? What was the "Septennial Act?" Who was John Law? Who sir Robert Walpole? Where, and how, did the king die?

31. GEORGE II.

1—What was the cause of the war with Spain? Who took Portobello? What feat did Anson accomplish?
2—Who was Maria Theresa? Whom did France espouse against her? Why did Walpole resign?
3—What about Dettingen? Saxe? Clementina Sobieski? Of Prestonpans? Give an account of the proceedings of prince Charles Edward in 1745? Where was he defeated? What do you know of his escape? Why was he called the *Pretender*?
4—Who defeated prince Charles? What about Kilmarnock and Balmarino? Who was Thurot? Wolf? Clive? What of *The Black Hole*? What was the manner of George the Second's death?

32. GEORGE III.

1—Whom did George III. marry? Who was his favourite minister? What policy did Pitt advocate? What places were taken from Spain?
2—Who commanded the English army in Germany? Mention the terms of the *Treaty* of 1763. What do you know of John Wilkes, and No. 45.?
3—What minister imposed the *Stamp Duty* on the Americans? Who the duties on tea and glass?

4—What counsel did Chatham and Burke give in the American War? Who was North? Washington? Burgoyne? When did Cornwallis surrender at Yorktown? Who was Franklin? What was his mission to Paris?

5— Who commanded the French auxiliaries sent to the Americans What European states acknowledged American Independence?

6—What is the date of the "Declaration of Independence?" By what treaty did England recognize American Independence? What is its date?

7—What do you know of Warren Wastings? Of Fox and Sheridan? When did the French revolution break out? When was England involved in it? What English officers were sent to the Continent?

8—In what battle did sir John Moore fall? In what Nelson? Who defeated the Spanish fleet off Cape St. Vincent? Who gained the battle of the Nile? Of Talavera? Of Thoulouse?

9—What do you know of Victor and Massena? What is the date of Waterloo? What was its immediate consequences? Who was the leader of the ministry called "All the Talents?"

10—Who was leader of the "Coalition Ministry? Who were the *Irish Volunteers?* What advantages did they procure for their country? How was the Irish Act of Union effected? What do you know of the *United Irishmen?* What led to the regency of the Prince of Wales? How long was he regent? When did the king die?

33. GEORGE IV.

1—Give an account of the Cato-street conspiracy. To whom was George married? Why was his coronation deferred? What proceedings were taken against queen Caroline? What excitement did they create? How long did she survive the king's coronation? What excursions did the king make immediately after the ceremony?

2—What do you know of Castlereagh? What foreign policy was observed by George Canning? What was the Holy Alliance? Who commanded the French army sent into Spain? For what purpose was that army sent?

3—What caused the insurrection of the Greeks? In what year did it occur? What English nobleman distinguished himself in the Greek cause? Who were parties to the Triple Alliance? When and where was it signed?

4—Who commanded the English fleet at Navarino? What was the result of the victory there? Give an account of the progress of the Russian war against the Porte.

5—Who commanded the expedition against Birmah? Give an account of the war. What places did we gain by the treaty of peace?

6—Who was Don Pedro? What were the aims of Don Miguel? What settlement of his empire did Don Pedro make? Under what circumstances did he leave Brazil? What body of auxiliaries did good service for Donna Maria?

7—In what year did the "Roman Catholic Relief Bill" become law? Whose talents and exertions mainly effected that measure? What beneficial effects may be traced to that measure?

34. WILLIAM IV.

1—What events led to the succession of William IV.? To whom was he married? What policy did Charles X. of France pursue? Who was his prime minister?

2—Who succeeded Charles X.? What do you know of the Belgian revolution?

3—What happened in Poland? What was the Algerine act? What declaration led to the fall of the Wellington ministry?
4—Describe the excitement that followed the rejection of the Reform Bill by the lords.
5—What changes were made in the Protestant establishment in Ireland? What was done regarding Negro slavery and the Bank of England?

35. VICTORIA.

1—How old was the queen when she came to the throne? Under whose guidance was she reared and educated?
2—To whom was Victoria married? Why was Hanover separated from the queen's authority?
3—What was the state of parties at the queen's accession? What occurred in Canada? What changes were made in the administration of Canada?
4—Who commanded the first expedition to Afghanistan? What do you know of Dost Mahommed? Of Macnaghten and Burns?
5—What victories were gained over the Mahrattas? Over the Sikhs, by Hardinge and Smith? Who won Chillianwallah?
6—State the causes of the war with China? What places in China were taken? What do you know of Admiral Stopford?
7—How did the designs of Russia transpire in 1853? What combination was formed against her? What about Silistria? Marshal St. Arnaud? The heights of Alma?
8—What engagements followed? Who commanded the fleet in the Baltic? What operations were carried on there?
9—Where did the Indian mutiny begin? Who was Haveloc? Sir Colin Campbell? What do you know of Cawnpore? Of Lucknow? Of Delhi?
10—To what causes may be assigned the wide and rapid extension of commerce? Who organized the two Great Exhibitions of Industry in London and Dublin? What social improvements chiefly engaged public attention?

www.ingramcontent.com/pod-product-compliance
Lightning Source LLC
Chambersburg PA
CBHW020900230426
43666CB00008B/1258